Chicken Soup for the Soul®

Our 101 BEST STORIES

Teens Talk Growing Up

Chicken Soup for the Soul® Our 101 Best Stories:
Teens Talk Growing Up; Stories about Growing Up, Meeting Challenges, and Learning
from Life by Jack Canfield, Mark Victor Hansen & Amy Newmark

Published by Chicken Soup for the Soul Publishing, LLC   www.chickensoup.com

The publisher gratefully acknowledges the many publishers and individuals who
granted Chicken Soup for the Soul permission to reprint the cited material.

Cover photos courtesy of iStockPhoto.com/aldomurillo

Cover and Interior Design & Layout by Pneuma Books, LLC
For more info on Pneuma Books, visit www.pneumabooks.com

Distributed to the booktrade by Simon & Schuster. SAN: 200-2442

Publisher's Cataloging-in-Publication Data
(Prepared by The Donohue Group)

Chicken soup for the soul. Selections.
   Chicken soup for the soul® : teens talk growing up : stories about growing up,
meeting challenges, and learning from life / [compiled by] Jack Canfield [and] Mark
Victor Hansen ; [edited by] Amy Newmark.

   p. ; cm. – (Our 101 best stories)

   ISBN-13: 978-1-935096-01-6
   ISBN-10: 1-935096-01-X
1. Teenagers--Conduct of life--Anecdotes. 2. Teenagers' writings. I. Canfield, Jack,
1944- II. Hansen, Mark Victor. III. Newmark, Amy. IV. Title.
BJ1661 .C293 2008
158.1/28/0835   2008928838

PRINTED IN THE UNITED STATES OF AMERICA
on acid-free paper
∞
16 15 14 13 12 10 09 08   01 02 03 04 05 06 07 08

Chicken Soup for the Soul

Our 101 BEST STORIES

for the Soul®

Teens Talk Growing Up

Stories about Growing Up, Meeting Challenges, and Learning from Life

Jack Canfield
Mark Victor Hansen
Amy Newmark

CSS

Chicken Soup for the Soul Publishing, LLC
Cos Cob, CT

Chicken Soup for the Soul

Contents

❶

~Being a True Friend~

❷

~Self-Acceptance and Self-Discovery~

❸
~Accepting Others~

❹
~Doing The Right Thing~

❺
~Insights and Lessons Learned~

❻
~Family Ties~

❼
~Special Memories~

❽
~Overcoming Obstacles~

❾
~Reaching for the Stars~

❿
~Making a Difference~

Chicken Soup for the Soul

A Special Foreword

by Jack Canfield & Mark Victor Hansen

For us, 101 has always been a magical number. It was the number of stories in the first Chicken Soup for the Soul book, and it is the number of stories and poems we have always aimed for in our books. We love the number 101 because it signifies a beginning, not an end. After 100, we start anew with 101.

We hope that when you finish reading one of our books, it is only a beginning for you too—a new outlook on life, a renewed sense of purpose, a strengthened resolve to deal with an issue that has been bothering you. Perhaps you will pick up the phone and share one of the stories with a friend or a loved one. Perhaps you will turn to your keyboard and express yourself by writing a Chicken Soup story of your own, to share with other readers who are just like you.

This volume contains our 101 best stories and poems about the challenges, lessons learned, and ups and downs of being a teenager. We share this with you at a very special time for us, the fifteenth anniversary of our Chicken Soup for the Soul series. When we published our first book in 1993, we never dreamed that we had started what has become a publishing phenomenon, one of the best-selling book series in history.

We did not set out to sell more than one hundred million books, or to publish more than 150 titles. We set out to touch the heart of one person at a time, hoping that person would in turn touch another person, and so on down the line. Fifteen years later, we know that it has worked. Your letters and stories have poured in by the hundreds of thousands, affirming our life's work, and inspiring us to continue to make a difference in your lives.

On our fifteenth anniversary, we have new energy, new resolve, and new dreams. We have recommitted to our goal of 101 stories or poems per book, we have refreshed our cover designs and our interior layout, and we have grown the Chicken Soup for the Soul team, with new friends and partners across the country in New England.

We have selected our 101 best stories and poems for teenagers from our rich fifteen-year history to share with you in this new volume. We know that being a teenager is hard—school is challenging, college or careers are looming on the horizon, family issues arise, friends and love come and go, you are getting to know your new body, and many of you experience the loss of a loved one too.

You are not alone. We chose stories written by other teenagers just like you. They wrote about friends, family, love, challenges, loss, and many lessons learned. We hope that you will find these stories inspiring and supportive, and that you will share them with your families and friends. We have identified the 25 Chicken Soup for the Soul books in which the stories originally appeared, in case you would like to continue your journey among our other books. We hope you will also enjoy the additional titles for teenagers in "Our 101 Best Stories" series.

With our love, our thanks, and our respect,
—*Jack Canfield and Mark Victor Hansen*

Chicken Soup for the Soul

Introduction: A Letter from a Reader
Common Ground

oward the end of high school, when it came time to start thinking about what colleges I was interested in applying to, there was only one thing on my mind: I wanted to get away from home. I was the older of two kids, and had begun to feel the urge to be on my own, that I was ready to take charge of my own life.

Even at the time of being accepted to Virginia Tech, I was excited at the prospect of starting over, with new faces and new things to see and do. I had no boyfriend at the time (in fact, I had just gotten out of a pretty bad relationship) and felt that I had no ties keeping me in my New Jersey hometown.

But as the time arrived to pack my bags and prepare to leave, the reality of what I was doing hit home hard. I cried as I realized that I was going to be eight-and-a-half hours away from everything and everybody that was familiar to me. I was leaving the town where I had grown up and all the things about it that I loved.

For the first few days after arriving at school, I thought that I was not going to make it through the year. I had yet to meet anyone besides a few random girls in my dorm, who I was fairly sure did not even remember my name. After a tearful call back home, I grabbed one of the few books that had made it into my suitcase, *Chicken Soup for the Teenage Soul*, and I headed down to the quad to read a few stories. They had always been able to cheer me up before, and I was hopeful that they would now.

On the way out, I passed another girl in the hallway. She saw the book in my hand and smiled, saying that she had the same book in her dorm room too. I took a chance and invited her to come and read with me. Being as homesick as I was, she agreed, and we found our way onto the quad.

Before we knew it, we were surrounded by girls, who like us had either read or owned the book, and who loved it as much as we did. As I watched the tears fall down everyone's faces and the smiles grow as we all read, I realized that I was not alone, and even if all we had in common was the love for the book, it was something to start with.

The days went on, and I still missed home—but the campus was beautiful, the people were kind, and it became better and better as the school year continued. I began to realize that there were many people who, like myself, were homesick and just wanted friends. The night we spent reading bonded a group of us together, and most of us still hang out now.

The binding of my book is now ripped and cracked from over-use, but I still feel amazing when I read each story. It is unbelievable to me how many souls and hearts have been touched by the book, and how many spirits have been raised and inspired. It gave me hope for a great new beginning, and the knowledge that sometimes all it takes is one small thing for many people to find common ground.

—*Megan Narcini*
Chicken Soup for the College Soul

Teens Talk
Growing Up

Being a True Friend

The most I can do for my friend is simply be his friend.
—*Henry David Thoreau*

Getting It Right

On the April morning I found out about Lucy's mother, it rained. A light, cooling sprinkle of tears that grayed the Texas sky. I didn't know what kind of cancer Mrs. Hastings had until later, but I knew her condition was serious—very serious.

Now don't get me wrong. I love Mr. and Mrs. Hastings almost as much as I love my own parents, and Lucy is my best friend. But I didn't want to go to school that day. And I sure didn't want to see Lucy.

What could I possibly say to her? What do people say to their friends at such a time? I was afraid to send Mrs. Hastings so much as a get-well card because I wasn't sure she was going to get well. I tried every trick I knew to get out of going to school. But Mom insisted.

"You have a history test this morning, Kristin," she said, looking at me as if she'd crawled into my mind and knew I was just making excuses. "Had you forgotten?"

"No, Mother, I hadn't forgotten."

She smiled. "Be sure to stay close to Lucy, especially today, because that poor girl is going to need your strength."

Strength? What was Mother talking about? I had no strength. I didn't even know what to say to my best friend.

I hid out in the choir room between classes in hopes of avoiding Lucy, but she was never out of my thoughts. I kept trying to come up with something appropriate to say to her because I really wanted to get it right. I even wrote out a dialogue between the two of us, but in the end, I tore it up because it simply didn't sound like me.

Lucy and I had last-period English in Mrs. Green's room. Though I'd eluded her all day, I was going to have to face her last period, and I still didn't have a plan. However, I worried needlessly because Lucy never showed up for class.

When English class was over, Mrs. Green said, "Kristin, I know Lucy Hastings is your best friend, and I would like to know how she is handling her mother's illness."

"I don't know how she's handling anything," I said, "because I haven't seen or heard from Lucy since yesterday."

"Well, you'll be seeing her shortly because Lucy is coming here in a few minutes to get her lesson assignments."

"Lucy is coming here?"

Mrs. Green nodded. My heart tightened into a hard knot and I trembled inwardly. I still didn't know what to say to Lucy, and time was running out.

"Excuse me, Mrs. Green," I finally said, "but I have to go now." I bolted from the classroom.

I raced down the hall and out the front door of school practically in one breath, joining the students who were headed for the campus parking lot.

It had stopped raining, and the air smelled clean and fresh. A rainbow cut across a sky still darkened by thunderclouds, and the wind tossed my hair in all directions until I pulled up the hood of my yellow raincoat.

In the distance I saw someone coming toward me. I knew it was Lucy even though I couldn't see her face. She had her head down, and she was wearing a yellow raincoat exactly like mine. She'd pulled her hood up, too; maybe she hadn't seen me. Maybe if I ran back inside and hid in the choir room again, she wouldn't find me.

Then I noticed how Lucy's shoulders shook with every step she took. And I knew she must be crying because I was. The rain came down again. Raindrops mingled with my tears. Lucy's heart was breaking, and I wasn't doing a thing to help her.

As I drew nearer to her, my throat tightened, making it impossible to speak, even if I'd known what to say. A deep ache filled my heart. I prayed for strength, the strength my mother claimed I already had, and I forced myself to move forward, arms outstretched.

"Oh, Kristin," Lucy cried. "I was hoping it was you."

We hugged then, but I still couldn't utter a sound.

Looking back, I learned something that day that I might never have grasped in any other way. You see, I'd been focusing on me: What should I do? How should I act? What will I say to Lucy?

But when we finally came face to face, I forgot me and centered on Lucy and her needs. When I did that, I was able to share Lucy's grief—let her know that she was special and that I really cared.

Since then, Lucy has told everyone she sees that I have the gift of saying just the right words at just the right time. I still don't think she realizes that on the day we hugged in the April rain, I never said a word.

—Molly Noble Bull
Chicken Soup for the Girlfriend's Soul

Understanding Jenny

The best way to mend a broken heart is time and girlfriends.
—Gwyneth Paltrow

I jumped into my mother's car, threw my cross country team bag into the backseat, slammed the car door and fought with my seat belt.

"I'm so sick of it!" I said and pulled my hair back into its frizzy ponytail.

"I can see that," my mom answered, then turned on the blinker, looked over her shoulder and pulled out into the traffic. "I'm guessing this isn't about your hair."

"It's Jenny, playing her mind games again. Training is less tiring than dealing with her and her feelings."

"Which one is Jenny?" my mom asked.

"She's been here about a month. She lives at the Timmers."

"Oh, yes, Gloria told me they had a new foster kid. Said she's been moved around, but she's getting decent grades and joining school activities."

"I just wish she hadn't joined my activity."

"Why's that?" My mom was pretty good about listening to me vent.

"I mean, we've been training for weeks: stretching, running, pacing, lifting weights and making ourselves into a team. Then in strolls Jenny, the goddess of cross country or something. A coach's dream.

She paces around the course with us, and suddenly she's so far ahead that she makes the loop and is running back towards us like we're standing in place. A smile on her face, her perfect hair swinging behind her."

"So are you upset because your team has someone who can earn you some real points, or because she has a talent that she enjoys or because her hair stays so perfect?" My mom leaned over and pushed my damp-curled bangs from my face.

"Mom, I'm not that shallow."

"I know, honey. Sorry. Just trying to see the problem here."

"Jenny's the problem. She helps all of us run faster by upping the pace. She cheers us on. She trains harder, and so do we. We were voted co-captains. Then, this week, she cops an attitude. I spent most of my time running after her."

"No pun intended!"

"Mom! Please! This is serious," I sighed and took a drink from my water bottle. "Our first meet is tomorrow. Jenny keeps saying she won't run with the team. She has all sorts of reasons from leg cramps to a headache. I have to beg her. I have to tell her over and over that she can't do that to the rest of the team. It goes on all day, between classes, at lunch, on the way to practice. She wears me out. What's her deal?"

"She ends up running though, right?"

"Yeah, but we're all tired of it. She's so needy."

Mom pulled into our driveway. Instead of rushing into the house to start dinner, she turned and looked at me.

"Cindy, you gave yourself the answer."

Great, I'm pouring it all out, and Mom's going to give me a pop quiz. "Make this easy, would you, Mom?"

"Well, Gloria told me a little about Jenny. She and her little brother have been together all this time in foster care. They're really close. Her caseworker said that Jenny took good care of her. My heart sank. "Please, don't tell me something happened to her little brother."

"No, he's fine. His father, Jenny's stepfather, earned custody of him. He came for him this week. He had gifts and hugs and big plans for their future."

"Really? That's good."

"Yes, but he had nothing for Jenny. She wasn't even a little part of his big plans."

My chest felt tight. "Why?"

"Well, Jenny's mom and stepfather weren't together that long. Jenny and her brother have been in foster care for a while now. I guess he didn't consider Jenny his."

"What about her mom?"

"Her mom wants her drugs and alcohol more than she wants Jenny."

"Poor Jenny, not to have a family." I was close to tears. "Not to feel wanted or needed."

My mother patted my knee. "That's it, honey. You got it."

And I did.

I didn't see Jenny during school the next day. I started to think I had understood too late, that Jenny wasn't going to show at all.

I was the last one to get on the team bus and was glad there were still a few empty rows. I could take up two seats, put on my headset and get some down time before the meet.

Then I spotted Jenny. She was sitting in the back, alone.

I started down the narrow aisle, causing quite a disruption trying to maneuver myself and my oversized bag to the back. By the time I got to my seat, most of the team was watching my progress.

"Can I sit by you?" I asked Jenny. She shrugged her shoulders. I took it as a yes. "I didn't see you today. I was afraid you weren't going to make it."

"I didn't think anyone would notice if I made it or not."

The girls around us groaned. Here she goes again.

I looked at Jenny. I saw past her attitude because I understood what she was really saying.

"We would've noticed if you weren't here, Jenny. We want you running with us. The team needs you."

Jenny seemed to fill up, to expand.

"Isn't that right, team?" I called. "Let's hear it for Jenny!"

There was silence. Please, I thought, for Jenny's sake, give her what she needs.

Slowly and then with building momentum, they cheered for their teammate. As they did, the atmosphere changed. They began to care more about Jenny.

Jenny felt it. The defiance drained out of her shoulders. Her face relaxed. She smiled and blushed with pleasure.

We didn't erase all the pain in Jenny's life, but neither had we added to it.

She ran with us that day. She won the individual blue ribbon and lifted our team to third place. She never threatened not to run again, and she led us to our best season record.

Through our simple offering of friendship and her willingness to accept it, we gave Jenny something more important to her than blue ribbons. We gave her what she desired the most: to know she was wanted and needed.

—Cynthia M. Hamond
Chicken Soup for the Teenage Soul IV

A House is Not a Home

My first year of high school felt awkward. After leaving junior high at the head of my class with all the seniority the upper grade levels could afford me, it felt strange starting over as a freshman. The school was twice as big as my old school, and to make matters worse, my closest friends were sent to a different high school. I felt very isolated.

I missed my old teachers so much that I would go back and visit them. They would encourage me to get involved in school activities so that I could meet new people. They told me that in time I would adjust and probably end up loving my new school more than I had my old one. They made me promise that when that happened I would still come by and visit them from time to time. I understand the psychology in what they were saying, but I took some comfort in it nonetheless.

One Sunday afternoon not long after I had started high school, I was sitting at home at our dining room table doing homework. It was a cold and windy fall day, and we had a fire going in our fireplace. As usual, my red tabby cat was lying on top of all my papers, purring loudly and occasionally swatting at my pen for entertainment's sake. She was never far from me. I had rescued her when she was a kitten, and somehow she knew that I was the one responsible for giving her "the good life."

My mother kept stoking the fire to keep the house nice and warm. Suddenly, I smelled something strange, and then I noticed it...

smoke pouring in through the seams of the ceiling. The smoke began to fill the room so quickly that we could barely see. Groping our way to the front door, we all ran out into the front yard. By the time we made our way outside, the whole roof was engulfed in flames and it was spreading quickly. I ran to the neighbors to call the fire department, while I watched my mother run back into the house.

My mother then ran out of the house carrying a small metal box full of important documents. She dropped the case on the lawn and, in a crazed state, ran back into the house. I knew what she was after. My father had died when I was young, and I was certain that she was not going to let his pictures and letters go up in flames. They were the only things that she had to remember him by. Still I screamed at her, "Mom! No!"

I was about to run in after her when I felt a large hand hold me back. It was a fireman. I hadn't even noticed that the street had already filled with fire trucks. I was trying to free myself from his grasp, yelling, "You don't understand, my mother's in there!"

He held on to me while other firefighters ran into the house. He knew that I wasn't acting very coherently and that if he were to let go, I'd run. He was right.

"It's all right, they'll get her," he said.

He wrapped a blanket around me and sat me down in our car. Soon after that, a fireman emerged from our house with my mom in tow. He quickly took her over to the truck and put an oxygen mask on her. I ran over and hugged her. All the times I ever argued with her and hated her vanished at the thought of losing her.

"She's going to be okay," said the fireman. "She just inhaled a little smoke." And then he ran back to fight the fire while my mother and I sat there dazed. I remember watching my house burn down and thinking that there was nothing I could do about it.

Five hours later, the fire was finally out. Our house was almost completely burned down. But then it struck me… I hadn't seen my cat. Where was my cat? Much to my horror, I realized that she was nowhere to be found. Then all at once it hit me—the new school, the fire, my cat—I broke down in tears and cried and cried. I was suffering loss, big time.

The firemen wouldn't let us go back into the house that night. It was still too dangerous. Dead or alive, I couldn't imagine leaving without knowing about my cat. Regardless, I had to go. We piled into the car with just the clothes on our backs and a few of the firemen's blankets, and made our way to my grandparents' house to spend the night.

The next day, Monday, I went to school. When the fire broke out, I was still wearing the dress I had worn to church that morning, but I had no shoes! I had kicked them off when I was doing my homework. They became yet another casualty of the fire. So I had to borrow some tennis shoes from my aunt.

Why couldn't I just stay home from school? My mother wouldn't hear of it, but I was totally embarrassed by everything. The clothes I was wearing looked weird, I had no books or homework, and my backpack was gone. I had my life in that backpack! The more I tried to fit in, the worse it got. Was I destined to be an outcast and a geek all my life? That's what it felt like. I didn't want to grow up, change or have to handle life if it was going to be this way. I just wanted to curl up and die.

I walked around school like a zombie. Everything felt surreal, and I wasn't sure what was going to happen. All the security I had known, from my old school, my friends, my house and my cat had all been ripped away.

When I walked through what used to be my house after school that day, I was shocked to see how much damage there was—whatever hadn't burned was destroyed by the water and chemicals they had used to put out the fire. The only material things not destroyed were the photo albums, documents and some other personal items that my mother had managed to heroically rescue. But my cat was gone and my heart ached for her.

There was no time to grieve. My mother rushed me out of the house. We would have to find a place to live, and I would have to go buy some clothes for school. We had to borrow money from my grandparents because there were no credit cards, cash or even any identification to be able to withdraw money from the bank. Everything had gone up in smoke.

That week the rubble that used to be our house was being cleared off the lot. Even though we had rented an apartment nearby, I would go over to watch them clear away debris, hoping that my cat was somewhere to be found. She was gone. I kept thinking about her as that vulnerable little kitten. In the early morning when I would disturb her and get out of bed, she would tag along after me, climb up my robe and crawl into my pocket to fall asleep. I was missing her terribly.

It always seems that bad news spreads quickly, and in my case it was no different. Everyone in high school, including the teachers, was aware of my plight. I was embarrassed as if somehow I were responsible. What a way to start off at a new school! This was not the kind of attention I was looking for.

The next day at school, people were acting even more strange than usual. I was getting ready for gym class at my locker. People were milling around me, asking me to hurry up. I thought it strange, but in light of the past few weeks, nothing would surprise me. It almost seemed that they were trying to shove me into the gym—then I saw why. There was a big table set up with all kinds of "stuff" on it, just for me. They had taken up a collection and bought me school supplies, notebooks, all kinds of different clothes—jeans, tops, sweatsuits.

It was like Christmas. I was overcome by emotion. People who had never spoken to me before were coming up to me to introduce themselves. I got all kinds of invitations to their houses. Their genuine outpouring of concern really touched me. In that instant, I finally breathed a sigh of relief and thought for the first time that things were going to be okay. I made friends that day.

A month later, I was at my house watching them rebuild it. But this time it was different—I wasn't alone. I was with two of my new friends from school. It took a fire for me to stop focusing on my feelings of insecurity and open up to all the wonderful people around me. Now I was sitting there watching my house being rebuilt when I realized my life was doing the same thing.

While we sat there on the curb, planning my new bedroom, I heard someone walk up to me from behind and say, "Does this belong to you?" When I turned around to see who it was, I couldn't believe my eyes. A woman was standing there holding my cat! I leapt up and grabbed her out of the woman's arms. I held her close to me and cried into that beautiful orange fur. She purred happily. My friends were hugging me, hugging the cat and jumping around.

Apparently, my cat had been so freaked by the fire that she ran over a mile away. Her collar had our phone number on it, but our phones had been destroyed and disconnected. This wonderful woman took her in and worked hard to find out whose cat it was. Somehow, she knew this cat was loved and sorely missed.

As I sat there with my friends and my cat curled up in my lap, all the overwhelming feelings of loss and tragedy seemed to diminish. I felt gratitude for my life, my new friends, the kindness of a stranger and the loud purr of my beloved cat. My cat was back and so was I.

—Zan Gaudioso
Chicken Soup for the Teenage Soul on Tough Stuff

We Promised

Ever since kindergarten, I had attended a small, private school. My class consisted of only nineteen kids, and we grew up with each other. Our class had become as close as a family, so as middle school approached, we suddenly realized that come eighth grade the unthinkable would occur. We would all be separated, scattered to different public schools—forced to meet new people, form new friendships.

When we finally reached eighth grade, we waited for graduation with terrified anticipation, excited to finally experience the fabled life of a public school student, frightened about not fitting in and saddened at the thought of abandoning the close friendships we had created within our small, comfortable community.

On June 23, we donned our blue robes and caps and participated in a long, sentimental graduation ceremony. Afterward we had a huge sleepover, filled with tears and promises of never forgetting each other or our wonderful years together.

Throughout the summer, we got together as much as possible. Discussions often turned to the dangers we would encounter at public high schools. Drugs. Drinking. Sex. Would we be pressured to submit to these temptations? "Probably not," we said. "We'd be too scared," we joked. But still the question hung in the air. What if? What if fitting in was more important?

That summer something else happened. Tiffany Parks, a senior at the public high school and my next door neighbor, died from a drug overdose. Her body was found at a friend's house where a bunch of high school kids were having a party. My parents were horrified. I was stunned. I couldn't believe it.

When I was younger, Tiffany used to babysit for me. I remembered how we would sit on the floor and play spit or watch movies. Since my family didn't have a microwave, Tiffany used to make popcorn at her house and then bring over the steaming, buttery bag for us to share as we watched. I still associate the delicious smell of freshly popped popcorn with her, remembering how it filled the house upon her arrival. One time we got locked out of the house, so Tiffany pulled a bunch of brightly colored nail polish bottles from her bag and we painted our nails on the porch until my parents got home.

As I got older, Tiffany stopped babysitting for me, but every morning as I stood at the end of my driveway waiting for the bus, she'd walk past on her way to school, blond curls bouncing. When she'd see me, her gloss-covered lips would form a genuine smile and she'd greet me by name.

The whole town mourned her.

When the summer ended, my girlfriends and I got together a couple of days before the first day of high school. As we sat on my friend's large bed, I told them Tiffany's story. We all sat in a circle, put our hands together and promised each other that we would never try drugs.

High school has been hard to adjust to. But eventually we all adapted to our new environments and met new friends. However, I'm still very close with my classmates from private school and I'm happy to say none of us have tried drugs. I think it's because we promised.

—Rachel A. Stern
Chicken Soup for the Teenage Soul: The Real Deal School

The Birth of an Adult

The doctors started to rush into the room. The delivery was going smoothly, but to me it felt like hysteria. The walls were a chalky gray like the wall of a jail cell. It wasn't the best setting for Jamie's labor, but it would have to do. Jamie was only a seventeen-year-old junior in high school. And now she was giving birth. She lay back in pain. Her only movements consisted of shaking her head from side to side, in an effort to escape the pain.

I took Jamie's hand, comforting her and trying to soothe her agony. Her eyes opened, and she looked at me. Our eyes met, and suddenly I felt every emotion I have ever known. I always knew Jamie would challenge me to better myself; however, I didn't think it would entail being her sidekick during her pregnancy.

All this began on the afternoon of New Year's Eve. I sat in Jamie's basement awaiting the urgent news she had to tell me. She collapsed onto the couch and told me how she had broken up with her boyfriend, Eric, who had left the country to study abroad. This came as something of a relief, although I did my best not to show it. I didn't think Eric, or any other guy she had dated, was good enough for her. Okay, I'll admit it, I was—how should I put it—a little jealous. But

I'd convinced myself we were better off as friends, anyway. And now she needed one.

Then the real news came: She was six weeks pregnant. Tears rolled down her face as she told me. I sat in shock and disbelief. The words were not registering in my head. She reached out and gave me a hug, which must have lasted only a few seconds but seemed like hours. My arms were still at my sides. We talked for a little while, and then I left her house and drove around in my car. I was in shock. I was upset about her lack of birth control because this whole ordeal could have been prevented. I was too young to deal with her pregnancy. Being a seventeen-year-old and a junior in high school was confusing enough without dealing with my own real-life afterschool special.

That evening I arrived at a party to drink my worries away. The air was filled with smoke and the partygoers reeked of alcohol. I could not take the atmosphere for long, so I left. I went to Jamie's house and stood on her front porch staring at the front door. What should I do? I asked myself. My foot started to turn from the door, but my hand reached out and pushed the doorbell. I wanted to run and go back to the party. I wanted to have fun this New Year's Eve. Suddenly, the door opened and Jamie stood in the doorway with her head down. "You can't spend New Year's Eve by yourself," I blurted out. She smiled, and we hugged in the doorway. This symbolized the beginning of the new journey that lay ahead for us. That night, we sat and laughed as usual while watching Dick Clark ring in the New Year. After that night, my life would change. I wouldn't be a crazy teenager anymore. I would become a young adult.

Weeks passed, and Jamie told her parents about the pregnancy. She and her parents made the decision to go through with the pregnancy, but to give the baby up for adoption. My parents talked with her parents and offered their support, almost like they were discussing our marriage; Jamie and I were growing and maturing together.

During her first trimester, I found myself at Jamie's house every day after school giving her a foot massage while she relaxed and watched her soap opera. She wasn't able to walk very much.

I made snacks for her and enough food runs to Taco Bell to last us both a lifetime. My friends were not considerate about what I was going through. While I was busy helping a friend, they were busy making fun of me. They would call Jamie's house wondering what I was doing. They already knew, but they just wanted to poke fun. At school, the jokes surfaced like, "Gonna be a good daddy?" and "What are you doing this weekend… Lamaze class?" I shrugged them off and ignored them. I went on with my daily chores and focused on Jamie. I tried to make her life as easy as possible.

Later, one Saturday afternoon as I was catching up on sleep, Jamie called.

"Did you want to do something today?" she asked.

"What did you have in mind?" I replied.

"I want you to help me choose the baby's family," she said.

My ears turned hot, and I felt uneasy. But I told her I would pick her up. As I drove to her house, I thought about how much I had changed. I was more responsible, but I still considered myself a child. I felt I had no business choosing a path for an unborn baby. I groaned and doubted myself. I arrived at her house and helped her into the car. As we were driving to the adoption agency, Jamie pointed out to me, "You're not speeding."

It occurred to me that I was no longer a crazy driver, thinking about how quickly I could get from one place to the other. I was now responsible for making sure we got there safely.

"I'm driving for three people now," I told her.

We arrived at the agency and were seated in a conference room. Fifty manila folders lay on the table, each containing a couple. One of these folders would be the lucky one. One of these couples would be the parents of Jamie's baby. The counselor and Jamie and I went through each folder discussing their spiritual, psychological, financial, genealogical and emotional backgrounds. I began browsing through one folder, which read "Jennifer and Ben." The folder was more like a booklet chronicling their life with pictures of where they'd been, who they are and who they wanted to become. Their explanation of why they wanted a baby caught my attention. This couple intrigued me. We kept narrowing down the couples, until we were down to two couples: Jennifer and Ben and Jamie's pick. We discussed both couples, finally agreeing on Jennifer and Ben.

As we were getting ready to leave, I took a picture of Jennifer and Ben out of the folder and slipped it into my jacket pocket without Jamie noticing. I wanted to have a record of them before their life was to be changed forever. I put on my jacket, and we left the agency.

It was a miserably cold spring day. After helping Jamie into the car, I walked around the car and a warm breeze struck me. I stood by the trunk of my car feeling the summer draft. I couldn't understand it. It was a cold day, but the wind was warmer than an August breeze. It felt like a sign, an anonymous thank you. We drove away and I thought about the decision we made. I thought about the families we didn't pick. How much longer would it take for them to receive the gift of a child?

A few weeks later we met Jennifer and Ben for the first time. They impressed me. They were a close couple, and I knew they would apply the love they had for each other to their child. Jamie told them that I urged her to pick them, which made this meeting even more overwhelming for me. I tried not to show it, though, as we bonded almost immediately. They urged Jamie to take a childbirth class so she would be ready for all of the upcoming events. She needed a partner for the class, so I agreed. She signed up for a class, and every Tuesday night Jamie and I attended together.

The first class was awkward. I had never felt so out of place in my entire life. Jamie and I sat down together, trying to ignore the seven married couples staring at us. We were too young and too ignorant to be going through a pregnancy and a birthing class. Nevertheless, Jamie had to do it, and I would not let her be alone. After time, we all began to bond and develop a tremendous amount of respect for each other. Everyone realized what a struggle it was for us to get this far.

During the "Mom Time," the dads and I sat outside talking about the babies' futures. The dads talked about peewee football, mutual funds and insurance. I talked about Shakespeare and Geometry. I was out of place, for sure, but I realized there is more to giving birth than nine months and a doctor. So much freedom was sacrificed, replaced with a huge amount of responsibility. The dads respected me and praised me for my humanity towards a friend, not to mention my maturity. I still just couldn't believe I was sitting around talking about babies. I wanted to be innocent again. I wanted to drive my car fast and go to parties, but more important responsibilities called me. I was maturing.

I was getting ready for school one morning when Jamie called me from the hospital. "Um, do you want to get over here?" she asked.

"It's only another sonogram. Besides, I can't miss class," I said.

"Well, I think you might want to get over here, 'cause I'm having the baby!" she shouted.

I ran out of the house and darted to the hospital. At the hospital, the nurse handed me scrubs and I entered her room. She lay there as I sat next to her.

"Well this is it," she said. "Nine months, and it's finally here." She grimaced with pain and moved her head back and forth. Doctors were in and out of her room every two seconds with medication. She was about to give birth. After a few hours of getting Jamie settled, she was fully dilated.

"Okay, here we go. When I say 'push,' you push," the doctor said.

She acknowledged him while grabbing my hands and nodding her head quickly several times. Jamie gave three pushes of strength and, with one final push, she breathed life into a new baby. The doctors cut the umbilical cord and cleaned the baby off. I sat in awe. Every possible human emotion struck me like a freight train.

"It's a boy," they exclaimed.

I smiled, and tears of joy ran down my cheek. No more fear, no more chores, just pure happiness. The baby was handed to Jamie, and she spent the first moments of the baby's life holding him in her arms. She looked up at me, and I looked at her.

"You did it, kiddo," I whispered in her ear.

The doctors left with the baby to run tests and weigh him. Jennifer and Ben came in with the birth certificate. "What's his name?" Ben asked. Jamie motioned for him to come closer, and she whispered in his ear. Ben smiled and went into a different room. I walked outside to get a drink. I came back in a few minutes and saw the completed birth certificate. It read Blake Jonathan.

I smiled and cried. The doctors brought Blake back in. They passed Blake to me, and I held new life in my hands. I thought about the dads in birth class. Then I thought about Blake's future. His first steps, peewee football games, the first day of school and his first broken heart. All the dads' talk finally caught up with me. Jennifer and Ben looked at me and smiled. Tears rolled down their cheeks. I gave Blake to Ben and received a gracious hug from Jennifer. They were his parents now. They were his keepers. Jamie still lay there, crying but filled with delight. I went over to her and gave her a big hug.

"Everything okay?" she asked.

"Fine. Absolutely fine," I whispered, and kissed her softly on her forehead. I would never be the same.

—Jonathan Krasnoff
Chicken Soup for the Teenage Soul on Tough Stuff

What Goes Around Comes Around

Aunique directive was initiated at a high school in northern Utah, in which students with a physical or mental challenge were fully integrated into the mainstream classes and curriculum. To make it work, the administration organized a mentor program that teamed up each special-needs student with a mainstream student who would help him or her along.

The athletic director presented the idea to the captain of the football team. John was a tall, strong, intense young man—not the patient, caring type needed for this kind of program. He made it clear this "wasn't his thing," and he didn't have time to be a mentor. But the athletic director knew it would be good for him and insisted that John "volunteer."

John was matched up with Randy, a young man with Down syndrome. Reluctant and irritated at first, John literally tried to "lose" Randy, but soon John welcomed the constant company. Randy not only attended every one of John's classes and ate with him at lunch, he also came to football practice.

After a few days, John asked the coach to make Randy the official manager responsible for the balls, tape and water bottles. At the end of the football season, the team won the state championship, and John was awarded a gold medal as the most valuable player in the state. Randy was presented with a school letter jacket. The team cheered as Randy put it on. It was the coolest thing that had ever happened to him; from that day forward Randy never took it off. He slept in his jacket and wore it throughout each weekend.

Basketball season started, and John was also the captain and star of that team. At John's request, Randy was again named the manager. During the basketball season they were still inseparable. Not only did John take Randy to special occasions—like dances as a joint escort for his girlfriend—but he also took Randy to the library to tutor him. As he tutored Randy, John became a much better student and made the honor roll for the first time in more than a year. The mentor program was turning out to be the most rewarding year of John's life.

Then tragedy struck in the middle of the state basketball tournament. Randy caught a virus and suddenly died of pneumonia. The funeral was held the day before the final championship game. John was asked to be one of the speakers.

In his talk, John shared his abiding friendship with and respect for Randy. He told how Randy had been the one who had taught him about real courage, self-esteem, unconditional love and the importance of giving 100 percent in everything he did. John dedicated the upcoming state finals game to Randy and concluded his remarks by stating that he was honored to have received the MVP award in football and the leadership plaque for being the captain of the basketball team.

"But," John added, "the real leader of both the football and basketball teams was Randy, for he accomplished more with what he had than anyone I've ever met. Randy inspired all who knew him."

John walked from behind the podium, took off the irreplaceable twenty-four-karat-gold state football MVP medallion that hung around his neck, leaned into the open casket and placed it on Randy's chest. He placed his captain's plaque next to it.

Randy was buried in his letter jacket, surrounded by John's cherished awards as well as pictures and letters left by others who admired him.

The next day, John's team won the championship and presented the game ball to Randy's family. John went to college on a full athletic scholarship and graduated with a master's degree in education. Today, John is a special-education teacher; he also volunteers ten hours a week for the Special Olympics.

—Dan Clark
Chicken Soup for the Sports Fan's Soul

My Guardian Angel

When I was fourteen years old, I met two people who would change my life forever. During the summer before ninth grade, I was at the beach with my friend, Nick, when he introduced me to his best friend. His name was Lee. We were instant friends. There was something about his smile that stayed with me for the rest of that weekend. We started talking to each other online, and then on the phone. We just clicked.

Over the next few months, I found myself falling in love with Lee. I don't know how or why it happened, but it did. By the time football season rolled around in mid-October, Lee and I were dating. Going out to eat after home games was a tradition for cheerleaders and football players at Central. And since I was a cheerleader and Lee played football, that's usually where we ended up on Friday nights. One night I was sitting with Lee eating my usual chicken fingers when this short, kind of pudgy kid walked in and strolled right over to our table.

"Meghan, this is Dan Welch," Lee said to me.

The kid looked at me with bright blue eyes, smiled the biggest, whitest smile I'd ever seen and said, "Hey, what's up?"

Little did I know that this was the beginning of the most important friendship I'd ever have in my life, and that I would grow to love that smile (not to mention that laugh) and depend on it to get me through some of my worst days. Dan made me laugh, made me cry, picked up the pieces when my life seemed to fall apart, and always managed to keep me smiling. We had staring contests that I always lost and wrestling matches that I usually won. He paged me when my favorite songs were on the radio and didn't care when I sang at the top of my lungs to them in his car.

For about a year, the three of us spent as much time as we could together. They were my life. Lee and I had our ups and downs, but no matter how many times Lee and I fought or saw other people or made each other mad, we always found our way back to each other.

Then at the end of August 1999, my heart was broken. Dan and Lee were going off to college. And even though they were only going forty-five minutes away to Boston where they would be roommates at Northeastern, I thought I was going to die without them.

But it wasn't as bad as I thought it would be. My parents didn't mind the phone bill too much, so I got to talk to them every day, and we talked online, too. They came home every weekend. On one of those weekend nights, they called me from Lee's house to tell me they were coming to pick me up so I could go play Laser Tag with them. As much as I wanted to go (I had been bugging them for a while now about going with them), I had to tell them no since I had to get up early the next morning. I was on my way out the door to the mall when the phone rang at 7:45. The last person I expected to hear from was Nick, who had gone with them. He sounded different, kind of shaken up. He told me they were just waiting for the game to start so I thought nothing of it. When I got home from the mall I found out he'd called again, right after I had left. I thought that was odd, so I called him back. As soon as he opened his mouth, my body turned to ice.

"I have bad news, Meg... Lee and Dan were in a car accident tonight on the way to laser tag."

I almost dropped the phone. This was not happening to me. Not to the two people I loved most in the world. I wouldn't believe it.

"No, Nick, I don't believe you. You would've told me when you first called... no, you're lying! How could you lie about something like that? I hate you!"

Right before I hung up, I heard Nick yell, "I'm coming over right now... wait for me..."

I went downstairs, still shaken, and waited by the door. I expected to see the three of them come up my steps laughing at how "gullible" I was. But when Nick walked up alone, I knew he had told me the truth. I could see it in his face.

"Nick, please tell me they're okay... they have to be okay! Nick, tell me!" I didn't know what I was saying; I could barely see straight I was crying so hard.

"Lee's in the ICU in Boston. I don't know if he's gonna be okay or not. No one would tell me anything."

"And...what about Dan?"

No answer.

"Nick, tell me he's okay!" I yelled.

"I can't, Meg...." Nick got very quiet and looked down. "Dan didn't make it. I'm so sorry, Meg... I'm so sorry. I was going to tell you earlier when I called you before, but I couldn't tell you... not like that, not on the phone." Nick was struggling for words, and I was struggling for breath.

"No!" I collapsed against him, crying. He pulled me into his arms and just hugged me. One of my best friends was dead, and my boyfriend was in intensive care. It was too much.

Nick got me into the living room and told my parents the details. Lee and Dan had been following Nick and a few other people in Dan's father's Blazer. Dan had lost control of the truck, and it crashed into the guardrail, flipping over and throwing them out. They didn't have their seat belts on. Nick had called me from the side of the road on his cell phone. He told me later that he had needed to hear my voice; he had needed to know that at least one person he cared about was okay.

Somehow I made it through that night. I went to see Lee at the hospital, and his mom told me he'd be okay. He had a broken cheekbone, a dislocated shoulder and some other injuries, but he would be okay. He didn't know about Dan yet, and everyone was worried about how to break the news.

I spent the next week in a daze, just going through the motions. Nothing mattered to me anymore. I cried myself to sleep every night, and even cried throughout the day. How do you go on without your best friend?

Telling Lee about Dan was the hardest. His parents told him, and he didn't believe it at first. Eventually he realized it was true, and when he did all he could do was cry and hold my hand. I didn't know what to say, so I stayed pretty quiet when they told him. It was a sad moment for all of us and a life-changing one for Lee.

It's now been almost a year and a half since Dan's death. Lee is fine now, physically, but emotionally we're both scarred for life. There is a part of us that will always be missing, a place in us that will always have Dan's name on it. I've been to his grave countless times, and I talk to him every night. I would give anything to have my best friend back. Nothing and no one will ever take his place. But I know he's watching over me. He once promised me that he would always be there for me and that he'd never let me down. I know Dan, and I know that he'll keep that promise forever.

—Meghan O'Brien
Chicken Soup for the Teenage Soul on Tough Stuff

A Healed Heart

It's not about losing the memories, but gaining the strength to let go.
—Jessica Leal

Dear *Chicken Soup for the Teenage Soul*,

I've always thought the name Chicken Soup for the Soul was cute and creative. However, I was unconvinced as to whether or not these books could really "heal" the soul. Don't get me wrong. I loved the stories in the Chicken Soup books, but I always just thought of them as light, heartwarming reading—until I broke up with my boyfriend of two years and discovered their true healing powers.

Brendan was my first serious boyfriend. I adored him. He didn't just have interests in life; he had passions. He loved to sing and play soccer. He was one of the funniest guys I had ever met. He had many friends and was very loyal to all of them. Most of all, he had goals for his life. I think these ambitions are what initially attracted me to him. He made me feel like I, too, could dream big.

When we first met in eighth grade, I hated his guts. He was annoying. All he ever talked about was this girl in our class, Tara, whom he had a crush on. He had followed her around for months trying to get a date until she finally agreed. He was ecstatic—and then she proceeded to publicly dump him two hours later. I felt sorry for him, and I let him talk to me throughout the whole ordeal. Over the next couple weeks we really got to know each other. And soon we were an item.

I smiled so much those first few months that I probably created wrinkles that will come back to haunt me when I'm fifty! I was in love. My friends told us all the time how cute we were together. I couldn't have agreed more. It wasn't always smooth sailing, but we always learned from our little quarrels and disagreements. The rough spots actually brought us closer together and made us grow. We were happy for two years.

A couple of weeks before our two year anniversary, Brendan started acting strange and distant toward me. I got a little worried, but I just figured we would get through it with a little effort, as always. A couple of days later I found out that I had mono. I was tired all the time and didn't feel like doing much of anything except sleeping. Talk about bad timing. Just when our relationship needed all the attention I could give it, all I could do was sleep.

I missed four weeks of school and during that time Brendan and I grew farther and farther apart. I started hearing rumors about him and Tara from our mutual friends. Finally one night I called him to talk about our relationship. I told him I thought that it might be time to end things between us. He agreed. And we were no longer a couple. I cried and cried that night and spent at least four hours sobbing on the phone with my best friend, Lindsay. I couldn't believe it was over.

Over the next few weeks, I was really depressed. I couldn't get over him. I kept telling Lindsay how much I still liked him and how much I missed him. I must have driven her crazy, but she was so patient and kept giving me subtle advice and kind words. One day at school she handed me a bag and told me to open it when I got home.

In the bag was her copy of *Chicken Soup for the Teenage Soul* flagged with personal notes from her on the stories she recommended. She also gave me a blank diary with this simple message written on the inside cover: "Who said being a teenager was easy?" Included in the package was also a heartfelt note that said she was there for me and that she wanted to help however she could. She told me that although I didn't believe it now, someday it wouldn't hurt me to think of him. Someday I wouldn't cry every time I looked at pictures of us. Someday I would remember our time together with a smile. Someday I would be over him.

Sure enough, as time wore on I slowly recovered. I let go of Brendan and learned to smile again. I later thanked Lindsay for all of her thoughtfulness and told her how much it had helped me. She said that someone had once helped her, too, and that I could repay her by helping someone else who needs it in the future. Since then I have been there for two of my closest friends through tough periods in their lives. A little Chicken Soup, some sticky notes and a few kind words from the heart can go a long way to make a friend feel better.

Thank you for creating the Chicken Soup for the Teenage Soul books. They are definitely the rattiest books on my shelf—well-read and well-borrowed—and have gone a long way to help heal the hearts of many.

Sincerely,
—Jackie Johnstone
Chicken Soup for the Teenage Soul Letters

Chapter 2

Teens Talk Growing Up

Self-Acceptance and Self-Discovery

Perfection is a trifle dull. It is not the least of life's ironies that this,
which we all aim at, is better not quite achieved.
—W. Somerset Maugham

Blizzards and Sweater Vests

So often time it happens, we all live our life in chains,
and we never even know we have the key.
—The Eagles, "Already Gone"

hile in middle school, students seem to have one goal: to be popular. More than anything, most of the students fervently hope to not be accused of going against the grain. These young teenagers would much rather conform and be accepted by the "in" crowd than focus on finding their own identity, style or path. Like most thirteen-year-olds, I succumbed to this need to fit in. One afternoon, however, I had a conversation with my father that made me think twice about following the rest of the lemmings over the proverbial cliff.

My dad and I were sitting in the dining area of the local Dairy Queen eating Blizzards on a dreary winter afternoon. We had run the gambit of usual conversation topics: school, orchestra, my plans for the weekend. Then, and I'm not quite sure how the discussion began, we started talking about popularity. I told him that I wanted to be popular, or at least accepted favorably by those who were. He looked at me and asked me why I felt that way. I shrugged my shoulders and looked back into my drink. I had never stopped to think about why

I felt the need to fit in... I simply did. I had been told by my friends that I should want to be popular, and since I had always trusted them, I was inclined to believe them.

My father proceeded to tell me a story from his college days. His mother, my grandmother Lorraine, had made him several sweater vests to wear at school. These sweater vests were practical and comfortable, but hardly "in style." Nevertheless, they became a staple of my father's wardrobe. He didn't care that he wasn't sporting the latest fashion. In fact, he didn't care what everyone thought of him, either. I was shocked. What was even more surprising was that after a few weeks, other students at my dad's school began wearing sweater vests. By deviating from the norm, my father had started a trend. What he wore became fashionable because the other students saw the confidence with which he dressed.

This information was a lot for a thirteen-year-old girl to process, especially one who had been carefully taught about what was "cool" and what was most certainly not cool. I found it hard to believe that going against the grain could have benefits for me, so I continued to wear the same clothes, listen to the same music and go to the same places that my peers did. Surely my father was mistaken. This is also, of course, the stage in which children think they know infinitely more than their parents. I had not yet seen the light, and I continued on my quest for popularity. However, our conversation that bleak winter day replayed over and over in my mind.

As the days passed and I mulled it over, I realized that my father's words might have some validity after all. I began to evaluate my wardrobe to find which items I had bought because they were cool and which items I'd bought because I truly liked them. I also looked back at my actions, attempting to determine how many of them I performed to please the crowd and how many of them I performed because I actually enjoyed them. I found myself caring less and less what people thought about me. It was wonderfully liberating.

I have come a long way since middle school. It no longer bothers me that those who still feel compelled to follow the herd do not accept me as one of their own. I do not strive to dress in the latest fashions; if anything, I attempt to create my own. The conversation I had with my father about wearing sweater vests and feeling the need to fit in sparked in me the desire to deviate from the beaten path and form one of my own. I have learned a valuable lesson in the process: Swimming against the current can only make me stronger.

—Esther Sooter
Chicken Soup for the Teenage Soul: The Real Deal School

My Worst Enemy

He used to look at me like I was the most beautiful girl in the entire universe. He often gazed at me, the corners of his eyes wrinkled by a sweet grin on his lips, and would tell me I was an angel who had swooped down from heaven just for him. There were many moments in our relationship when I convinced myself that Brian and I were destined to spend our lives together. When he looked at me with his adoring eyes, I felt, for the first time ever, like I was beautiful.

When I was with Brian, I was at peace with myself. Unfortunately, things were not so tranquil without him. My self-esteem was terribly low, and by the time I was seventeen, I was painfully aware this was a serious problem. Instead of solving the problem, I opted to hide it and pretend like I was perfectly content with myself. I let Brian give me the love that I couldn't give myself. I didn't want him to know that my reflection was my own worst enemy. I didn't want him to know that I spent nights crying because my hips were too wide and my thighs were too fat. I didn't want him to know that the girl he loved didn't love herself.

"Emily, you're amazing," he would whisper softly, tickling my ear while my heart threatened to burst from happiness.

As the months wore on, my lack of self-confidence began to show through. Brian would say, "Emily, why don't you wear that shirt?" And I would argue, "It makes my hips look too big." He would shrug, as boys often do when they can't understand the reasoning of a female mind, and the subject would be dropped. The problem was, moments like that began to show up more and more often in our relationship, and Brian started to get frustrated.

"Emily, you're beautiful! Why do you have to get so jealous? You know I love you!" And even though I knew this, every time I saw Brian talking to other girls, my mind instantly feared he had finally realized that I really wasn't as gorgeous as he had thought.

"I can't deal with this anymore," he announced one day. "How can you love me if you can't even love yourself! I love you for you. But you have to find out what it is that makes you so scared of who you really are. You have to stop being so negative about yourself." He left after that, and I was stuck, all alone, with my own worst enemy.

In time, I realized my relationship with myself is just like a relationship I share with anyone else. In order to make it better, it was necessary to nurture it. Just like I spend time with the people I love, I had to spend time with myself. I had to learn and grow and hold my own hand instead of slapping it away.

Of course, it took me many painful months to discover this truth. I took the breakup really hard and verbally bashed myself time and time again. Ironically, I was punishing myself for not loving myself. I actually believed that I was a plague to society who didn't deserve to live on the same earth with loving and accepting people like Brian. When I looked in the mirror, I absolutely despised the person with the puffy, red eyes and unwashed hair who stared back at me.

Developing self-acceptance was a process that occurred slowly, but gradually I began to smile at my reflection. Little things like a guy in chemistry calling me cute, shopping for clothes that were more fitting and flattering, and discovering new interests and talents contributed to the foundation for my whole new perspective on me. Giving myself a hard time hurt me. Accepting and loving myself nurtured me. I began to feel more energetic, and I was excited about even the smallest things. It's incredible how my worst enemy turned out to be my best friend once I made some humble yet necessary changes. I can honestly say I like myself now. And I've got a feeling things are just going to keep getting better.

—Emily Starr
Chicken Soup for the Teenage Soul IV

Kissing the Bully

looked down at my skinny body and turned to the side. I was awkward; my knobby knees led down to thin, bony legs. I looked around, enviously watching as the other girls pulled on their bras and hooked the back. I pulled on the bra I barely fit into, the one I had forced my mom to take me to buy, just so you could see the outline through the back of my shirt. I was a late bloomer; there was no questioning that.

I walked home from school with my equally skinny best friend Laura at my side; she had hidden her embarrassment of her not-yet-developed body with a larger-than-life attitude. It was the normal walk home: She and I were taunted by Ben and a few other boys our age who inevitably found a way to make me cry.

I reached my house, knowing that the phone would ring later that night with some crank call and muffled sounds of prepubescent boys' laughter. I knew that the same pattern would be repeated the next day: They would walk behind us on the way to school, laughing about the "wall," Ben's less-than-endearing reference to my chest.

To ease my despair, I was told, "They only do that because they like you." My dad reassured me that once I blossomed, they'd be begging to go out with me. I hadn't had a boyfriend yet, and it seemed like everyone else was well on his or her way to awkward handholding and spin-the-bottle games. I pined for some sort of attention from the opposite sex. I didn't realize at the time that the torture from Ben and his friends was actually attention.

By the ninth grade, Laura and I were no longer walking to school; we caught the number three bus on our corner to the local high school. Ben, by this point, had moved on to hitting us with spitballs. So every morning, I had to clean the wads of gross spit-covered paper from my hair, making sure the evidence was gone. I would yell at him to stop, which only provoked more torture. I had known him for four years at this point, and the funny thing was we considered each other friends. He would talk to me, if the other boys weren't around, and I knew, despite his tough exterior, that he actually enjoyed my company.

Throughout middle school, Ben maintained the ritual of Rollerblading to my house after school, but I'm sure he never told his friends that in the seventh grade he had held my hand down the street, teaching me to use the Rollerblades I had just received for my birthday. It seemed that the nicer he was to me in private, the meaner he had to be to me in public.

I vowed that once I "blossomed," he would want to be my boyfriend, that the group of boys who tortured me in middle school would long for me in high school. I had a cruel fantasy of one of them asking me out and my rejecting him coldly, in front of everyone. I wanted to make them feel the embarrassment I had felt during all those walks home, and on all the bus rides with spitwad-filled hair.

High school finally came along and, better late than never, I did blossom. I grew out of my awkward, bony body. My wavy red hair grew longer and straightened itself out. Although I didn't transform, I grew up, more in mind than in body. I started to accept the freckles and felt blessed to be naturally thin. I even wore a little makeup. And my dad was right, it did happen. I finally had a boyfriend. He was from a different middle school than I had attended, and he was unaware of my uncomfortable beginnings.

I still saw Ben; we attended the same high school parties and shared the same group of friends. He teased me a bit, but it didn't really bother me as much. I went through a few boyfriends in high school, and it seemed that the awkward years were finally over.

This summer I returned home from my first year of college. Ben and I ran into each other. He stood about a foot taller than I did, and I realized how much he had grown up throughout our eight years of friendship. He lives on his own now and invited me over to see his new apartment. The walls were sparse; it looked like a college boy's room, which struck me as odd. I knew so many college boys, but it was hard for me to picture Ben as one. I still saw the skinny blond boy who sat behind me in eighth grade snapping my bra straps.

We started talking about those years, and we both laughed. A few other old friends filled the apartment, and one of Ben's old partners-in-crime leaned over and said, "You have gotten so pretty." I thanked him, smirking at the same time. It seemed like I had waited eight years for this, for my revenge.

I found myself sitting outside with Ben, and then, it happened. He leaned over, and he kissed me, something that had never happened between us before. For a second, I thought, "This is it, I can finally tell him off and embarrass him for all the times he belittled me." But I didn't. I no longer needed revenge. I continued to look at him, and I asked, "Did you ever have a crush on me?"

And he responded, "I had a crush on you the whole time. I was just too embarrassed to tell you."

—Lia Gay
Chicken Soup for the Teenage Soul III

I Am Loni

*To be nobody but yourself in a world that's doing its best to
make you somebody else is to fight the hardest battle
you are ever going to fight. Never stop fighting.*
—e. e. cummings

Why do I even try? If there's one thing I should have learned, it's, try or not, I'll probably screw up. Mom says, "Loni, a lady shouldn't say things like 'screw up.'" That just proves my point. I even screw up how to tell you that I screwed up.

I know; I have so much going for me. Don't even go there. Dad brags about my grades, and Mom's proud of the person I am and all my activities. Grandma goes on and on about my pretty face. Yeah, too bad about the rest of me, I think to myself.

I'm not, like, big enough to be featured as The Amazing Amazon Teen in The Guinness Book of World Records, but I am big enough not to like shopping with my friends. "How cu-u-u-u-ute!" they squeal over every rack of clothes. They know they'll fit into anything. I can't commit until I scan the plastic circle dividers to see how high the sizes go.

I pretend that clothes don't matter to me. That explains my semi-grunge look everyone takes for my chosen style. No outfit is complete without a sweater, flannel shirt or sweatshirt tied around my waist to cover up... oh... everything.

So, when we go to the mall, I'm the designated shopper. You know, like the designated driver who goes to a party but doesn't partake. I stand outside the changing rooms to ooh and aah when they emerge for the three-way mirror check. Only after a careful inspection do I reassure them that their thighs, legs, waist or bottom do not look too big in that outfit; otherwise, it would be taken as insincere.

It takes all I have not to roll my eyes when they hand me a piece of clothing and plead, "Can you see if this comes in a smaller size?" Give me a break. Where should I look? The children's department?

I really did screw up, though. Being a self-appointed good sport, I tried out for the volleyball team with my friends. Here's the bad part: I made it.

It seems I have a killer serve. I use it for self-defense. The harder I ram the ball, the less likely it will be returned and force me to clod around the court keeping it in play.

To make matters worse, we keep winning. This is the first winning season of any girl's sport in our school's history. Volleyball fever took over, and attendance soared. Just my luck. And those pep rallies. There's a thrill. Jumping around high-fiving while my name echoes over the PA system.

In our small town, making it to State Finals is newsworthy. Our team was pictured sitting in the bleachers in a "V for Victory" formation. I was the connecting bottom of the "V," front and center in all my glory.

"Loni Leads the Charge to State!" read the headline. Not bad. I didn't even pretend to protest when Mom bought copies for the relatives. I was pleased when the team framed the picture and hung it in the tunnel between our locker room and the arena. It soon became our team gesture to blow kisses at our picture every time we passed it.

It was the night of the final game, and we had home court advantage. The series was tied two games to two. I led the team's run for our triumphant entrance. Cheers stormed down the tunnel to meet us. We glanced at the banners posted along the walls, taking energy from the words.

YOU GO, GIRLS! YES YOU CAN! WE'RE #1!

We were ready to blow kisses at our picture when shock froze me. Two words were written in red on the glass. Two words that totally changed the headline.

"Loni THE BULL leads the charge to State!"

The horns drawn on my head completed the insult.

I felt myself emptying until I wasn't me anymore. I was nobody. The team bunched behind me.

"Who did this?"

"Who would be so mean?"

Their questions had no answers. They thought they were as upset as I was, but they were wrong. I wasn't upset at all. I was in shock.

So this is the truth, I thought. This is who I am.

And all the words around me didn't heal the hurt because nobody said the three words I needed to hear most: "That's not true."

The team moved me down the tunnel. There was no time to sort myself. What was real seemed like a dream, and I couldn't shake myself awake. The chants of "Loni! Loni!" sounded hollow. I let the cheers of the many be muted by the jeers of the few.

We won the coin toss and took to the court for my first serve. Around me the team was pumped and ready to go. I rolled the volleyball in my palms to get its feel and mechanically went into my serving stance. All I could see were the words... THE BULL. THE BULL. THE BULL.

I tossed the ball up, but before my fist made contact the shout "OLE!" hit me. I stutter-stepped and missed the ball. I told myself not to look, but my eyes were drawn anyway. I couldn't pick out who it was. The team tried to buck me up with back slaps and "that's okays." But it didn't help.

I went through the rotations until I was at the net. My concentration scurried between the game and the bleachers. When the ball skimmed the air above my head, a loud snorting sound came from the front row.

"That's taking the bull by the horns!" someone yelled. The player behind me made the save and set up the ball for me to spike. But I wasn't looking at the ball. I was staring into the faces of the five high school guys who were mocking me. My humiliation only fueled their taunts.

"Give me a B, give me a U, give me a double L, too. What's that smell? LONI! LONI! LONI!"

Why didn't someone shut them up?

The coach called a time-out. "Loni, can you get your head in the game?"

I shrugged.

"Why are you letting a few people who don't even know you decide for you who you are?"

I shrugged again.

"Loni, you're valuable as a person and to your team. Unkind words don't change who you are unless you decide they change you," she said.

Sounds good in theory, I thought, but this is the real world.

"I'm keeping you in, but if you can't work through this I'll pull you."

I nodded.

I walked past the boys to take my place in the game.

With each step I took, they stomped their feet to shake the floor. I got the point. Very funny.

I also had to walk past my teammates, and in spite of my weak showing, they were still rooting for me. "You can do it." "You're the best."

Something in me gave way. The quote on a magnet on my grandma's refrigerator popped into my thoughts: "God don't make no junk."

I knew what I knew, and I knew myself—I wasn't junk. I felt my value to the very depths of my soul. Who was I anyway? What did some immature boys know about me? There were so many people who loved and supported me, and it was time to do my best for them and for myself.

And just like that, I was free of them. Oh, they continued to stomp their feet with each of my steps. I didn't like it, but it didn't matter. They were powerless over my life.

The game was close, and we played hard. The winning serve fell to me. It was my moment, and I took it. The ball went up, my fist came forward and hit it right on. It was a perfect power serve unreturnable by the other team. The crowd went wild. The pep band started beating out our school song. The team huddled around me.

Shouts of "Loni! Loni!" vibrated the arena. The funny thing is, the cheers didn't feed me like they used to. They were great, but the joy I felt, the freedom I felt, the sense of myself I had filled me more than any cheers.

There was more than one victory that day, and the game was not the most important one.

—Loni Taylor as told to Cynthia Hamond
Chicken Soup for the Teenage Soul on Tough Stuff

14

Perfection

Skinny legs, bigger breasts
Is all they want to see
Tiny waists and thinner arms
The opposite of me.
The pressure to be perfect
Is slowly closing in
An utter suffocation
That doesn't seem to end.
Society is telling me
Beautiful is thin
And if I choose to starve myself
Perfection's what I win.
Shoving something down my throat
Will get me what I want
Bring me closer to that goal
Of a body I can flaunt.
Society is telling us
Beauty is a prize
Measured in the size of your breasts
In weight and clothing size.
But let me tell you here and now
No good will come from that
It seems okay at first
But soon becomes a trap.

A disease that clouds the mind
And believes what is untrue
Believes you're never good enough
No matter what you do.
There is one beauty that I know
It's the greatest prize of all
It's learning to accept yourself
Imperfections, flaws, and all.
The beauty that really matters
Lies in our heart, our soul, our core
Because when you love what's inside
You love what's outside even more.

—Brittany Steward
Chicken Soup for the Teenage Soul IV

15

Losing Becky

You have within you, right now, everything you need to deal with whatever the world can throw at you.

—Brian Tracy

I didn't see it coming, the day I lost my best friend. Becky and I were eating our bag lunches at some benches out by the school tennis courts. We were alone; our other friends weren't with us, which was unusual in those days—we almost always ate lunches in a group, the eight of us—so this should've tipped me off. It's true that Becky had been acting strangely for the past few weeks, alternately ignoring me and snapping at me. When I'd asked her what was wrong, she'd said, "Nothing!"

"Then why are you acting so weird?"

"If I'm so weird, maybe you shouldn't hang around with me."

So I was glad today to be hanging out with her, just the two of us, like old times. We'd been best friends for almost two years. We'd met soon after we started the seventh grade and quickly fell into being best friends in that mysterious way friends sometimes do. We'd shared countless phone calls and school lunches and sleepovers. We'd spent many weekends together, laughing gut-strengthening laughs, playing records and the radio; I played piano while Becky sang in her light, high voice. We shared lots of inside jokes and goofiness, like our hilarious games at the tennis courts. Neither of us were any good at tennis, so as we hit the ball wildly off the mark, we'd yell to each other, "It's still going!" laughing helplessly and scrambling to retrieve the ball, no matter how many times it had bounced.

But today at the tennis courts, neither of us was laughing or even smiling. And suddenly, I realized that this lunch alone together had been planned. Becky wanted to talk to me.

"You wanted to know what was wrong," Becky said. Her tone was overly kind and condescending. "For awhile now, we've felt you haven't been having a good time with us." Why was she saying "we"? I had a sinking feeling. She was right about my not having a good time lately hanging out with our friends. Really, they were Becky's friends, and I hung around with them for her sake. They were nice enough girls, but I didn't have much in common with them. They liked Top 40 music, which increasingly bored me. They thought the music I liked was too weird. During lunch, they'd chat on and on about thirteen-year-old boys, gymnastics, TV shows and how stupid the popular girls were. More and more, I'd tune out their chatter, daydreaming about the bands I liked, feeling profoundly bored by Becky's friends—but not by Becky. I endured my boredom because of her. Besides, there was a certain security in having these girls to sit with at lunch, having them if you wanted them.

Becky went on with her speech: "I want to be... popular." Her voice was quavering and ruthless. "You don't seem to want to, but we feel it's important." I couldn't believe I was hearing this. They'd gone on and on about what lame idiots the popular girls were. But what Becky had to say next sent my world spinning. "We think maybe you ought to have lunch with some other girls from now on."

"But who?" I asked, panicking. I couldn't think of a single person. It suddenly sank in that I no longer had a best friend.

"What about those older girls? You seem to get along with them," she suggested with a trace of what sounded like jealousy. It was true that I did get along with some of the older girls—like Lisa, who we'd met in an after-school creative writing workshop, who wrote strange, impassioned poems, and who'd loaned me a tape with some equally strange, impassioned songs on it, songs I listened to over and over again. The older girls were more interesting than Becky's friends. But at that moment, all I wanted was for Becky to say we were still best friends. I felt as though no one could possibly want me around.

The next day at noon, I put my books in my locker, grabbed my lunch, slammed the locker shut, then headed automatically for Becky's locker as I had every day for what seemed like forever. Just as I saw her—small, thin girl with shoulder-length black hair—I remembered. She saw me, and we both stood frozen for a moment. Then I made myself turn and walk in the opposite direction. It was like a divorce.

At first, I wandered around school close to tears all the time—in class, in PE, everywhere. But I did start getting to know some of the older girls better. I began to eat lunch with them, to sit with them during free period. We talked about the music and the movies we liked, and I found myself having fun. No longer did I have to tune out—I wasn't bored anymore. I still missed having a best friend. But by the time I got to the ninth grade, I had many friends and several close ones—and a number of them had also been dropped by their previous cliques for being "too weird." They liked the same music I did, and some of them even went to see live bands. Soon I was going out, too, and my whole world seemed to open up.

Becky and I were never friends again, although I still talked to her from time to time at school. Sometimes I tried to tell her about the fun I was having, but she didn't seem to understand. She and her friends hadn't become any more popular than when I was part of their crowd. I didn't know whether that continued to matter to her.

She apologized to me one day in the school lunchroom for the way she had treated me. "I can't believe I did that to you!" she said. But I told her I had long since realized that she had done me a favor. I had found my true friends, friends who could really understand me, friends I could be completely myself with, while the pain of Becky's rejection has become a distant memory.

—Gwynne Garfinkle
Chicken Soup for the Teenage Soul on Tough Stuff

16

Like Water

I'm in phys ed class, freshman year. I'm wearing my stupid fuchsia gym pants. I feel self-conscious. I'm the short, nerdy girl in the ugly clothes. I'm embarrassed by myself. I scratch my head and yawn. More than anything, I wish this class were over. For good.

I stare at the clock and wonder if its hands could move any slower. The teacher comes in and we automatically start running around the gym. That is our routine exercise. We only stop when the teacher blows his whistle, but he's really slow today. I wonder if he forgot to look at the time or if he's just torturing us on purpose. A little while longer and I might start hyperventilating. Finally, the shrill sound pierces the air.

We sit down in our squads as the gym teacher and his student instructors take attendance. Today is elective day. We have a choice between basketball and volleyball. I stand up and walk toward the cart of basketballs. I reach in and take a good, bouncy one. Suddenly, a pair of hands seizes the ball from me, and maniacal laughter sounds. I look up to see a big, scary sophomore girl. She grins evilly at me. "My ball!" she says. Her big, scary posse cackles.

I've seen lots of movies where the bullies pick on nerdy kids. I just never thought it would happen to me. I've always liked to think of myself as brave. Not daunted by anyone. So here's my chance. That girl stole my basketball. Am I just going to let her bully me like that? I take a deep breath. What am I supposed to do? Tell her off? Steal my ball back? Punch her in the face?

Talk about a slow reaction... the mean girl and her posse have already run off laughing before I even have a chance to do anything. By now, half the gym class has seen what happened. I feel like a horrible coward. I tell myself to think happy thoughts. Stay calm. Be like water. Don't let the ripples disturb you. I imagine myself punching that girl in the face. I feel a little better.

I'm dribbling another basketball. It is very flat and hardly bounces. I look up and I wonder if my eyes are deceiving me. That mean girl is running toward me. Maybe she's coming to apologize, beg for forgiveness. Suddenly, she comes up and grabs my basketball. Again. I clench my teeth. Enough is enough. The time has come for her to get what she deserves.

"Hey," I said. My brilliant comeback. "Stop!" She rolls her eyes psychotically at me and runs off to her friends, who are roaring with laughter. The other kids laugh, too.

I try not to cry. If I were someone else, someone who actually had courage, this would have turned out differently. Only a nerd would get pushed around like that.

Someone tugs at my arm. It is Sarah, my gym partner. Silently, she hands me another basketball. Gym class goes on. I survive it.

What happened in gym that day might not seem like a big deal. And no, it wasn't necessarily one of those crucial, life-changing moments. But I did learn something. I realized that no matter what kind of person you are, there are bound to be hard times in life when others are mean to you. No one is perfect; no one is immune to teasing and bullying. There are bound to be people bigger and tougher than you. It is how you deal with them that matters. When you learn to respect yourself, others will get the message to do the same.

Today, I'm a junior in high school. I don't think school is that bad anymore. The psycho girl and her gang have not given me any trouble since freshman year, and I hardly see them. I still wear my fuchsia gym pants. They've come a long way, and I've grown attached to them. I don't care what I look like or what I wear. I'm not embarrassed that I'm short, or that I don't have name-brand clothes, or that yes, sometimes I have acne flare-ups. Isn't that part of life? I realize that feeling self-conscious and pressured to fit in is not healthy at all. I have learned to be glad of who I am.

—Jean Huang
Chicken Soup for the Teenage Soul: The Real Deal School

17

Happiness from Within

Having been raised Catholic by parents who worked hard for every penny they earned, I was taught at an early age that money cannot buy happiness. As much as my parents and the church tried to teach me these values, I had to learn through my own experiences that happiness comes from within and cannot be measured by material possessions.

As a child, I would sit in church, trying to concentrate on the words of the priest, but my attention was soon diverted by the sparkle of the gold and diamonds worn by the Sunday churchgoers. As my eyes began to wander, I noticed men dressed in their tailored suits and monogrammed shirts, accompanied by women in their designer dresses with matching handbags and shoes.

My family, on the other hand, was the opposite of glamorous. Our hand-me-down clothes had been washed so many times that the colors had become dull and lifeless and the material frayed around the seams.

Although our clothes revealed the money struggles of our large family, our faces were always washed, our hair neatly combed, and we each tossed our twenty-five cents in the basket even when there was a second collection. As my family piled into our big green and white VW bus after the service, I fantasized about the glamorous lives led by those driving their brand new BMWs, wishing I were more like them.

I continued these fantasies when I was an adolescent attending

Catholic school. Since it was a private school, most of the children came from wealthy families. As a result, I constantly felt inferior to the rest of my classmates. Although I could hide my lack of wealth at school by wearing our mandated school uniforms, my poverty was embarrassingly apparent on weekends when my classmates wore designer jeans, and I had no choice but to wear my sister's outgrown jeans.

Once, because I could not afford a birthday gift, I gave one of my own used CDs to a friend in school. When she opened the gift, her face twisted into a strange look as if she did not know whether to laugh or say thank you. It was times like these, when the other kids laughed at me and talked behind my back, that convinced me that if I only had the new clothes, the nice house and other such material possessions, then maybe I would have a chance to fit in. Then I would be happy.

I began to believe so much in the material world that I started my first job when I was fourteen so that I could afford those "things" that were going to make me happy. Soon I was working two jobs in order to fulfill my needs. I began to purchase the clothes, the jewelry and the perfume. Each purchase was a sign of hope. Each time I thought, "This is it, this is really going to make me happy." Within a few days, sometimes as little as a few hours, that feeling of emptiness came over me again. I would dream bigger and set my goals higher to purchase something even better. Each time I thought it was going to be different, but it never was.

Unfortunately, it took many of these disappointing and painful experiences, not to mention the amount of money spent, for me to realize that what I admired in other people was not their clothes, their hairstyles or the cars they drove. It was their self-confidence. I admired the way they carried themselves, their ability to take on new challenges and the way they looked people in the eye during conversations instead of staring down at their toes as I often found myself doing. I began to notice that it was the qualities that they possessed inside themselves that I was lacking. I knew then that I would never be a complete person until I started to do some work on the inside.

There was no lightning bolt or voice from God that brought me to this realization. I had to go all the way down the wrong road in life to realize that I was headed in the wrong direction. As a result, I now possess those qualities that I had always admired in other people. Long gone are the days of remedying my problems with new clothes and makeup. I confess I still get caught up in the excitement of shopping sprees, but there is a difference today: I know each time I put on a new outfit and look in the mirror, the same person will be underneath it all. I now carry myself with an air of confidence, and I can look people in the eye, for I have no reason to look down.

—Dianna McGill
Chicken Soup for the Teenage Soul III

18

Why I Have to Take U.S. History Again

I think of myself as an intelligent, sensitive human being with the soul of a clown, which always forces me to blow it at the most important moments.
—Jim Morrison

What was I thinking? Why couldn't I have left well enough alone? Stupid, stupid Valentine's Day. I had to write that dumb poem, and I had to go and put it in Lisa's locker. Why do they have those vents on lockers anyway? What needs to breathe in your locker? I don't keep puppies in my locker, and I don't know anyone who does. And my textbooks are just as stale as ever, with or without air. But they have to put those vents on, just big enough to stick a stupid valentine with a stupid poem inside.

It all started at the beginning of last year in U.S. History class. I was walking into class with my friend Dave, minding my own business, talking about some play in some game that we both watched the night before, when I saw something bright out of the corner of my eye. I looked over. Actually, it wasn't a bright spot at all, but a head of brilliant blond hair. Beneath that hair were two amazing, beautiful blue eyes. I didn't know it then, but that moment was the beginning of the end for my chance of a good grade in U.S. History.

I spent the next twelve weeks staring at that beautiful head (or at least the back of it). Seating was alphabetical, but I was fortunate enough to be three rows back and four seats over from Lisa so that if

I stretched my neck in just the right way, I could see that head. When the bell rang, I would try to get up at just the right time so that I could bump into her or catch her glance as she left the room. I'm sure Mr. Houston, our teacher, must have given his lecture every day, but all I can remember is something-something Appamatox and something-something Battle of the Bulge (although that last one might have been from *Saving Private Ryan*).

We broke for the holidays, and all I could think about was Lisa. I would go play video games or hang out at the mall and hope to see her. Surely Lisa shopped at the Gap. Maybe I'd see here there. I think I once heard her say she liked movies. Maybe I'd catch her at the movie theater. I saw a girl at the mall that I thought I once saw talking to Lisa at school so I followed her around for about twenty minutes, but it turned out she was with her mom and she looked at me like I was a little creepy, so I gave that up.

So anyway, the next semester started. Lisa never made her move, and so I somehow decided it was a good idea to write a stupid poem and put it in Lisa's locker, through those evil vents. I knew when Lisa's next class got out, and I somehow got a hall pass so I could sneak out of my class early and position myself at the wall around the corner from her locker before she did. My plan worked, and I was there in time to see Lisa open her locker. The bright red envelope came flying out and nearly poked her in the eye. It hit the ground, and Tyler Coleman picked it up.

"What's this?" he asked. "Did someone send you a valentine? Who's your boyfriend?" Lisa's friends suddenly gathered around. Tyler opened the envelope and began to read my poem.

Dear Lisa:

You may not know much about me
So I'm sending you this little plea
Today is Valentine's Day
And I have something to say

I have admired you from afar
I wish I had a car
So I could take you out on a date
To the movies or maybe to roller skate

Because I think you are cool
The best in our dumb school
So please hear what I have to say
It's really important, okay?

The words resonated in my head, each one striking me with the force of a sledge hammer. And there was my name at the bottom of the page—for all the world to see! What was I thinking? Everyone laughed. The force of their laughter caused me to move, ever so slightly, and someone noticed me. I had nowhere to run and had to walk past them all on my way to my next class: U.S. History. They saw me.

"Look, Lisa, it's your boyfriend." "Why don't you give him a big kiss?" "Hey, superdweeb, come over here and give your girlfriend a big old kiss."

Tyler grabbed my arm and tried to shove me toward Lisa. She turned away with a look as though someone had just shoved dog poop in her face. I think I turned a new color of red that's not even available in the Crayola 64 box of crayons. All I could hear was the laughing. Other kids started coming around to see what was so funny, and Tyler handed over the card so they could pass it around. I tried to move, but Tyler had a firm grip on my arm. How could this possibly get any worse?

I looked to Lisa for some support, some sign that she wasn't part of this ugly mob. But her expression had changed from a look of disgust to laughter, too. She had joined in with the rest. This was clearly the single worst event of my entire life.

If I was distracted in U.S. History before, now multiply that by ten. I couldn't even look at the back of Lisa's head because everyone was looking at me to see if I was looking at the back of Lisa's head. I could only wallow in self-pity. The whole rest of the year I was either Lisa's boyfriend or superdweeb. Everyone forgot my name.

That day, I went home and tried to hide under the covers of my bed. My mother came in and asked me what was wrong. I couldn't possibly tell her. But I had to tell someone.

She eventually managed to get the story out of me. I told her everything—about Lisa, the blond hair, the blue eyes, the attempts to accidentally bump into her, the staring contest and, finally, the evil locker slots and how they forced me to put that card with the poem inside.

She just looked at me and smiled. She smiled. She didn't laugh; she didn't cry. She didn't pat me on the head and tell me everything was going to be okay. She didn't try to turn the whole experience into some kind of lesson. She didn't scold me, and she didn't compliment me. She just smiled.

At first I thought maybe she was possessed, or maybe she had been cooking with wine again. But then she took my hand and asked me a question: "If you could go back and do it again, what would you have done differently?" I thought about it. I could have not stared at Lisa's big, blond head. I could have not tried to bump into her. I could have not put that card in her locker. Sure, I could have avoided the whole ugly mess, and people would still remember my first name.

"And so then where would you be?" my mom asked. I'd be a happy, anonymous ninth grader. "Is that how you think of yourself?" she asked. How did I think of myself? Right then, I didn't think much of myself. I felt like a big loser. She must have known.

"You aren't a loser. How do you think any boy ever got to meet any girl? By hiding in the corner? By letting boys like Tyler decide who you can like and who you can't? In my opinion, this is Lisa's big loss. I think your poem is sweet."

She said all that because that's what mothers are supposed to say. I knew that. And I still felt bad, but I started to see things from her point of view. How could I have not taken the chance? In that moment when I put the card in Lisa's locker, I had felt brave and adventurous and strong. How dare they laugh at me? I had dared to take my shot.

That moment didn't last very long because the next day I got my report card, and it turned out I failed U.S. History. So now I have to go to summer school. But it's okay, because there's this new girl, Carolyn, who just transferred in and she has to go to summer school, too, and you should see the back of her head....

—Tal Vigderson
Chicken Soup for the Teenage Soul on Tough Stuff

The Party That Lasted a Lifetime

"It's just a party," Alicia said. "Come on, it'll be fun."

I was both panicked and excited by my cousin's words. My parents had gone to Europe on vacation for two weeks that summer, and I was thrilled at the opportunity to stay with my Aunt Sarah and my favorite cousin, Alicia. I absolutely idolized Alicia, who was everything I wanted to be—seventeen years old, athletic, a popular cheerleader and beautiful.

"Sure, I'm cool with that," I said. I was honored that she wanted me to go with her, even though I knew my parents wouldn't approve of me going, since I had only just turned fourteen.

"What do we tell your mom?" I asked, hoping I sounded like I really didn't care.

"We'll just tell her we are going to the movies with some of my friends." Alicia started talking about the party and who was going to be there, as she stood in her closet and began throwing out some of her clothes for me to try on.

"Okay, we need two outfits, one for Mom to see us leaving in—and the other to change into for the party. Pick out what you want to borrow, and I'll help you get ready. We can do your makeup in the car," Alicia said while we tried on a dozen different outfits. My emotions seesawed between not believing my good luck and being nervous. I wondered what a high school party would actually be like.

I had been to boy/girl parties before, and I had even made out with Joey Razzone in the back of the skating rink, but that was all junior high stuff. This was a high school party. The thing I was most worried about was that everyone would think I was just a stupid little kid.

"Alicia, everyone's going to know I'm barely fourteen," I whined, while trying my favorite outfit on again. It was a lime green tank top (not very well filled out) and a blue jean miniskirt Alicia had decided against wearing, with a pair of white sandals.

"No, they won't... here...," Alicia responded as she tossed me one of her strapless bras and a box of Kleenex.

"Oh my gosh, Alicia, I can't do that!" I said.

"Why not?" she answered as she shoved a few tissues in her own bra. Then she crammed our party clothes, makeup, hair spray and a brush into her bag. "All right, little cousin, it's time to go!"

I felt a small pang of panic. I was going to my first high school party, and Alicia wouldn't dare take me with her if she thought I would embarrass her—right?

We parked Alicia's Honda down the street from the house where the party was. Real butterflies had started in the pit of my stomach. Don't you dare throw up, I scolded myself. Ugh, I thought, how did I get into this?

"Let's go!" Alicia said excitedly, after we had changed our outfits and completed our makeup. I followed her from the car. "Don't forget to smile," I kept repeating to myself. I don't really know why I felt that was so important—maybe I didn't want anyone to notice how scared I was, but more likely it was because Alicia's smile seemed to be cemented on her face.

As we walked up the sidewalk toward the house, I noticed small groups of people on the front lawn. They were all laughing and talking, and most had a beer in their hand. I heard music coming from inside the house, and I looked over at Alicia, who didn't appear to be nervous at all.

"Cory! Hey, how's it going?" she yelled across the lawn to a group of guys in football jerseys.

"Hey, Alicia!" the boy shouted, as my cousin bounced across the yard.

"Leigh! Over here!" Alicia called. I walked over to where my cousin was standing with the group of older-looking boys—men almost. I couldn't believe this is what the boys at my school were going to grow into. Alicia introduced me to Cory and the others, and although they really didn't include me in their conversation, thankfully, they didn't laugh at me either. Maybe this won't be so bad, I thought.

After a while in the front yard, we made our way into the house. It was packed with people. The sound system was on full volume. There were groups of teenagers everywhere—most drinking, some kissing and quite a few doing both. I was amazed. This was not like any boy/girl party I had been to before.

Everywhere I went, I was offered a beer that I didn't want, and when I refused it, whoever I was talking to would just shrug, turn around and walk off. No matter how hard I tried to fit in, I kept finding myself alone, and after a few hours, I was very ready to go home. Finally, I walked up to Alicia, who was talking to a boy, and said quietly, "Alicia, I'm ready to go." I didn't really want to be a pain in the you-know-what, but I was tired and not enjoying myself at all.

"Who's this?" Cory asked, nodding his head in my general direction.

"It's my cousin, Leigh. You met her earlier," Alicia answered, never taking her eyes off Cory.

"Well, make her go away," he snapped, as he started kissing Alicia right in front of me.

Devastated, I didn't even wait for Alicia's response. I just turned and quickly walked away. I felt tears welling up in my eyes and didn't want anyone at the party to see me cry—especially Alicia. I felt so alone and stupid. I was embarrassed about coming to the party in the first place, much less letting those idiots get to me. I walked as fast as I could to the bathroom, then closed and locked the door.

The first thing I did was look in the mirror. I was so disgusted with myself for the way I looked. As my tears fell, the mascara Alicia had caked on my eyelashes was now thick, black streaks on my face. My hair was a huge blob of hairspray, and—thanks to the tissues— my breasts were two times larger than they should have been. I didn't look like a seventeen-year-old—I just looked like a clown. I stood there, staring at my awful reflection and cried for what seemed a really long time. Then I started scrubbing. I washed all the makeup off my face and found a brush in the medicine cabinet to brush out my hair. I took the wads of tissues out of my bra, threw them in the toilet and triumphantly flushed. I regretted the tank top and miniskirt now too, and I wanted to go get my other clothes in the car, but I didn't want to have to interrupt Alicia again to ask for the keys.

When I finally felt presentable—and more like me—I left the bathroom. My face was a little puffy from the tears, but that was okay. I knew I couldn't look any worse than I had looked all night long. I found a comfy spot on the couch and sat down to wait. Alicia had disappeared somewhere with Cory, and I didn't know where she was. I sat there for a long time, hoping I was really as invisible as I felt.

"Hey, are you okay?" came out of nowhere. I looked up, and there was a boy standing in front of me. His blue eyes seemed to plead with me to ask him to sit down.

"Yeah, fine… you?" I managed nervously. I was shocked that someone was actually talking to me, and truthfully I was slightly disappointed that my invisibility had worn off.

"Can I please sit down?" he asked, while fidgeting with his hands in his pockets. He looks harmless, I thought.

"Sure." This was really not going well. Conversation seemed so easy for Alicia, why couldn't I squeak out more than one word at a time?

"So, what's your name and how do you know Brian?" The boy was staring straight into my eyes now. Does he know I've been crying? Is this some sort of pity chat?

"Who's Brian?" I asked, trying to sound as cool as I could.

"The guy who lives in this house, dummy!" he began to chuckle. "What's your name, anyway?"

"I'm here with my cousin, Alicia, who has left me alone for the millionth time tonight. I don't know anyone here, and for your information, I'm not a dummy," I said defiantly, now somewhat angry at him for laughing at me.

"I didn't mean that! I'm sorry if I hurt your feelings. I was just trying to lighten you up, girl. My name is Anthony; it's nice to meet you," he said, and as he sat down, he flashed a brilliant smile and stuck his hand out toward mine. Wow, he's kind of cute, I thought.

I reluctantly put my hand into his. When I could, I finally spoke, "My name is Leigh... nice to meet you, too." My face was blazing red now, and my heart was pounding so loud I was afraid he could hear it.

"Leigh, that's a really pretty name," he said as he gently squeezed my hand before letting it go.

Anthony and I sat and talked on the couch for a while. I was starting to feel a little more comfortable. I was happy to be talking to Anthony. He was fifteen, a freshman at my cousin's school and played drums in the high school band. His older brother was Brian, so this was his house, too. He hardly knew anyone either—these were all Brian's friends—and he was pretty upset that his brother was having this party while their parents were out of town.

"I'm going to the kitchen. Want a beer?" Anthony asked.

"No, thanks, I don't drink," I mumbled, praying this wouldn't be the wrong answer.

"That's cool... me neither! How about a Coke?" he asked, as he got up from the couch. Miraculously, he was back in just a few minutes with two cans of soda pop. I had truly expected him to take advantage of this perfect escape.

"Where's your cousin, anyway?" he asked as he took a big gulp of his soda. I just stared at him—he really was cute.

I suddenly realized I didn't care at all where Alicia was. I was finally having a good time in my own element and, most important, acting my own age—not hers. I had spent so much time trying hard to walk in her footsteps (and fill her bra) that it had been hard for me to even think about walking in my own. In that one night, my wise and gentle friend Anthony taught me a lesson that some people need a lifetime to learn: Just being yourself is the best you can ever hope to be.

—Leigh Hughes
Chicken Soup for the Girl's Soul

Image Isn't Everything

Decorate yourself from the inside out.
—Andrei Turnhollow

On the first day of school, after I got out of my mom's car and mumbled a goodbye, I stared in awe at the huge buildings that seemed to tower over my head. This high school was definitely bigger than the one I had previously attended. Over the summer I moved from Midland, Texas, to St. Louis, Missouri. I had lived in Midland all my life, until the move.

This was my second year of high school, but my first year of school in St. Louis. I was really nervous about starting a new school and having people like me. I had decided the night before, while lying in my bed trying to fall asleep, that I would be much happier in a new school if I made friends that were so-called "popular." Getting in with the right group of people would make my life a whole lot better.

I had to project the right image to the people at this school. I didn't care how much money it cost, I was determined to buy an outfit everyone else would want to have. I bought a new outfit, new makeup, got a manicure and had my hair styled just so the first day would be perfect. I had the chance to start over in a new school, make new friends and build an image for myself. I wasn't going to waste this opportunity.

Scared, yet anxious to begin my new life, I walked up the stairs to the front door. The halls were packed with kids yelling and laughing and telling stories of their summer adventures. I found my way to the main office where I was to receive my schedule and fill out forms. I was on my way. My first class was geometry, but where was that?

I was standing in the hall looking confused, when a short, blond girl wearing glasses came up and asked, "Are you new? You look lost. Do you want me to help you find your class? My name is Diane. What's yours?" Even though she seemed a bit strange, definitely not the kind of person I wanted to be associated with, I decided to answer her anyway. I was, after all, lost.

After exchanging names, I followed her up the stairs and down a hallway on the right, making polite conversation the whole way.

When we reached my room she said, "Well, here you are. It was nice meeting you. I hope I see you again. Welcome to JFK, and I hope your day goes all right."

I said thanks and waved goodbye. Once inside the classroom, I saw one big group of people huddled around someone who seemed to be telling some sort of story. I walked over and got close enough to overhear. All eyes were glued to the guy in the middle of the circle who was wearing a letter jacket covered with patches. I decided that this guy was popular. He was talking about how he and some of his friends had gone up to someone's ranch outside of St. Louis and done some pretty wild and crazy things. A few minutes later the teacher told everyone to break it up and go find a seat. I managed to get one right next to the guy wearing the letter jacket. I said, "Hi, my name is April and I'm new here." He said, "Hi, I'm Johnny."

That class dragged on and on. Finally the bell rang. I turned to him and asked, "I'm not sure where my next class is, could you help me find it?" He looked at me and then said a quick no, turned back to his friends, and walked out of the classroom. As they were walking out I heard him say, "Did you guys see that new girl trying to get into our group? That outfit was way too weird." They all laughed and some of them turned around and stared at me. I slowly gathered my stuff, not believing what had just happened. I walked out of the classroom and found my next class, bewildered that I could have cared so much.

The same type of thing happened all day in all of my classes. At lunch, I ended up sitting by myself because I had snubbed people who had been nice to me and I had been snubbed by people who I had tried to be nice to. I didn't realize it then, but I had been really shallow just wanting to be friends with popular people.

Finally, sixth period came around and I was ready to go home and never come back. Before class started, someone came up behind me and said, "Hi, again. How was your first day?" It was that same girl who had showed me to my first class.

I told her my day had not been so great. She said she was sorry and offered to walk me outside. At that moment I realized how wrong I was in wanting to only be friends with popular people. Those people weren't even going to consider being my friends, but there were some other people who I'd already met today and liked and they liked me.

Maybe I shouldn't decide whether a person is worth being my friend or not by their reputation, but by who they are. I said, "Thanks, I'd like that. I'm sorry I was kind of rude this morning." She said it was okay, she was new at school once, too. Walking with Diane made me realize how nice it would be to have a friend like her. On the way to class she asked me if I wanted to go out after school to hang out with some of her friends and get to know them better. I did go out with Diane and had a lot of fun.

As time went on I made friends with lots of different people, some of them from "the popular crowd" and some not. My standards were different though. The people I sought out for friends were the nice ones—period.

—Jamie Shockley
Chicken Soup for the Teenage Soul II

What One Boy Can Show a Girl

I was never fat nor was I ever skinny. I always had some meat on my bones, which made me look healthy, not scrawny. But when I entered middle school, the first thing I pointed out to myself was how fat I was.

I came from a small elementary school, where no one wore name-brand clothes and everyone liked to have fun regardless of how they looked. We were not worried about guys or what other people thought of us; we were merely being kids. So middle school was a shock to me. There were so many different groups to hang out with. There was one that was considered "bad," one with girls whose moms still dressed them, one that was really smart, and the one that required name-brand clothes and lots of makeup. Of course I wanted to be cool, have the boyfriends and be a part of the in-crowd.

I would only wear my name-brand clothes, which meant my wardrobe consisted of two pairs of jeans and four shirts. I begged my parents to let me wear makeup, but they wouldn't budge. I tried to hang around the popular girls and win them over by complimenting them on their clothes and looks, but they just looked past me and pretended I wasn't there.

My self-confidence dwindled. I gave up on my popularity quest and soon found myself back with my friends from my previous school. They were great. They were there for me and liked me for me, but I still didn't like myself. I thought I was fat, and no one could convince me that I wasn't. At the beach when all my friends would be playing volleyball in their bathing suits, I would be in my clothes. When we went swimming, I would make sure I had shorts on over my bathing suit bottoms to cover up my thighs. I was no fun to hang around because I was constantly worried about how fat I looked.

At the start of eighth grade I was faced with another issue: boys. I became interested in them and even had middle school boyfriends. But now not only did I worry about how fat I looked, I worried about everything else that went along with my appearance. I became so consumed with my looks that nothing else seemed to matter. Wherever there was a mirror, I was there fixing my hair. Wherever there was a scale, I was weighing myself to see if I had lost any weight. I wasn't worried about grades, family and homework—only me. The world revolved around me and my appearance. My parents were concerned about how I was acting. I was not confident in my body, and it showed.

On the last day of school, my class was to take a trip to a local water park. I cringed at the prospect of having to walk around and stand in lines in just my swimsuit. I wouldn't even do that in front of my friends, much less all the guys and other girls in my school. I was dreading it, but I couldn't miss the last class trip. And I'm glad I didn't.

With the help of one very special person, Adam, I was able to open my eyes and see what I had not been able to see for so long. Adam was what all the girls considered a "major hunk." Blond hair, blue eyes and a great body. So you can imagine my surprise when he asked if he could hang out with me and go on all the rides together. Things like that just didn't happen to me, so I was thrilled, to say the least.

We had a blast together. At first I was noticeably uncomfortable with just my two-piece on, but after I realized that Adam wasn't gawking over how "fat" my thighs were or how "big" my butt was, I settled into my skin. For the first time in nearly two years, I was beginning to feel comfortable with my body. Being with Adam gave me the confidence I needed to start appreciating and accepting myself.

The next day, as I was looking through a picture album, I questioned why Adam wanted to hang out with me when he could have spent the day following one of the popular blond girls parading around in her skimpy bikini. Then I spotted a recent picture of a friend and me at school. I looked closely at the picture and studied how I looked. I discovered that my butt wasn't that big and my thighs weren't really that huge. I had always compared myself to girls with other body types, and that only left me feeling sorry for myself.

I turned the page and found a picture of my mom when she was in high school. It's one of my favorite pictures because she looks so pretty. I cherish the picture because my mom died of brain cancer when I was in grade school. I compared the picture of my mom with the picture of my friend and me, and the resemblance shocked me. I had always been told that we looked so much alike, but I never really realized it until then. We share the same thick brown hair, the same body structure and the same facial features. I realized that if I can't be skinny and tall like a model, then at least I can look like one of the most beautiful people I know: my mother.

—Sarah Erdmann
Chicken Soup for the Teenage Soul IV

Whatever I Want to Be

Dear Chicken Soup,

My name is Renee Tanner. I am fifteen years old and an interracial child. My father is black, and my mother is white. I do not consider myself either black or white. I won't even say that I am mixed. I like to define myself as me, for skin color is really of little importance. It is part of the exterior, not the interior. I believe that what matters most is what's inside your heart, not what color skin you have. However, I have not always felt this way.

From the age of six, I did what every kid did. I went to school and learned, came home, played and just had fun. But there was something inside me that was never quite right. I never felt complete. I felt different in a way. It didn't really affect me until I was older. As time passed, it became harder and harder to just be me.

All through elementary school my best friends were white. The kids at my school seemed as if they did not know that I was both black and white. But once I got into seventh grade I realized that I was different because some of the black kids at my school started to make fun of me, I think because I wasn't entirely black. Also, some of the white kids from the other elementary schools looked at me in a weird sort of way. I was an outcast to them. My best friends never knew how upset I was, because I couldn't tell them. I knew they wouldn't understand. One day I was crying hysterically, and I called a friend of mine. I told her that I didn't fit in. That nobody understood me. And nobody would ever understand me. I said that I was different and that it was impossible for me to just be me. She asked me where I had come up with all of this. I told her that my mother was white and my father was black and I didn't know what I was. Was I mixed? Was I black? Was I white? I didn't know.

She said to me, "Renee, you are Renee Elizabeth Tanner. That is who you are. You are everything and anything you want to be." I didn't believe her, but she kept trying to tell me that it didn't matter what I looked like. However, it didn't work, and I continued to believe that I was different.

I couldn't talk to the black people at school, for I was not fully black, and I couldn't talk to the white people because I was not fully white. It hurt inside to not know who I was, to not be able to fit into a perfect category. For almost a year I cried every night. I wrote poems and stories. I kept everything either inside or on paper. Never once did my friends know how much pain I was in. And some of them still don't know.

One day after crying for hours, I picked up the book my mother had given to me for my birthday, *Chicken Soup for the Teenage Soul*. I began to read it, hoping that it would lift my spirits. Not even ten minutes into the book, I stopped crying. By the time I had finished, I felt something incredible. I felt a sense of belonging. I called my friend again and told her that I no longer felt so alone. Again she said, "Renee, you are whatever you want to be." Finally it hit me.

After all those years of feeling different, I finally came to terms with who I am. My name is Renee Tanner. My parents are black and white. And I, well, I am both of them. I no longer care what color my skin is, or whether black or white people talk to me. The people who are my friends don't care what I look like.

Sincerely,
—Renee Tanner
Chicken Soup for the Teenage Soul Letters

Teens Talk
Growing Up

Accepting Others

It takes courage to grow up and become who you really are.
—E. E. Cummings

Answering Critics

23

An A for Mrs. B

What we see depends mainly on what we look for.
—John Lubbock

I was sitting next to Missy in my ninth grade world history class when Mrs. Bartlett announced a new project. In groups, we were to create a newspaper around the culture we were studying.

On a piece of paper, we wrote the names of three friends we wanted in our group. After collecting all the requests, Mrs. B. informed us that she would take into consideration the names we chose and would let us know the results the next day. I had no doubt I would get the group of my choice. There were only a handful of sociably decent people in the class, and Missy was one of them. I knew we had chosen each other.

The next day, I anxiously awaited the class. After the bell rang, Missy and I stopped talking as Mrs. B called for our attention. She started to call out names. When she reached group three, Missy's name was called. So I'm in group three, I thought. The second, third and fourth members of the group were called. My name was not included. There had to be some mistake!

Then I heard it. The last group: "Mauro, Juliette, Rachel, Karina." I could feel the tears well in my eyes. How could I face being in that group—the boy who barely spoke English, the one girl who was always covered by skirts that went down to her ankles, and the other girl who wore weird clothes. Oh, how badly I wanted to be with my friends.

I fought back tears as I walked up to Mrs. B. She looked at me and knew what I was there for. I was determined to convince her I should be in the "good" group. "Why...?" I started.

She gently placed a hand on my shoulder. "I know what you want, Karina," she said, "but your group needs you. I need you to help them get a passing grade on this assignment. Only you can help them."

I was stunned. I was humbled. I was amazed. She had seen something in me I hadn't seen.

"Will you help them?" she asked.

I stood straighter. "Yes," I replied. I couldn't believe it came out of my mouth, but it did. I had committed.

As I bravely walked to where the others in my group sat, I could hear the laughter from my friends. I sat down and we started. Different newspaper columns were assigned according to interests. We did research. Halfway through the week, I felt myself enjoying the company of these three misfits. There was no need for pretending—I grew sincerely interested in learning something about them.

Mauro, I found out, was struggling with the English language and his lack of friends. Juliette was also alone, because people didn't understand that she was only allowed to wear long skirts or dresses because of her religion. Rachel, who had requested to do the fashion column, wanted to be a fashion designer. She had a whole barrel of unique ideas. What a walk in another person's shoes did for me! They weren't misfits, just people that no one cared enough about to try to understand—except Mrs. B. Her insight, vision and thoughtfulness brought out the potential in four of her students.

I don't recall what the newspaper's headline was or even the culture we wrote about, but I did learn something that week. I was given a chance to see other people in a new light. I was given the opportunity to see in myself a potential that inspired my actions in later years. I learned that who we are is more important than what we are or seem to be.

After that semester ended, I always received a friendly hello from my group. And I was always genuinely happy to see them.

Mrs. B gave us an A on that assignment. We should have handed it right back, for she was the one who truly deserved it.

—Karina Snow
Chicken Soup for the Teenage Soul II

24

The Slam Book

*You can tell more about a person by what he says about others
than you can by what others say about him.*
—Leo Aikman

I stared at the page so hard I thought my eyes would pop out. There was my name, and scrawled right underneath it the words "The Mop." My heart pounded, my face and ears burned red hot. I wanted to run, hide, anything to get away from the destructive words of this cruel creation by some of my classmates. They called it the "Slam" book.

I couldn't imagine anything worse than being thirteen, living in a new town, going to a new school, trying to make new friends and then having some unknown person write this in a book for everybody to read.

I'd watched during math class as the black book circulated from desk to desk. Each time the teacher turned toward the blackboard, the book was swiftly passed to the next person and hidden until it could be opened, read and written in. When it landed on my desk, I opened it and saw the vicious anonymous comments scribbled across each page.

Who are these people? Why would someone say these things? "Barbara—The Mop." I'd only been at the school a month. I didn't even know them. My fragile confidence was shattered. I'd tried to make new friends, but it hadn't been easy. It was a small town, and they'd all known each other for years. I wondered, Will I ever fit in?

I turned the pages to other names. Amanda, "conceited, big lips, hairy eyebrows." I thought she was nice and even pretty. Courtney, "witch's pointed nose, thick glasses." I was just getting to know Courtney. She lived around the corner from me, and we walked to school some mornings. She was kind to me and had a good sense of humor.

I hated school for the next few days and did whatever I could to not be noticed. But that didn't last long. It couldn't. The vicious book kept circulating and gathering more anonymous slander. Somehow I knew the cycle had to be stopped—but how? Determining right from wrong is usually not all that difficult. The scary part is doing it, and I had to dig deep to muster my courage. I wasn't all that brave.

I didn't tell the teachers or rant and rave at the students, although I wanted to scream at a few. Instead, I did the only thing I could do—I refused to participate.

"No," I stammered, pulse racing. "I won't read it, and I won't write in it," I said the next time the book came my way. The boys mocked anyone, especially a newcomer, who refused to participate. Standing alone against them took all the courage I had, at a time when I needed friends.

Suddenly, I noticed other girls saying no, and one even ripped out the page with her name on it. Finally, when all the girls refused and there wasn't an audience, the book faded away into oblivion. The old saying, "If you extinguish the reward, you extinguish the behavior" proved true. We eliminated the reward.

There was, however, another lesson I learned from this experience—one that proved more valuable than just affirming right from wrong. I learned to make up my own mind about people. I learned to understand and welcome their differences, to not accept someone else's shallow criticisms or petty observations, but to see people for who they really are.

Amanda was proud of her full mouth, thick dark eyebrows and olive skin, all of which were beautiful attributes of her Italian heritage.

Courtney's poor vision didn't diminish her wit and intelligence. She made me laugh, and eventually we became best friends.

And as for me; I learned to laugh when "The Mop" stayed with me as a nickname. I looked at my tangle of naturally curly hair that wanted to go its own way and eventually came to love it. It wasn't going to be tamed, and neither was I.

The "Slam" book showed up another year, but its history was short lived, and its impact minimal. The girls refused to be intimidated, refused to participate, and the reward was once again extinguished.

—Barbara J. Ragsdale
Chicken Soup for the Girl's Soul

My Best Friend Mike

A friend is one of the nicest things you can have,
and one of the best things you can be.
—Douglas Pagels

"Hi. It's Mike..."

"Hi, Mike, what's the matter?" Mike had been going through a lot lately, and it was not unusual for him to sound upset.

"I need to tell you something, but I'm not sure if I should," he said. Curiosity got the best of me, and I convinced him to let me in on his big secret. "I can't tell you on the phone. Come over." I walked for five minutes around the block, rang his doorbell and followed his mother's instructions to go up to his room.

Mike had been my best friend for the past two years. At first I thought he was weird. We met during our freshman year of high school and soon became inseparable. The summer after that year was the highlight of our friendship. I never had more fun with any other person. We spent every night and every day together. Time flies when you are having fun, however, and we soon found ourselves back in school. I began to notice a change in Mike. The fun ceased, and I felt a strain in our friendship.

Mike was suffering from depression, and I could not understand why. He seemed to have everything going for him. He was doing well in school, there were no problems at home, and he had many friends who loved him. I soon found myself spending every weekend in his bedroom, trying to convince him to cheer up. Nothing seemed to work. His parents became worried and decided to seek professional help.

Mike began to take medication to counteract his depression, and things seemed a little better, but they were not what they used to be. I was still clueless as to what had been causing this change in his behavior. I did not want to give up on my true best friend, so I continued spending painful hours trying to drag him out of his house.

It was one of those weekends, and there I was, sitting on his bed, waiting to hear what he had to say. I had a sense that he was about to tell me something serious. There was a strange look in his eyes, and he would not focus them on me. The silence was overbearing. He finally looked up at me.

"I'm gay." It hit me like a bolt of lightning. I was shocked. "Okay" was all I managed to utter. Silence followed for minutes afterward.

It took some getting used to, but I decided right then and there that I was not going to lose my best friend over it. Mike seems to be back to his normal self these days. We're seniors now, and I still spend a large portion of my time with him and his friends.

A smile comes to my face every time I think back to the first day we met, and the first thought that came to my mind as I approached the bus stop that day: Who is that weird kid? That weird kid is my true best friend, Mike, and there is nothing weird about him.

—Brian Leykum
Chicken Soup for the Teenage Soul III

Chicken Soup for the Soul

The Dark Gift

he look on her face was one of numb disbelief. "It can't be," she says. "Why me? Why now?"

"It's not as bad as you're making it out to be," I said to my good friend Alex, as she sat there staring vacantly at the heavy cast on her leg. One moment she was running about, preparing for college, worrying about books, her car and which classes to take. Now, she was sitting here with a broken ankle. It all happened so suddenly.

This was the first time Alex had collided with an indifferent world. Everything else had been negotiable, arguable. Everything else up to now could be avoided, escaped, bought off, laughed away.

I tried to comfort her and tell her it would be all right. But this was real; this was hers. No one could change it, make it right, make it fair. It was life—an absolute without explanation—that was indifferent to her plans and dreams.

"My life is ruined," she sighed, feeling utterly depressed.

"No, your life isn't ruined. Just consider this one of those dark gifts. A bad circumstance can teach you something valuable, maybe even change your life."

Suddenly, I remembered the time several years ago when I, too, had broken an ankle. It was March. The streets were slushy paths, and corners were precarious hard-packed trails, through mounds of ice and snow. I struggled on crutches, trying to balance on uneven surfaces of ice. People pushed past me, muttering about how they had to get through, about how I was taking so long. I tried gingerly to make my way up over the snowpack without slipping or letting my cast drag in the slush. My arms ached from the tension, my shoulders were rigid and numb from the digging pain of the crutches. I tried to block out the others around me, not to feel them brushing brusquely past me.

Crutch by crutch, I made my way down to the street. Cars flew by, splashing slush on my cast. I hobbled into the street. The approaching cars were not slowing. I tried to hurry, but the icy ground was too precarious. Cars slid to a stop, and drivers leaned on their horns. I was consumed with my own fragile balance, ashamed of my deliberate pace, frustrated at others' lack of concern.

I looked across at the snow bank I would have to negotiate on the opposite side of the street. There, making her way down through the small uneven pathway of ice, was an old woman with a cane. People were standing behind her muttering. She was feeling with her foot, trying to find solid ground. No one could help her; there was not enough room for two abreast. I saw her frantic look, her shaking hands. Then, for an instant, she looked up. Across the distance of that icy, slush-filled street, our eyes met. The fear, the sadness, the frustration, the utter aloneness of our respective plights, were mirrored in our respective gazes.

I wanted to help her, but I could not. I could barely make my way across the street myself. The other pedestrians rushing past us were no help either. To them we were impediments to the necessary pace of daily living. To the drivers in the long line of cars that was backing up in the street, we were insufferable obstructions. We approached each other from opposite directions. As we passed, we glanced at each other.

"Hi," I said, not knowing what else to say.

She, who had the added fear of being elderly and alone on a city street, did not know whether to answer. Finally, she said, very softly, "Hello." Cars honked at the further slowing of pace that had been caused by our brief conversation. Other walkers brushed against us in their rush to get to the other side.

We looked again at each other, then went on. The cars revved and drove past in anger as soon as we were out of their path.

When I got to the other side, I turned to see how the woman was doing. She was feeling for the path through the snow with her cane. When she found her footing, she stopped as if she had accomplished a huge feat. She turned to look at me, and she smiled a sweet and tender smile. She knew I understood. For a moment she didn't feel so alone, and neither did I.

I wanted to tell Alex this story. But she was lost in her own world. I watched her as she put her backpack on and moved on unsteady crutches down the hallway. She had an evening class that she had to attend. "I never knew that doorknobs could be so much work," she said as she balanced on one leg and tried to open the door.

"Steps, revolving doors, taking baths, crossing streets. You've got a lot of fun ahead of you," I said. "But make sure to keep your eyes open for those dark gifts. They will be some of the best lessons you will ever be fortunate enough to learn."

Her pack slipped off her shoulder and almost pulled her over. I wanted to help her. But there was nothing I could do. "I'll never make fun of old people again," she said.

With that, I remembered the sweet smile of that woman. "Neither will I."

—Kent Nerburn
Chicken Soup for the College Soul

A Lesson for Life

I don't like that man. I must get to know him better.
—Abraham Lincoln

"Look at fatso!"

Freshmen in high school can be cruel and we certainly were to a young man named Matt who was in my class. We mimicked him, teased him and taunted him about his size. He was at least fifty pounds overweight. He felt the pain of being the last one picked to play basketball, baseball or football. Matt will always remember the endless pranks that were played on him—trashing his hall locker, piling library books on his desk at lunchtime and spraying him with icy streams of water in the shower after gym class.

One day he sat near me in gym class. Someone pushed him and he fell on me and banged my foot quite badly. The kid who pushed him said Matt did it. With the whole class watching, I was put on the spot to either shrug it off or pick a fight with Matt. I chose to fight in order to keep my image intact.

I shouted, "C'mon, Matt, let's fight!" He said he didn't want to. But peer pressure forced him into the conflict whether he liked it or not. He came toward me with his fists in the air. He was no George Foreman. With one punch I bloodied his nose and the class went wild. Just then the gym teacher walked into the room. He saw that we were fighting and he sent us out to the oval running track.

He followed us with a smile on his face and said, "I want you two guys to go out there and run that mile holding each other's hands." The room erupted into a roar of laughter. The two of us were embarrassed beyond belief, but Matt and I went out to the track and ran our mile—hand in hand.

At some point during the course of our run, I remember looking over at him, with blood still trickling from his nose and his weight slowing him down. It struck me that here was a person, not all that different from myself. We both looked at each other and began to laugh. In time we became good friends.

Going around that track, hand in hand, I no longer saw Matt as fat or dumb. He was a human being who had intrinsic value and worth far beyond any externals. It was amazing what I learned when I was forced to go hand in hand with someone for only one mile.

For the rest of my life I have never so much as raised a hand against another person.

—Medard Laz
Chicken Soup for the Teenage Soul II

Terri Jackson

O n the first day of sixth grade, I sat in my quiet homeroom class and observed all the people who I would eventually befriend and possibly graduate with. I glanced around the room and noticed that the majority of the middle class kids were dressed in their nicest first day of school outfits.

My glance stopped on a shy-looking girl in the back of the room. She wore a stained, yellow plaid shirt with a pair of frayed jeans that had obviously had several owners before her. Her hair was unusually short and unwashed. She wore dress shoes that were once white, and frilly pink socks that had lost their frill with too many wearings. I caught myself thinking, "That's disgusting. Doesn't she know what a bathtub is?" As I looked around, I figured others were probably thinking the same thing.

The teacher began checking the attendance, each person casually lifting his or her hand as names were called in turn.

"Terri Jackson?" the teacher asked, following the roll with her finger. Silence. "Um, Terri Jackson?"

Finally we heard a meek answer from the back of the room, followed by the sound of ripping cloth. We all shifted in our seats to see what had happened.

"Scary Terri ripped the armpit of her shirt!" one boy joked.

"Eww, I bet it's a hundred years old!" another girl commented. One comment after another brought a roar of laugher.

I was probably laughing the loudest. Sadly, making Terri feel insecure made me feel secure and confident. It was a good break from the awkward silence and uncomfortable first day jitters.

Terri Jackson was the joke of the whole sixth grade that year. If we had nothing to talk about, Terri's trip through the lunchroom was an entertaining conversation starter. Her grandma-looking dress, missing front tooth and stained gym clothes kept us mocking and imitating her for hours.

At my twelfth birthday party, ten giggly, gossipy girls were playing Truth or Dare, a favorite party game. We had just finished a Terri Jackson discussion. It was my turn at the game.

"Umm... Sydney! Truth or Dare?" one of my friends asked.

"How about a dare? Bring it on. I'll do anything." Oh, if only I'd known what she was about to say.

"Okay, I dare you to invite Terri Jackson over to your house next Friday for two whole hours!"

"Two whole hours?! Please ask something else, please!" I begged. "How could anybody do that?" But my question was drowned out by a sea of giggly girls slapping their hands over their mouths and rolling on the floor, trying to contain their laughter.

The next day, I cautiously walked up to Terri as if her body odor was going to make me fall over dead. My friends huddled and watched from a corner to see if I would follow through with the brave dare.

I managed to choke out, "Hey Scary—I mean Terri—you want to come over for two hours Friday?" I didn't see her face light up because I had turned to my friends and made a gagging expression. When I was satisfied with their laughter of approval, I turned back to Terri. Terri's face was buried in her filthy hands; she was crying. I couldn't stand it. Half of me felt the strongest compassion for her, but the other half wanted to slap her for making me look so cruel and heartless. That was exactly what I was being.

"What's got you all upset? All I did was invite you over," I whispered, trying not to show my concern.

She looked up and watched my eyes for what seemed like forever. "Really?" That was all she could say. Her seldom-heard voice almost startled me.

"I guess so, if you're up to it." My voice sounded surprisingly sincere. I'd never seen her flash her toothless smile so brightly. The rest of the day I had a good feeling, and I was not dreading the two hour visit as I had before. I was almost looking forward to it.

Friday rolled around quickly. My time with Terri passed by in a flash as the two hours slipped into four hours, and I found myself actually enjoying her company. We chatted about her family and her battles with poverty. We discovered that we both played violin, and my favorite part of the afternoon occurred when she played the violin for me. I was amazed by how beautifully she played.

I would love to tell you that Terri and I became best friends and that from then on I ignored all my other friends' comments. But that's not how it happened. While I no longer participated in the Terri bashings and even tried to defend her at times, I didn't want to lose everyone else's acceptance just to gain Terri's.

Terri disappeared after the sixth grade. No one is sure what happened to her. We think that she may have transferred to a different school because of how cruelly the kids treated her. I still think about her sometimes and wonder what she's doing. I guess all I can do is hope that she is being accepted and loved wherever she is.

I realize now how insecure and weak I was during that sixth-grade year. I participated in the cruel, heartless Terri-bashing sessions because they seemed kind of funny in a distorted way. But they were only funny because they falsely boosted my own self-confidence; I felt bigger by making someone else feel smaller. I know now that true confidence is not proven by destroying another's self-esteem, but rather, by having the strength to stand up for the Terri Jacksons of the world.

—Sydney Fox
Chicken Soup for the Teenage Soul III

Thirty Cents Worth

All God's angels come to us disguised.
—James Russell Lowell

Whispering voices and laughter fill the hallways of my school as I walk with my friend toward our next class. I resist the impulse to become yet another person using these few moments to judge others in order to make myself feel better. I repeat to myself, Thirty cents, as I continue to walk in silence, something I rarely do. My friend digs her elbow into my side and grumbles, "That's just gross. Why would anyone want blue hair? That's so nasty!" I think before my tongue springs into action. Ordinarily, I would just give the expected giggle and nod—but for some reason, I hesitate.

My thoughts turn back to the previous Sunday afternoon. After flying through the house grabbing and tossing things into my soccer bag, I discovered that I was out of Blister Block Band-Aids, an essential for the next day's game. After some persuasion, I coaxed my mom into taking me to Walgreen's. She dropped me off and assured me she'd be right back. I rushed inside and snatched the goods.

There was a line at the register, as usual, and I waited my turn. I slowed down for a minute and examined the man in front of me. I was appalled.

He was old and reeked of gasoline and cigarettes. His hair was unkempt and reached below his shoulders. He wore a red vest matted in dust and jeans faded beyond recognition. His blue eyes were glassy and tired, and his dark mahogany face was etched with deep wrinkles carved by hard times.

He reached the counter and greeted the saleswoman with a nod. She averted her eyes as he pointed to the cigarettes behind the counter. She grabbed the carton he was pointing to and quickly rang him up. He grabbed the plastic bag and slowly ambled away.

I gave her four one dollar bills and the Band-Aids as she nodded in agreement with my disgust. "Sorry," she said. "You're thirty cents short."

"Oh, no... I don't have thirty cents! My mom isn't here.... She'll be right back. Can I run out to the car real quick?" As I was pleading my case, the cashier was visibly annoyed by the delay I was causing. I could feel the blood rush to my face as the people behind me in line started looking at each other with the same judgmental eyes I had just shared with the cashier. Just as I was about to run out of the store without my Band-Aids, I got a strong whiff of cigarettes and gasoline.

A dirty hand with yellow fingernails placed four nickels and a dime on the counter. I was awestruck and at a loss for words. I quickly offered to pay him back.

"That's okay. It's only thirty cents," he said with a warm smile and a wink. The man I had just judged as a foul creature had done something amazingly kind.

Now when I start to judge somebody based on their looks, I stop and repeat "thirty cents" to myself as a reminder to look beyond appearances. When I do that, I see beauty in everyone I meet.

—Trish E. Calvarese
Chicken Soup for the Christian Teenage Soul

Adult Teeth

Judgments prevent us from seeing the good that lies beyond appearances.
—Wayne W. Dyer

As a young girl, two of my wishes were to have glasses and to have braces, items that I associated with the magical pre-teen world of growing up. I got the glasses in second grade, and quickly realized that I had been wrong—I did not want to wear glasses, after all.

Still though, I clung to the romantic vision of braces, the metal and plastic that would transform me into someone older and infinitely more appealing.

As my adult teeth started to grow in, I was horrified to realize that my neat little rows of baby teeth were being replaced by a mouthful of mismatched, overlapping grown-up teeth.

In sixth grade, at last, I got my braces. And again, I found that the reality was far different than I'd imagined. I didn't like the way that the braces looked on me, but far worse was the way they felt.

The first night after I got my braces on was the worst. My teeth felt as if a world-class bodybuilder was yanking them apart. Hard. My mother made hamburgers for dinner, and I was starving, but I could only eat slowly, miserably, with a minimum of chewing and a maximum of pain.

Two excruciatingly long years later, after months and months of those agonizing torture sessions called "getting your braces tightened," I was finally, finally, scheduled to have my braces removed. I was also, my orthodontist mentioned in an offhand way, going to need gum surgery.

My mother immediately made an appointment with an oral surgeon whose office was in a nearby city, an hour away from our small town.

I sat in the passenger seat of the car, staring out the window as we drove.

"You'll be fine," she assured me.

"How do you know? You'll be out in the waiting room reading *Cosmo*," I muttered sourly.

As she had predicted, I did survive the procedure.

Afterward, since we were in the city already, my mother decided to do a little shopping. I should mention that she is not a cruel woman, and that this was toilet-paper-in-bulk kind of shopping, not just felt-like-another-new-dress shopping. Also, neither one of us realized at first that my mouth had been numbed to the point where I could no longer swallow.

I followed her into a large retail store with my jaw drooping and my own drool hanging from my mouth. I had never realized how many times a day I swallowed automatically, without ever giving it a thought.

Distracted by the immediate problems at hand—trying to avoid slobbering on the floor, periodically sopping up the spit with a handkerchief—it took me a few minutes to notice what was going on around us. As we walked, everyone we passed was staring at us. Their expressions ranged from curiosity to pity to revulsion. They didn't know what was wrong with me, but whatever it was, they weren't sticking around long enough to see whether it might be catching. No one knew that I had just undergone gum surgery.

Mom and I finished our errands and drove home. The anesthetic wore off, and I went back to involuntary swallowing. With my gums healed and my braces removed, I used my now smooth, even teeth to eat whole hamburgers and grin like a Cheshire cat at every person I saw.

When I was alone, though, I spent a lot of time thinking about how people had looked at me when I was in the store that day, when they had thought that perhaps I was a mentally or developmentally disabled teen. I was fourteen years old and, I had never in my life been looked at that way. I also thought about how my mom (who could have walked ahead and pretended that she didn't know me) stood by my side talking to me as she always did, and ignoring the stares.

This experience didn't drastically change me or my life. What it did do, though, was to alter my perception of the world just a little. It changed the way I thought about appearances, making them seem a little less important. It also gave new weight to the clichés my mom had been repeating ever since I was little: "Don't judge a book by its cover," "Everyone has feelings," and "You have to walk a mile in someone else's shoes."

I knew that I had only walked a few steps in someone else's shoes, but I was newly determined to treat other people—regardless of their appearance—with more compassion and respect.

And that, I realized, was something truly grown-up.

—Leah Browning
Chicken Soup for the Preteen Soul 2

Respecting Others

$\mathcal{D}$ear Jack, Mark and Kim,

I am such a huge admirer of your books. They have literally changed my way of thinking and how I act. I never used to really think twice about making rude comments to people in my school who I thought were weird. I want to share how a story in your book changed the way I treat people.

When it comes to the social structure, my school, like most typical high schools, has all kinds of different groups of friends. My group of friends is a tight group, and we consider each other best friends. Unfortunately, someone always seems to get left out of a group and in our group that was Jessica. For some cruel reason we liked to make fun of her. We thought it was actually pretty hilarious. We constantly made jokes about the way she dressed and how her hair always looked like it was never clean. It wasn't that she didn't wash it, but there never seemed to be any life to it, like it was straw. We just couldn't figure it out. We would make up poems and silly little songs about her hair. We knew we were being immature, but it was a way to get a cheap laugh here and there, not really realizing what it could be doing to her inside.

One day, my English teacher read us a story from *Chicken Soup for the Soul* titled, "A Simple Gesture." It was about a boy named Mark who was on his way home from school with all his books and everything else he had stored in his locker. He had fallen and a fellow classmate named Bill helped him up. Mark was going home to commit suicide because he was having a difficult time in school and in life in general. But because of Bill's kindness towards Mark, he decided not to hurt himself, realizing what other good things he might miss later on down the road.

When she finished reading the story, I immediately thought about Jessica and what we were doing to her and how horrible she must feel when we make fun of her. It made me wonder if all the jokes we told about her caused her to think about suicide.

My next class with Jessica was in ten minutes and she sat in front of me. This was where we usually made fun of her hair, but this time I didn't nor did I ever again. Instead, I wrote her a letter apologizing for the way I had treated her. I told her I couldn't apologize for the rest of the girls, and that maybe they just didn't realize yet what they were doing to her and the pain they were probably causing her. This letter was the most sincere apology I had ever given to anyone in my life. When I handed it to her she wanted to throw it away, but I stopped her and begged her to read it. She said, "Why, so I can just read all the insults that you wrote to me? I don't feel like putting up with this anymore."

So I took the letter from her hands and started reading it out loud to her in front of the entire class. My friends gave me the strangest looks, but I didn't care at that point. I wanted them and the rest of the students to hear what I had written. When I came to the end of the letter I said, "I'm so sorry for what I've done to you. I hope that somehow you can find it in your heart to forgive me." She ran up to me with tears in her eyes and hugged me. I cried with her. I could see my friends whispering to each other, but it didn't matter.

I had gained a new friend that afternoon. I will always be forever grateful to my English teacher for reading us that story and to you for publishing such amazing stories. You have helped open my eyes and to realize that everyone deserves to be treated with respect, no matter what. Keep up the great work you guys are doing.

Sincerely,
—Jennifer Lirette
Chicken Soup for the Teenage Soul Letters

Teens Talk
Growing Up

Doing the Right Thing

The time is always right to do what is right.
—Martin Luther King, Jr.

32

The Graduation Dance

I watched as my son walked purposefully toward the car with a look on his face that I knew so well. He was bursting to tell me some news about the eighth grade graduation dance he'd just attended. As I waited in the parking lot with the windows open on that warm summer night, I had to smile. Adam had always been the type of kid to come home from school spurting out exciting or unhappy experiences about his day before the screen door had even slammed behind him.

"I did the best thing I ever did in my whole life tonight," he blurted out as soon as he put one foot in the car. The smile on his face spread from earlobe to earlobe. Pretty strong words for a person who has only been in existence for fourteen years.

The story spilled out of him like a hole in a bag of coffee beans.

"I was standing with Justin, Mark, Kristen and Britney," he began. "It was noisy and dark and everyone was dancing and laughing. Then Britney pointed out a girl to me who was standing off into a darkened corner, kind of crying to herself.

"She told me, 'Go dance with her, Adam.'

"I told her she was crazy. First of all, I didn't even know the girl. I mean, I've seen her around, but I didn't know her name or anything. It's not like I'm friends with her or anything.

"But then Britney started bugging me. She told me how I have a responsibility to people because I was voted Most Popular. She said I should be a role model, and that I had the chance to do something special by dancing with this girl. She said we're here to make a difference in other people's lives, and if I danced with this girl, I'd make a difference."

"Did you dance with her?" I asked him.

"No, Mom. I told Britney she was really crazy, because she didn't even know why the girl was crying. That's when she said something that really made me think. She said, 'You know why she's crying, Adam. We both do. Look at her. It's her eighth grade graduation dance, and she's standing alone in a corner. She's a little overweight, and she's in a room full of teenagers who only care about what kind of clothes they're wearing and what their hair looks like. Think about it. How long did you spend trying to decide what you were going to wear tonight? Well, she did the same thing. Only no one is noticing, and no one cares. Here's your chance to prove you deserve to be voted Most Popular.'"

"So did you then?" I asked.

"No," he said. "I told Britney she was right, but that everybody would laugh at me if I danced with her. So I told Britney I didn't want to look weird and I wouldn't do it."

"What happened?" I asked.

"Well, Britney wouldn't stop bugging me. She told me that if people laughed at me because I danced with an unpopular girl, then they weren't people I needed to care about. Then she asked me if I saw any guy dancing with her, would I laugh? Or would I secretly have a lot of respect for that person?

"I knew she was right. But it was still hard to go over and ask her to dance. What if I walked all the way across the room in front of everyone and she turned me down? But Britney said, 'She won't turn you down, but even if she does, you'll get over it. I promise you, if you dance with her, she'll remember you for the rest of her life. This is your chance to make a difference.'

"So I went over to the girl and asked what her name was. Then I asked if she wanted to dance. She said yes and as we walked out to the dance floor, the music changed to a slow dance. I felt my face turn all red, but it was dark and I didn't think anyone noticed. I thought everyone was looking at me, but no one laughed or anything and we danced the whole dance.

"The weird thing is that Britney was right. It was three minutes out of my life, but it felt so good. And for the rest of the night, a lot of the guys danced with her and with anyone else they saw who hadn't danced yet. It was like the greatest eighth grade graduation dance, because no one got left out. I really learned something tonight, Mom."

So did I, Adam, so did I.

—Linda Chiara
Chicken Soup for the Teenage Soul on Love & Friendship

33

How Much Does It Cost?

> *Good decisions come from experience,*
> *and experience comes from bad decisions.*
> —Author Unknown

The six teenagers sank onto their beanbags in the group counseling room. Today there was none of the usual raucous punching and good-natured exchange of insults. I knew they didn't want to be at school this week any more than I, their counselor, did.

For three days they had received counseling, comfort, sympathy and lectures. Ministers and psychologists had come to the school at a time when the kids' world seemed to have ended. It had indeed ended for four of their schoolmates, who had died in a car accident on the way home from a keg party in celebration of graduation.

What was there left for me to say? Only that these six would go on living, barring a tragedy like this one—a tragedy that didn't have to happen.

My mind searched for words to fill the silence. Finally I said, "I remember a day when I was about your age, seeing a fancy Levi's jacket and jodhpurs in a store window. Since I was to be riding in the girls' rodeo competition the following month, I figured I simply couldn't live without that outfit. I went into the store, found the garments in my size and bought them without asking how much they cost. I practically had a heart attack when the clerk told me the price.

There went all the spending money I had saved practically forever. In fact, I had to go home and rob my piggy bank and then go back to the store for my purchase."

At that point in my story, I paused long enough to note that the group members were staring at me with questioning eyes. After all, what did a stupid rodeo costume have to do with their grief?

So I babbled on. "Was the outfit worth that much? No way, I concluded during the following months, when I had to do without several things I needed or wanted, including a class ring."

My counselees continued to look at me with a so-what? expression.

"I did learn from that experience," I said finally. "I learned to ask, 'What does it cost?' before buying. During the years following, I've learned that looking at price tags is a good idea when it comes to actions, also."

I told them about a time when I went on a hike with friends without telling our parents where we would be. The price was heavy. My fellow hikers and I got lost, and it was many terrifying hours before we straggled back to town to face our frantic parents and the drastic punishments they decided we deserved.

Now it was the kids' turn to talk, and they did, relating some of the times when their bad judgment had not been worth the cost of the consequences.

I gently reminded the students at this point that their friends' graduation celebration had cost too much. I mentioned the frequency of teen tragedies, many involving alcohol and other drugs. Then I read them parts of an editorial about an accident that had occurred a few months earlier. The article had been written by the town's chief of police:

> Close to a thousand people were there that day, all sitting in front of a smooth casket topped with flowers and a high school letter jacket. Jason was president of the senior class, a star athlete, a popular friend to hundreds, the only son of successful parents, but he drove into the side of a fast-moving freight train at

the city square on a beautiful Sunday afternoon and was killed instantly. He was eighteen years old. And he was drunk.

You never get accustomed to or forget the horror on the faces of parents when you break the news to them that their child is forever gone from this earth.

We know there will be both youth and parents who don't like our enforcement posture. There will be verbal and maybe physical abuse against the officers. Some parents will complain about our enforcement of underage drinking laws. But we can live with that a lot easier than telling parents that their son or daughter has been killed.

Four of the six students were crying by the time I finished reading the editorial. Crying for Jason, crying for their dead schoolmates and their families, crying because of their own loss.

Then we talked about the four friends they had just lost.

"Can any good come out of our tragedy?" I asked. "Or do we just let it end like a sad movie?"

It was Mindy, the shyest member of the group, who suggested in a wispy voice, "Maybe we could make a pledge or something."

Ordinarily, the three boys in the group would probably have ridiculed the idea, but this day was different.

"Hey!" Jonathan said. "Not a bad idea."

"Something like pretending there's a price tag on things grown-ups think we shouldn't do, then maybe deciding if we're ready to take the chance anyway," Laurel added.

Paul said, "The problem with that is, we can't know for sure what that price would be. Maybe nothing bad will happen even if we take the risk."

"That's a point," I admitted. "Suppose instead of 'How much will it cost?' we asked ourselves, 'How much might it cost?' Then we'd at least look at the possible outcomes."

"I'll buy that," Kent said.

A week ago, these kids would have shrugged off such suggestions, but today—well, today they weren't quite the same people they had been last week.

—Margaret Hill
Chicken Soup for the Teenage Soul II

34

Another Statistic

I don't want to be another statistic
Some suicidal teen
Who makes a choice to kill herself
When the world just seems too mean.
She can't go on with life
Or so to her it seems
Reality has fallen short
And so have her many dreams.

I don't want to be another statistic
Some pregnant little girl
Who met this great guy
And then gave sex a whirl.
She was only fifteen
But it felt so right
She thought they'd be together
For more than just a night.

I don't want to be another statistic
Some kid strung out on crack
Who started at a party
And now he can't turn back.
First cigarettes and alcohol
Now meth, crack and cocaine

He's been smoking it so long
That now he's gone insane.

I don't want to be another statistic
Some girl left in the rain
Who was walking home from school
Then raped and left in pain.
She can't tell her parents
And it hurts to tell her friends
She doesn't know what she'll do
To make this nightmare end.

I don't want to be another statistic
Some kid out of school
Who dropped out really early
And was acting like a fool.
He thought that it was boring
He thought that it was dumb
He doesn't have an education
But lives on the streets like a bum.

I don't want to be another statistic
Some stereotypical teen
I'm gonna make a difference
I'll finish with my dream.
I won't end up pregnant
On drugs or even dead
I won't drop out of school
Because I'll use my head.

I don't want to be another statistic
To fit into some mold
Of what society thinks of kids today
Because it's getting kind of old.
Not all of us are bad

In fact most of us are good
When will the world see us
And give us credit like they should?

—Amanda Parmenter
Chicken Soup for the Teenage Soul on Tough Stuff

35

Dear John

It was the last day of school; the last day I would ever walk down those halls as a student. I had a few things to take care of before the rehearsal for our graduation ceremony. I had to return my school library books and pay a shop-class fine from my sophomore year when I had broken Seth's project and was supposed to pay to replace his kit.

I was always clumsy around him, and that time I had knocked over the birdhouse he had made. It had tumbled and shattered at our feet.

We were on our knees picking up the pieces when our hands brushed against each other. I felt the same electricity I had first felt in fourth grade when he grabbed my hand for a Red Rover game.

I looked into his eyes, and he looked into mine. I thought that maybe this time he would notice me. My heart fluttered. I flushed with embarrassment and anticipation. Just an inch closer and he could kiss me.

Seth parted his lips and said, "Hey, why are you all red? It's not that hot in here." I guess it wasn't.

Seth and I had a different circle of friends. His were the outgoing, athletic, school council, homecoming court, merit scholar type. Mine weren't.

As our class assembled in the gym for graduation rehearsal, I couldn't help but feel sentimental. My mood lifted when Seth sat down in front of me, until I remembered that this would be the last day he would be part of my daily life.

The announcements droned on and on. Yearbooks started circulating for last minute signings. When Seth's was handed to me, I autographed my senior picture and was about to pass it to the next person when the thought hit me. What did I have to lose by telling him now?

I tapped my pen on my teeth while I composed the note in my head. It had to be perfect. My hand shook when I began to write.

Dear Seth,

I have been in the background of your life since elementary school. You have meant more to me than I have to you. I wished that we could have known each other better and spent some time together. I will always remember you and wish you a great life.

Forever,

Cindy

I closed his book and passed it on before I could change my mind. As I scribbled my name in other books, I began to imagine and then to hope that maybe, just maybe, my yearbook would come back to me with a similar message from Seth.

It wasn't until the bus ride home that afternoon, that I finally had the nerve to open my book and look for Seth's picture. In its corner he had written, "To Cindy, whoever you are, Seth."

I can't say that I was crushed. I didn't expect anything more, really. I could've worried about what I wrote in his book, but I guessed he wouldn't know or care who I was, anyway. Still, his terse message did hurt. He didn't have to prove that I was invisible to him.

I was one step away from a "what a jerk" conclusion, but I just couldn't go that far after years of holding his perfect image in my mind.

I was putting my book into my backpack when the guy behind me tapped me on the shoulder. "Sign my book?"

"Sure," I said and handed him mine. I found my picture again and scribbled, "Good luck, from Cindy."

With the whirl of graduation and the activity of early summer days, it was a week before I thought to open my backpack. My yearbook was on top, and I sat down on the edge of my bed to thumb through it. I cringed when I reread Seth's message to me.

What a sorry thing that a guy could just overlook someone, no matter how nice she might be or how much she cared about him, just because she wasn't part of his circle.

It was then that I noticed another inscription. The friendly smile in the picture looked vaguely familiar.

Dear Cindy,

I was new this year. You are the first person I noticed. I've been sitting behind you in English Lit and I looked for you to come in every day. I wished we could've gotten to know each other and spent time together. I will always think of you and remember you.

Forever,

John

My heart sank as I realized the truth. I had done to John what Seth had done to me. I hadn't taken the time to know him, because, well, I didn't already know him. I had dismissed him without really seeing him.

I still feel a pinch of remorse when I remember that moment. Ever since that day, I have tried to notice and acknowledge the people in my daily life.

I had barely taken a thought to scribbling my name in John's book, but his message to me has been written across my life.

—Cynthia M. Hamond
Chicken Soup for the Teenage Soul IV

My Most
Embarrassing Moment

[Author's note to her mom and dad: I'm sorry you have to find out about this at the same time all of America does. I never told anyone.]

Honor student, tennis team player, Spanish Club president. Sunday school teacher assistant, Swing Choir piano accompanist. Although these publicly recognized accomplishments of my teenage years went on to influence my life in many ways, there was one particular group activity I participated in that had an even greater impact on me: Mustard Gang Member.

The fall of 1977 found me enrolled as a freshman in the school system I had attended since kindergarten. My student file over the last ten years could be summed up with positive comments such as "consistently above average," "enjoys extracurricular activities" and "cooperates with teachers and fellow classmates." No suspensions. No detentions. Basically, a model student. However, within a total time period of approximately one hour, this trademark behavior would fly right out the window (at the speed of sound).

Three of my lifelong girlfriends—who would fall under a fairly close ditto description of that above—caught up to me after school on a Friday afternoon. One of them had just received her driver's license and was going cruising in a nearby town to celebrate. She asked if I would like to come along. (Rhetorical question.) The final bell was sounding as we piled into an older model Dodge Charger on its last legs. Regardless of its condition, it had a full tank of gas and the ability to get us from Point A to Point B.

Within minutes of leaving the school parking lot, we were on the open highway. As I look back now, that highway was pretty significant. It not only separated two towns, it separated those of us in the car from the people who knew us and the people who didn't. We became daring.

When the novelty of just driving around wore off, someone suggested it might be fun to squirt mustard on parked cars as we drove past them. (Author's sensible reaction twenty years late: WHAT?!) A unanimous agreement must have followed, because all four of us stood beside each other in the checkout line where the bottle of mustard was ultimately purchased.

Loading back into the car, each of our faces looked as though we couldn't believe what we were doing. We couldn't. Four kids, four clean records. Lost time was about to be made up for.

We decided that the person sitting by the passenger's side window would be the Designated Squirter, while the others in the car would be responsible for choosing the target ahead. Since I was cowardly, trying to hide in a corner of the backseat, I thought this sounded swell. Feeling my guilt would be somewhat lessened if I didn't actually touch the mustard bottle, I thought I was off the hook. A nervous sigh of relief was escaping me until the words "and we'll pull over every other block and switch seats so it will be fair." Hook re-inserted.

The "talk" in the car proved to be more productive than the "action" as the first and second girls took their turns in the passenger seat, both chickening out at the last second, squealing, "I can't!" Before I knew it, the car had stalled and it was me who was climbing in beside the driver. Sliding my sweaty palms up and down the bottle's sides, the target was being pointed out to me, loudly and with demanding encouragement. The attack was to be launched on a little red Volkswagen up ahead, fast approaching. "Do it! Do it! Do it!" my friends chanted.... And I almost did. But, as was the case with the girls before, feathers grew from within me and we soon sped past the car, leaving it as solid red as it had been when first spotted.

Since the driver couldn't take a respective turn as the shooter, we headed for home, the mischief supposedly ended. Just when we were nearing the highway, we passed two girls jogging, their hands moving up and down in front of them. Still looking for trouble, we interpreted their innocent actions. "Hey! They just gave us the finger!" And of course, if we had been needlessly insulted, they certainly would have to pay. Simple as that.

Within seconds, they were jogging into a Kmart parking lot.... And we were right behind them. Jumping out of the car, we ran toward our unsuspecting prey yelling, "Get 'em!" We did. Well, I did. After all, there was only one bottle and it was my turn. Silently they just stood there.

My hearing must have been the last of my senses to fail, for the car door did not slam shut behind me without the words from one of these mustard-covered strangers ringing in my ears: "That wasn't very funny, Rochelle." Clear words. Echoing words. Rochelle. Rochelle. Rochelle. Not only had I just left two people covered with mustard back in a parking lot, but at least one of them wasn't a stranger.

Although no one in the car physically recognized either victim, there was no doubt among any of us that the voice that just spoke was a familiar one. But whose? The longest minute of my life followed until I figured it out: Miss Greatens, MY TYPING TEACHER!

Miss Greatens, fresh out of college, was committed to making a strong professional impression on the business class students she taught. Her hair was always gathered on top of her head, large glasses covered her eyes and crisp business suits were her chosen attire. And yet outside of her work environment, she suddenly changed. Drastically. Her hair looked as though it grew a foot or so (since just this afternoon), she shrank a solid two inches (heels removed), contact lenses replaced glasses and her business suit was traded in for a sweatsuit. She no longer looked like Miss Greatens; she looked more like...well, us!

Situation assessment: WE HAD A PROBLEM. The Dodge

Charger immediately went chasing back to the parking lot, but the joggers were nowhere in sight. Plan B was implemented. A telephone booth directory could provide her home address. Success. She lived right across from Kmart in an apartment complex.

Little did we know that Miss Greatens was doing some of her own phone referencing while we were trying to find her. First she called the school principal at home, then she called my parents. (My life, as I knew it, was about to end.) However, she hung up after the first two rings before anyone answered either call. She had decided to speak to us first.

And here we were.

Miss Greatens answered the door graciously, standing before us with mustard-stained clothes and tear-stained cheeks, wanting to hear what possible explanation warranted her pain. There was none. Absolutely none. What we had done was uncalled for. Our consciences made that perfectly clear as we poured out a flood of genuine remorse and tears to equal her own.

Then something extraordinary happened: She forgave us. Fully. Right there on the spot. She could have spoken to all of our parents about what happened, but didn't. She could have contacted school officials and sought stern reprimands for each of us, but didn't. And she could have held the incident over our heads for a very long time and reminded us of what we had done at will, but didn't.

Will we ever do anything like that again? NO WAY. You see, that is the power of forgiveness.

—Rochelle Pennington
Chicken Soup for the Teenage Soul II

37

Deep Inside

Standing on the beach,
Sand between my toes,
What lies in my future?
Who will come and go?
The sun beams down upon me,
As I raise my head and look
At the vast ocean before me,
Its size, which I mistook.
I feel so insignificant,
Compared to this great expanse.
What difference can I make?
Will I even be given a chance?
I realize then while standing there,
That all I have to do,
Is listen to my heart,
And it will pull me through.
For strength and inspiration,
Are not material things,
They come from deep inside of you,
They give your soul its wings.
So whenever you're in doubt,
And you begin to stray,
Take a look down deep inside,
And the answer will come your way.

If you only believe in yourself,
You can make your dreams come true,
For no one else can do it,
The power must come from you.

—Stephanie Ives
Chicken Soup for the Preteen Soul 2

38

Mary Lou

*Every time I've done something that doesn't feel right,
it's ended up not being right.*
—Mario Cuomo

It was my first day as newcomer to Miss Hargrove's seventh grade class. Past "newcomer" experiences had been difficult, so I was very anxious to fit in. After being introduced to the class, I bravely put on a smile and took my seat, expecting to be shunned.

Lunchtime was a pleasant surprise when the girls all crowded around my table. Their chatter was friendly, so I began to relax. My new classmates filled me in on the school, the teachers and the other kids.

It wasn't long before the class nerd was pointed out to me: Mary Lou English. Actually she called herself Mary Louise. A prim, prissy young girl with a stern visage and old-fashioned clothes. She wasn't ugly—not even funny looking. I thought she was quite pretty, but I had sense enough not to say so. Dark-eyed and olive-skinned, she had long, silky black hair, but—she had pipe curls! Practical shoes, long wool skirt and a starched, frilly blouse completed the image of a total dork. The girls' whispers and giggles got louder and louder. Mary Lou made eye contact with no one as she strode past our table, chin held high with iron determination. She ate alone.

After school, the girls invited me to join them in front of the school. I was thrilled to be a member of the club, however tentative. We waited. For what, I didn't yet know. Oh, how I wish I had gone home, but I had a lesson to learn.

Arms wrapped around her backpack, Mary Lou came down the school steps. The taunting began—rude, biting comments and jeering from the girls. I paused, then joined right in. My momentum began to pick up as I approached her. Nasty, mean remarks fell unabated from my lips. No one could tell I'd never done this before. The other girls stepped back and became my cheerleaders. Emboldened, I yanked the strap of her backpack and then pushed her. The strap broke, Mary Lou fell, and I backed off. Everyone was laughing and patting me. I fit in. I was a leader.

I was not proud. Something inside me hurt. If you've ever picked a wing off a butterfly, you know how I felt.

Mary Lou got up, gathered her books and—without a tear shed or retort given—off she went. She held her head high as a small trickle of blood ran down from her bruised knee. I watched her limp away down the street.

I turned to leave with my laughing friends and noticed a man standing beside his car. His olive skin, dark hair and handsome features told me this was her father. Respectful of Mary Lou's proud spirit, he remained still and watched the lonely girl walk toward him. Only his eyes—shining with both grief and pride—followed. As I passed, he looked at me in silence with burning tears that spoke to my shame and scalded my heart. He didn't speak a word.

No scolding from a teacher or preaching from a parent could linger as much as that hurt in my heart from the day a father's eyes taught me kindness and strength and dignity. I never again joined the cruel herds. I never again hurt someone for my own gain.

—Lynne Zielinski
Chicken Soup for the Teenage Soul III

39

Making Sarah Cry

He stood among his friends from school,
He joined their childhood games
Laughing as they played kickball
And when they called poor Sarah names.
Sarah was unlike the rest;
She was slow and not as smart,
And it would seem to all his friends
She was born without a heart.
And so he gladly joined their fun
Of making Sarah cry.
But somewhere deep within his heart,
He never knew just why.
For he could hear his mother's voice,
Her lessons of right and wrong
Playing over and over inside his head
Just like a favorite song.
"Treat others with respect, son,
The way you'd want them treating you.
And remember, when you hurt others,
Someday, someone might hurt you."
He knew his mother wouldn't understand
The purpose of their game
Of teasing Sarah, who made them laugh
As her own tears fell like rain.

The funny faces that she made
And the way she'd stomp her feet
Whenever they mocked the way she walked
Or the stutter when she'd speak.
To him she must deserve it
Because she never tried to hide.
And if she truly wanted to be left alone,
Then she should stay inside.
But every day she'd do the same:
She'd come outside to play,
And stand there, tears upon her face,
Too upset to run away.
The game would soon be over
As tears dropped from her eyes,
For the purpose of their fun
Was making Sarah cry.
It was nearly two whole months
He hadn't seen his friends.
He was certain they all must wonder
What happened and where he'd been
So he felt a little nervous
As he limped his way to class.
He hoped no one would notice,
He prayed no one would ask
About that awful day:
The day his bike met with a car,
Leaving him with a dreadful limp
And a jagged-looking scar.
So he held his breath a little
As he hobbled into the room,
Where inside he saw a "Welcome Back" banner
And lots of red balloons.
He felt a smile cross his face
As his friends all smiled, too
And he couldn't wait to play outside—

His favorite thing to do.
So the second that he stepped outdoors
And saw his friends all waiting there,
He expected a few pats on the back—
Instead, they all stood back and stared.
He felt his face grow hotter
As he limped to join their side
To play a game of kickball
And of making Sarah cry.
An awkward smile crossed his face
When he heard somebody laugh
And heard the words, "Hey freak,
Where'd you get the ugly mask?"
He turned, expecting Sarah,
But Sarah could not be seen.
It was the scar upon his own face
That caused such words so mean.
He joined in their growing laughter,
Trying hard to not give in
To the awful urge inside to cry
Or the quivering of his chin.
They are only teasing,
He made himself believe.
They are still my friends;
They'd never think of hurting me.
But the cruel remarks continued
About the scar and then his limp.
And he knew if he shed a single tear
They'd label him a wimp.
And so the hurtful words went on,
And in his heart he wondered why.
But he knew without a doubt
The game would never end, until they made him cry.
And just when a tear had formed,
He heard a voice speak out from behind.

"Leave him alone you bullies,
Because he's a friend of mine."
He turned to see poor Sarah,
Determination on her face,
Sticking up for one of her own tormentors
And willing to take his place.
And when his friends did just that,
Trying their best to make poor Sarah cry,
This time he didn't join in,
And at last understood exactly why.
"Treat others with respect, son,
The way you'd want them treating you.
And remember, when you hurt others,
Someday, someone might hurt you."
It took a lot of courage
But he knew he must be strong,
For at last he saw the difference
Between what's right and wrong.
And Sarah didn't seem so weird
Through his understanding eyes.
Now he knew he'd never play again
The game of making Sarah cry.
It took several days of teasing
And razzing from his friends,
But when they saw his strength,
They chose to be like him.
And now out on the playground,
A group of kids meets every day
For a game of kickball and laughter
And teaching their new friend, Sarah, how to play.

—Cheryl L. Costello-Forshey
Chicken Soup for the Teenage Soul II

Never Cool Enough

*I was always looking outside myself for strength and confidence,
but it comes from within. It is there all the time.*
—Anna Freud

Why was it so easy for my blond-haired, blue-eyed twin sister, Allie, to make friends? She didn't even try, but they gravitated to her. It was so hard for me to be noticed when she was around. I didn't know why I wasn't like that. Her charming outgoing personality was too much for me to compete with.

I was the shy girl who sat in the corner. Why didn't people stop to think that maybe the person who doesn't talk the most might have the most to say? Why didn't any of the kids think that maybe I was just like them, but too intimidated to say anything? I was just as fun to be around as Allie was... if you got to know me. Yet I struggled all through elementary school trying to find friendships. I spent years lacking one of the most meaningful relationships a child can have.

Growing up is hard for everyone. For some it's harder than for others. Especially the scramble we go through to find the right best friend—or just to find a friend at all.

By the time I reached eighth grade, I was lost. I had tried everything to become "cool" and to fit in. I changed how I dressed, talked and presented myself. I copied other people's style, thinking that if I did, I would fit in with them and their friends. I tried the sporty look, then the preppy look—then came any other look you could think of. For a while, all my shirts were black and my jeans hung on my hips three sizes too big. You name it, I tried it.

I even changed the way I talked. I'd speak in a well-thought-out manner, very articulate. When people didn't notice that, I would speak like I had trouble putting a sentence together. I would change the tone of my voice. High pitched, different accents or just silly tones: Nothing could get me noticed. I just knew that if someone paid attention to me, I could win them over.

If that wasn't bad enough, there was the dreaded lunchroom where you can become very vulnerable to what others think and say about you. If you didn't sit with anyone, you were automatically a loser. Once one person thought you were a loser then everyone thought you were a loser. No one gave me a chance. There was also the constant fear of getting things thrown at you or in your general direction. I was struck many times with flying food. It was not an enjoyable experience. I ate lunch with my sister in elementary school because she felt sorry for me, but once we got to middle school, I wasn't cool enough to sit with her and her friends. I was forced to face what I thought was my destiny, sitting all alone at lunch over a tray of uneaten pizza.

So I felt horrible about myself. I continued to reinvent myself constantly in hopes I would be liked by at least one person. Surely someone wanted to hang with me. Allie blended in perfectly with the popular kids. She projected confidence, and people really responded to that.

Going through something like what I was going through was very difficult without Allie. Like perfect strangers, we didn't talk at school. We talked at home though, which was awkward. It became a hassle to try to make it seem like we were fine when both of us knew we weren't. We were twins. We have the same sense of humor. We talk the same, and most of the time, we think the same. We don't dress or act alike, but that isn't what matters. We went through everything together. I remember when I broke my arm, she went out of her way to make sure I had everything taken care of. I wouldn't even have to ask her to do something because it was already done. And when we moved, she stuck by me when I was having a hard time. Through thick and thin, it had always been the two of us. Having our relationship on the rocks made going through eighth grade anything but easy.

The only way I could cope with the ever-apparent reality of my situation was to act as though it didn't bother me. I pretended I didn't want to be popular. I acted like I hated everyone. I even became disruptive in class. I constantly made fun of the stupid things the popular kids did or said. I was all over it, mocking them in every way. Oddly enough, acting so rudely toward the popular kids attracted the attention of the self-declared rebels. Apparently being incredibly rude is a quality some people like. I decided it was easy to be rude, and it was finally going to be easy to make friends with these kids. All I had to say was that I hated "preps," and I was in. Way in.

I became a big part of that little group before I realized it was happening. The more mean and belligerent I became, the more these kids wanted to be around me. Inside, I was torn. I didn't want to be mean, but I wanted friends. I decided to do what at the time I thought was right. I had to start rolling with that crowd. Looking back, I realize it was a big mistake.

I bought into their whole punk thing. I started dressing in a way that sent a message that didn't portray me, but portrayed what I had to be, to be in this group. Band T-shirts, leather wrist bands, studded belts—the whole nine. I took notes from my friends; I changed my way of thinking. Anything having to do with my family was no longer cool. The government was all wrong. Nothing was right.

I was becoming a completely different person, all for these people who I thought would never like me for me. When my friends started getting into drugs and other illegal activities, I felt really alone. I had no idea I was going to have to deal with these things at the tender age of fourteen. I had no idea how these people, my friends, could do this. Over the course of about six months, my friends started drinking and smoking. At first, they'd drink or smoke once a month. Gradually, it escalated into a weekly, then a daily, occurrence. They were constantly coming to school under the influence. I was dumb-struck by this, especially because the teachers didn't seem to notice or care. I prayed for the day when they would get caught. I thought then maybe they would shape up, and I would have my friends back. That day never came.

So I stood by, while my friends got trashed in their basements while their parents were upstairs. I stood by while they ditched class to go outside and smoke. But I was firm in my belief that participating in those activities was simply unacceptable. Finally, these friends began to distance themselves from me. Apparently, I wasn't cool enough for them because I didn't want to get high or wasted. At least that's what I thought. Maybe they just resented me for my values and couldn't stand the fact that they were weak enough to fall into that—and I wasn't.

I realized those kids weren't my real friends. It was hard to deal with that. I thought I had found a group that I could stay friends with for a long time, but I wasn't about to throw my morals out the window for a few people. It was extremely difficult to face the fact that I had to choose between my morals and going back to being called names and always being alone. No one to eat with. No one to talk to.

At the beginning of ninth grade, I was flying solo again. Then something strange happened that year. I simply put my true self out there, which is what I should have done to begin with, but I had been too afraid. Finally, I was just being myself. I hadn't ever done that before.

Soon, I made friends with all kinds of kids—"preps," "punks," "nerds" and "losers." I looked at them individually instead of as being part of a group, and they began to respect me for that. I also started to get to know people instead of saying I couldn't be friends with them because they didn't think the exact same things as me. It didn't matter to me if they didn't dress like I did.

I became known as someone you could have fun with without doing anything illegal. I wasn't out every Friday night, but it had nothing to do with my popularity and everything to do with my values.

Finally, things at lunch are all good. I have yet to have a day this year when I have gotten pelted in the head with a grape or have nowhere to sit. People come and find me at lunch because they want to sit with me. They want to sit with me. I never thought that would be my reality. I was even voted Lady for the freshman class in the Homecoming Court!

I would have never guessed in eighth grade that I would be living the life I'm living today. I never knew it, but not once did I need to change a single thing about me.

I became cool by being myself.

—Natalie Ver Woert
Chicken Soup for the Girl's Soul

China's Story

China was fourteen, she gave what she got
She had many friends, who loved her a lot.
She loved them back, too, and would always be there,
But at prettier girls, she could not help but stare.

You must understand, that this group was a sight,
With their Cover Girl masks, and their shirts way too tight.
The guys hung around them, as though in a trance,
They were always the first ones who were asked to dance.

They seemed so secure, knowing just what to say.
And they said what they said in the coolest of ways
They never were seen without smiles on their faces.
Their clothes were real tight in all the right places.

You can see what I mean, when I say they were cool.
They were by far the sexiest girls in the school.

So China dreamed on, by day and by night,
Wishing her shirts would fit her as tight.
She wondered what contest she would have to win.
For, she'd give up the world, and her life to fit in.

She kept it a secret, hoping nobody knew,

But her friends caught on fast, and they found it was true.
They tried to warn her of their pretentious way.
But China grew more and more stubborn each day.

As cool as they were, and as hot as their show,
They struggled in school and their grades were quite low.
The groups of girls smoked, and were known to drink beer,
But this was not stuff China wanted to hear.

So China tried hard to fit in with the clique,
She giggled at jokes that she knew were just sick.
She gave her attention to these cool girls alone,
She dressed just like them, in a style not her own.

China's old friends feared her drifting away,
They were losing her slowly, and didn't know what to say.
They told China the truth, that the group was all fake,
But their words of advice, China just wouldn't take.

Why aren't they happy for me? China thought,
I don't act like myself, but now look where I've got.
She thought her old friends were jealous and tart,
She was truthfully happy, deep down in her heart.

China laughed at her old friends, along with her new,
They made fun of so many and smiled at so few.
China's new friends were cool, she was in with the clan,
She was treated like they were, she was happy again.

China's old group of friends sadly melted away,
They left China alone, but watched close every day.
They longed for her friendship, the warmth in her smile.
And hoped she'd miss them, and come back in a while.

But the jokes kept on coming, so the group with a sigh,

Turned their backs on harsh China, and walked silently by.
The pain was too deep and the torture too hard,
Her old friends' poor hearts had been torn out and scarred.

As all this did happen, the cool did their thing,
They giggled and gossiped and made actions sting.
They mutated China, the best that they could,
And taught her to be like a glamour girl should.

China went to parties, she got into fights,
She became really cool, but during the night,
She tried to discover just what was the scoop,
Why she wasn't content in her newly found group.

Then one day it hit her, came into her head,
That the answer was one that she truly did dread.
She had run ahead quickly and back round the bends,
She had left her companions, she had ditched her true friends.

China realized her error, "This group's not a sight,
With their makeup done perfect and hair fixed just right.
That's not what they look like, it's a lie what you see,
It's the Maybelline models they wish they could be."

Then early one night, around seven o'clock,
A girl opened her door to the sound of a knock.
Out in the cold, standing there in the rain,
Stood teary-eyed China, her old self again.

Neither one spoke, as she ushered her in,
The girl knew from experience, where China had been.
She had also once felt that those girls were the best,
But those long-ago thoughts, she had put down to rest.

The girls sat up talking for a good length of time,

China knew in her heart that she would be just fine.
She couldn't believe just how much she'd been blessed,
That her loving dear friends would forgive her like this.

This tale ends happy, but not all stories will,
Some friends aren't so forgiving, they go in for the kill.
China was lucky, but you may not be,
So choose your friends wisely, and help others see.

The moral is not to have one group of friends,
From a particular table, with particular trends.
It's to teach of the truth, that those girls tried to hide,
You will always be cool if it comes from inside.

—Libby Barnes
Chicken Soup for the Teenage Soul III

42

Learning the Hard Way

*D*ear Chicken Soup for the Teenage Soul,

My name is Kim, and I am from Ohio. I have really enjoyed reading your books. My friend Chelsea introduced me to them, and I've been reading them ever since.

I am fifteen years old—and five months pregnant. One subject I haven't read much about in your books is that of teenage pregnancy and its consequences. Girls and guys my age do not realize how serious it is to have sex. My mom always tried to warn me about making better choices for myself. She warned me about the serious things that could happen to me like getting pregnant, and contracting an STD or AIDS. But I never listened.

I've made a lot of mistakes. And now I'm pregnant. The father is not going to be in my life—or the baby's life, for that matter. I would give anything to be able to take it all back, but I can't. My only hope is that I can help to prevent it from happening to someone else by sharing with teens the extent of my remorse.

The stories in the book have helped me to do the right thing in other areas of my life. Last weekend my friends who had been drinking told me they would take me home. But having read the story about a guy who was killed when he let his friends drive drunk, I decided to call my mom and ask her to pick me up. My friends didn't think I was a dork or anything, because I was just looking out for myself and my baby. I felt very positive about my decision. My mom was proud of me, too.

I hope your books continue to teach us lessons and open our eyes. It's hard to listen to our parents all the time. Sometimes it helps to be able to take our life lessons in the form of a story, rather than the bitter medicine of our parents' lectures. Thank you.

Sincerely,
—Kim Lowery
Chicken Soup for the Teenage Soul Letters

43

The Crash

Dear Chicken Soup,

Today I bought *Chicken Soup for the Teenage Soul II*. I am already on page twenty, and I can't put the book down!

I recently watched a boy a few years older than me die on the side of the road because he and his friends had been drinking and took a turn at ninety miles per hour and crashed into another car. I was the first one at the scene and called 911. My boyfriend and I were going home after Homecoming, an unforgettable night. We were just talking and laughing when we both saw the crash. I heard screeching and screaming. We drove up to where the cars had hit, and I got out of the car.

While I was dialing 911, I looked down and realized I was standing barefoot in glass and gasoline. My boyfriend went to the cars to see if everyone was all right. In the car that got hit by the teenagers were three older ladies. They were all okay at the time. But, unfortunately, one of the ladies died about a week after the accident.

The boys in the other car were both unconscious. I stood there watching paramedics try to keep the driver of the car alive. Ten minutes later they put a body bag over him. I will never forget the boy who died or the blood and glass everywhere and the bottle of alcohol the police took out of the car.

To this day I will never let any of my friends drive drunk or drive with someone who has been drinking. I do not want to lose someone

I love. Watching that boy die made me realize how easily life can be taken away. This really proved to me how stupid drinking is.

I just wanted to tell you my experience and how reading your book really helped me think about the whole situation. I hope I can share it with others.

Sincerely,
—Elizabeth Young
Chicken Soup for the Teenage Soul Letters

Teens Talk
Growing Up

Insights and
Lessons Learned

Never look down on anybody unless you're helping him up.
—Jesse Jackson

44

Courage

Forgive all who have offended you, not for them, but for yourself.
—Harriet Nelson

The excited sound of seventh grade laughter and voices tumbled down the hallway as the students filed into the gym. I scanned the room, searching for my friends, and soon spotted them near the door to the restroom. I weaved my way through the mass of people and sat down next to my best friend, Lauren.

"So, what exactly are we doing here?" she questioned.

"Well, according to Mrs. Marks, we're supposed to be listening to a speaker about bullying, peer pressure and put-downs." I said this somewhat sarcastically, because the entire year our grade had been lectured over and over again on these topics. We were earning the reputation as the worst class in the school, which was not a reputation that my friends nor I were particularly proud of. As our science teacher stood in front of the entire grade level, attempting to get our attention, my friends and I sat back, prepared to sit through another monotonous speech full of harsh remarks about "Kids these days..." and "Your maturity level when you put someone down is no greater than that of an eight-year-old."

But as soon as she started talking, I snapped to attention. She had this way about her, as if she knew how to reach into our minds and souls and make us think. And for once, I actually began to think about what it was she was preaching about. I thought about all the kids who came to school every day, despite knowing that they would have to face cruel comments and sneering faces all day long.

One boy, in particular, came to mind. Every day, this boy came to first hour late, and I suspected it was because he needed to get medicine from the nurse. But this didn't stop the kids in the class from making fun of him. They punched him in the shoulder and said, "Hey, man! Where have you been?" And then another would add, "How's that girlfriend of yours? Oh sorry, we forgot. You don't have a girlfriend. You only have boyfriends." This harassment would continue until the teacher cut in, forcing the boys to stop. But it was too late—it always was. The boy would put his head down on his desk in shame. The worst, though, was when he tried to retaliate. His attackers only laughed and continued the cruelty until the entire room was laughing at his expense.

As I sat in the auditorium, absorbing everything the speaker had to say, thoughts of this poor boy crept into my head. I sighed, thinking how sorry I felt for him, not that there was anything I could do. I tuned back into the speaker and listened intently to her words of wisdom.

"Now, before I leave today, I would like to give everyone here an opportunity to say anything he or she wants to on the subject of bullying or peer pressure. You may apologize to a friend, thank someone for his or her kindness, anything. And this is the one time I can promise that no one, but no one, will laugh at you."

The stillness in the room made me believe her. Slowly, I saw a few hands raise tentatively in the air behind me. One girl wanted to apologize to a friend she had been ignoring recently. Another thanked a boy for his kindness when she slipped on the steps the other day. It was then that my moment of courage happened. The speaker called on me, and with shaking hands and clammy palms, I began to talk.

"What you said today really made sense. I know that it's true, because I see it every day in class. There is one person who is always made fun of. It doesn't matter why—it could be the way he looks, talks or even takes notes." My voice shook. "I think that everyone here has made fun of him at one time or another. I know I have. And now I really regret it. To us, it may just be a game, but to him, it must hurt. And I think... well, I think we need to stop."

Scared of my classmates' reaction, I felt like the silence that followed lasted forever. But then, soft clapping started in the front of the room, quickly spreading through the entire crowd. By the time I looked up, the soft pitter-patter had turned into a thunderous roar of applause. I had voiced something that everyone was feeling.

Later on that day, the boy whom I had been talking about came up to me privately and said thank you.

I noticed that from that day on, people began to treat him a little better. The teasing stopped, and people greeted him in the halls with a friendly, "Hi!" It was those little, everyday things that I noticed, and I'm sure he noticed them, too.

—Ruth Ann Supica
Chicken Soup for the Teenage Soul III

Illusion of Perfection

This perfect little princess
No one sees her pain
The way she bottles it up inside
She'll most likely go insane.

She has everything she could want
There is nothing else she needs
How could she feel so unhappy
In this perfect life she leads?

She has all the material things
She can even get the guys
But she's searching for internal happiness
In this perfected life of lies.

If people only knew
The thoughts that go through her head
Maybe they'd reach out to this princess
Before she ends up dead.

Luckily she's afraid of death
The thought of never awaking again
Hopefully this fear stays with her
So her life does not come to an end.

Everyone sees the small things
They don't make the connection
If they were to look at the big picture
They'd see it's all an illusion of perfection.

—Alicia A. Vasquez
Chicken Soup for the Teenage Soul: The Real Deal School

Sweet Lies

There is a wisdom of the head, and... a wisdom of the heart.
—Charles Dickens

I moved from Massachusetts to North Carolina the summer before eighth grade. It didn't take me long to notice that my new classmates were a lot more interested in dating than my old friends had been. Girls on the bus continually talked about who was "going with" who. At first I didn't know what they meant. Having a boyfriend at twelve or thirteen? I was totally not ready for that!

Still, I was all ears when it came to other people's love lives. A boy named Garth was a major subject of gossip. Every other day, the rumors had him going out with a different girl. He was a year behind me, but he rode my bus so I knew who he was. He was blond and cute and very smooth. I thought he was a little too in love with himself, but I could see why he was popular.

Garth never seemed to pay much attention to me. Not that I expected him to—I was a new kid, sort of a nerd and not what most people would call pretty. So I was totally surprised when he called me up at home one day in February. He called to say he liked me. A lot. Me!

A day or two later, he took the seat behind me on the bus and started talking in a quiet, serious voice. He talked about himself, about the hard life he'd had.

"We moved a lot when I was a kid," he said. "So I never had a best friend. And maybe because of that, I've always been a loner. I can act friendly on the outside, but I always keep the real, deep parts of me hidden."

He leaned closer to me. "I guess I'm just too sensitive," he said. "I feel things, I take things really hard... so, I don't want people to get close."

I got off the bus thinking that I hadn't really been fair to Garth. He wasn't stuck up. That was just a face he put on, so people wouldn't know how sensitive he was. I felt sorry for him. He was so nice—and so unhappy!

A few days after that, Garth came by my house after school. We stood around on my porch talking for a long time. It was cold, but we didn't care. Actually, we didn't notice. We were too involved in our conversation.

"I have to tell you," he said. "I think I'm falling in love with you. You're just so amazing, so perfect—"

"No, I'm not!" I said, blushing.

"You are!" he insisted. "You're beautiful, you have great manners...."

I'm not good with compliments even when I know they're true. But when they're not true, and I wish they were... "I'm not beautiful," I said. "I'm not even pretty."

"You are beautiful," said Garth. He put his arm around me. It felt strange, but I didn't try to stop him. "Look," he said. "I've gone with a lot of girls, and I know. You're special. You really are."

I shook my head, but I didn't try to argue.

"Listen," said Garth. "Tell you what—I'll help you stop saying bad things about yourself, if you'll help me stop being so sensitive. Okay?"

I smiled at him. "Okay," I said.

He held me closer and bent his head like he was going to kiss me. I didn't know what to do. I turned away suddenly, and his face just brushed my cheek. I felt kind of clumsy, but I was glad he'd missed. I wasn't ready for kissing, and I honestly didn't like him "that way."

I felt all mixed up inside. I was happy and excited and totally flattered, but something still felt wrong. For one thing, I felt like I was pretending to love him when I really didn't. Shouldn't I tell him the truth? But how? And how could he be in love with me, anyway? He hardly knew me!

Just then my mom turned on the outside light, and Garth let go of me fast. He said, "See you tomorrow!" and took off down the road.

The house felt stuffy and warm after all that time outside. I dropped my books in the kitchen and ran up to my bedroom to think.

I really only liked Garth as a friend, but his arm did feel nice around me. And it was kind of cool having someone in love with me. I told myself it wasn't like I had to do anything about it. What did "going out" with someone mean anyway, besides just spending time together? I could just tell him I wasn't ready for kissing—couldn't I?

The next day on the bus, Garth acted like nothing had happened between us. He acted like we were just friends. I told myself he wanted to play it down so the other kids wouldn't tease us. But his acting seemed a little too good.

For the next few days, whenever we were alone, Garth talked about how he loved me. But when other people were around, he acted like we were just friends. Of course, I was just friends with him, but the whole thing was starting to bother me. Was he ashamed of liking me? Or was he lying about it in the first place? Why would he lie?

A week went by, and after that, I hardly saw Garth at all. That was okay. I didn't exactly miss him. I was so confused about him, about what had happened and about what it meant. Then about a month later, I heard something that helped me understand.

I was on the bus when I heard a girl mention Garth's name. "It's disgusting," she said. "They actually brag about how many girls they've kissed! Garth's got the most, of course."

"Yeah," said her friend. "Like every seventh- and eighth-grade girl in the school! I hear he's working on the ninth-graders now."

I felt like I'd been hit in the stomach. I just wanted to crawl under the seat and die. How could I have been so stupid? How could I have believed a single one of his ridiculous lies?

It took me a while, but eventually I got over it. After all, he fooled a lot of girls, not just me. I just wished I'd listened to that voice in my head that said something was wrong. Now I know better. I know that you should always listen to that little warning voice, because it's usually right.

—Laura Gene Beck
Chicken Soup for the Girl's Soul

I'm Sorry...

I'm sorry for all the times I lost my temper
For the times when I was rude
For all the gifts that were given
And never received thank yous.
For all the love you've given me
And I haven't given back
For all the times you were patient
A virtue that I lack.
I'm sorry for all the people
To whom I was so cruel
To all the people I laughed at
I acted like a fool.
I couldn't see past your imperfections
I couldn't see past my pride
Your feelings I trampled all over
On my high horse I would ride.
I'm sorry for all the times I lied
For the people I hurt along the way
Not a day goes by that I don't regret it
And I'd take it back any day.
The only person I cared about
Was me and only me
And now I'm truly sorry
I only wish I could make you see.

I'm sorry for everything I've done
For all the people I let down
I'm only asking for a second chance
So I can turn things back around.
I know that it's a little late
My deeds can't be undone
I realize now that I was wrong
And I'm sorry everyone.

—Teal Henderson
Chicken Soup for the Teenage Soul on Tough Stuff

The Long Road Home

Continuity gives us roots; change gives us branches,
letting us stretch and grow and reach new heights.
—Pauline R. Kezer

I find myself packing again. Well, let's be completely honest, this isn't really packing—it's shoving three weeks' worth of dirty clothes into a suitcase and having my roommate sit on it so I can get it to close.

This time is different; this isn't the same nostalgic trip down memory lane as when I packed before college. This is the "night before my first trip home frantic pack." So you get the idea—my plane leaves in two hours, and no, college didn't teach me to procrastinate. I was experienced in that art long before I stepped onto my college campus.

So now that I'm packed, I have a minute to examine my emotions about my first trip home. I'm excited. My best friend, Matt, picks me up, groggy, for our 4:00 A.M. drive. My expectations are that I am going home to what I left: my parents, home-cooked meals, friends with whom I shared distinctive bonds and my long distance boyfriend, whom I have been dying to see. I am happy at college, but a trip home, to my family and friends, sounds like just the thing I need to prepare me for the prefinals crunch.

I think I will catch up on the missed hours of sleep on the plane. Instead, I look around and realize that most of the exhausted passengers are students just like me. Below us, in the cargo bin, sits a year's worth of dirty laundry at least.

I miss my connecting flight, so I am later than expected. I step off the plane to find my mom frantic, thinking I had been "abducted" on the trip home. I look at her puzzled. I guess in a mother's eyes there is no logical explanation for being late, such as the obvious flight trouble. I assure her that I am fine and that I don't need to fly as an "unaccompanied minor" on the way back.

A few hours later, I'm back at the airport, waiting for my boyfriend's arrival home. He steps off the plane with the same groggy but excited look I wore hours before. We drive over to see my dad, who seems calmer than my mother had been. I ask to see my room, expecting to find my shrine, my old pompoms, prom pictures, candid photos of friends and dolls scattered about. To my surprise, everything is gone; there's not even a trace I had ever lived in the room. I'm starting to wonder if I really had been abducted on the way home. It's as if the second I became a "college" student, I had ceased to exist.

I start to wonder what else had changed since I'd been gone. My parents are in an awkward transition, wondering how to treat me now. They wrestle with whether to treat me—still their daughter—as one of them, an adult, or as the child they feel they sent away months earlier.

I run into two of my best friends from high school; we stare blankly at each other. We ask the simple questions and give simple, abrupt answers. It's as if we have nothing to say to each other. I wonder how things have changed so much in such a small amount of time. We used to laugh and promise that no matter how far away we were, our love for each other would never change. Their interests don't interest me anymore, and I find myself unable to relate my life to theirs.

I had been so excited to come home, but now I just look at it all and wonder: Is it me?

Why hadn't the world stood still here while I was gone? My room isn't the same, my friends and I don't share the same bond, and my parents don't know how to treat me—or who I am, for that matter.

I get back to school feeling half-fulfilled, but not disappointed. I sit up in my bed in my dorm room, surrounded by my pictures, dolls and mementos. As I wonder what has happened, I realize that I can't expect the world to stand still and move forward at the same time. I can't change and expect that things at home will stay the same. I have to find comfort in what has changed and what is new; keep the memories, but live in the present.

A few weeks later, I'm packing again, this time for winter break. My mom meets me at the curb. I have come home accepting the changes, not only in my surroundings, but most of all in me.

—Lia Gay
Chicken Soup for the College Soul

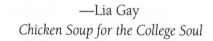

49

Perfection Is Just an Illusion

We don't see things as they are, we see them as we are.
—Anaïs Nin

I didn't mean to stare, but I couldn't help it. She was just so perfect. There, across the room, sat Stephanie, the most popular girl at school. History class was just about over and my notes thus far consisted of my name and the date. I had spent the entire class admiring the qualities that made her the crush of all the boys and the envy of all the girls. She had everything I ever wanted—beautiful blond hair, a twenty-four-inch waist and the most extensive wardrobe of anyone I knew. Most important, though, she had Craig, a guy I had had a crush on for the past three years. He was the most popular guy at school, so it was only natural that he and Stephanie would be dating. Stephanie led the most perfect life imaginable for a sixteen-year-old girl, or so I thought.

One rainy Monday afternoon, I sat in the locker hallway catching up on some biology homework. Stephanie suddenly walked in, sobbing uncontrollably. Her best friend, Alyssa, was desperately trying to console her. I wondered what could have possibly gone wrong in Stephanie's "perfect" life. Maybe the rain made her hair a little frizzy, I thought. As I listened to Stephanie and Alyssa's conversation, I discovered that Stephanie's life was not nearly as perfect as

I thought. She explained that her mother had been diagnosed with breast cancer over the weekend. She also said that she turned down the opportunity to go away to her dream college because she refused to leave her mother's side during this difficult time.

I had been jealous of popular girls like Stephanie all throughout high school. After all, they had everything they wanted and absolutely nothing to worry about. That Monday afternoon in the locker hallway, I came to realize that I couldn't have been more wrong. It's easy to assume that popular people lead perfect lives, but in reality, they have problems just like everyone else.

—Valentina Cucuzza
Chicken Soup for the Teenage Soul: The Real Deal School

50

Firmer Ground

'd had a crush on him for as long as I could remember. His sandy blond hair was to his shoulders. His eyes were brown, his skin pale. He was quiet, mild-mannered. Most of all, I was drawn to his smile—when I could coax it out of him. I was in junior high. He was in high school.

He was my friend's brother and, for some reason, I believed he was taboo. Maybe because I knew instinctively my friend would be angry if I ever started to see him. Or maybe I knew the age gap of three years would not sit well with my parents. Or maybe, more than anything, I was terrified he'd reject me.

So I kept my feelings as quiet as a cat hiding from a pack of dogs. But every time I saw him at my friend Tina's house, my heart beat hard and I could barely breathe. When I saw him walking up the street alone, I'd rush over to him and glow in his warmth. He'd wave, smile a weak hello and ask me how I was doing.

He was an artist and a good one, and the day he gave me a pen drawing of a seagull soaring through the sky, I was in my glory. I saw it as a symbol, a sign perhaps, of affection shown by an older boy who felt it wise to keep his love for me inside. Of course, it was more likely that he just felt sorry for such a gangly kid.

It didn't matter. I cherished his artwork and truly believed that he would be a great artist someday. If only I had such talent, I'd moan. He'd always tell me that I probably did have a lot of talent. I just hadn't found it yet.

Somewhere as we were growing older and suffering the pangs of adolescence, Mike lost his ground. I'm not sure if he knew where to put his feet anymore. His family life was a disaster: a mentally ill mother, a father with a wicked second wife (at least that's how the children saw her) and a new baby who took all the interest away from three other kids.

Whenever I walked by his home, there was always a man—often a different man—parked in a car across the street from Mike's house. It happened so often that I began to wonder what was going on. I began to ask questions of my friends. I learned that my sweet, reserved Mike had turned into a high school drug dealer. Not the small kind of drug dealer. He was a big fish and according to my friends, he was in trouble. Someone was closing in on him—the police or the creeps who got him involved in the first place.

I knew that a lot of kids dabbled in drugs—mostly marijuana. But no one, and I mean no one, took the risk of dealing. The odds of getting hurt or busted were far too great in this middle-class neighborhood. I often wondered what led Mike there. Did he hate his parents? Did he feel lost? Did he want payback time for his dad remarrying and leaving his mom? Who knows what went on in his brain. I just wished he had talked to me because I really cared about him. The problem was that he didn't care. And I was too afraid to go to Mike and confront him about whether he was selling drugs.

When the knock on the door came, I looked out the balcony of my house and saw one of my neighbors standing there. "I thought you and your family should know I found Mike in the canyon this morning. My sons and I were walking there and I saw Mike bowing as though he were praying. It didn't look too good."

Our neighbor had held his young boys back as he investigated. Mike was dead. He had hung himself from a tree, and had died in a kneeling position on the ground, his head slumped forward. The news pounded my face as if a block of cement had struck. I thought I would pass out, but instead, I was sobbing. Within the hour, I raced up to Mike's to see how Tina was.

She was sitting on her bed, just staring out at empty space. I would learn later that she was in shock. In a dull voice, she explained that she and her older brother, Gary, had known that Mike was dealing drugs. After Mike's body was discovered, Gary went into Mike's room and cleaned out Mike's top drawer before the police came. There, tucked underneath a few shirts, was every drug imaginable: LSD, cocaine, pot and an abundance of colorful pills. Soon after, Tina ran away. It took us hours to find her.

My parents tried to explain why Mike died. But they couldn't. They didn't even know he was a dealer. They didn't know the ugly things we kids faced going to school every day. It was a trying time not only because Mike died, but because I was shocked to peel away the layers and find a Mike I had never known. Or maybe he was that kind, sweet boy who let his difficult life suck him into a world of deceit, fast bucks and danger.

To this day, I always wonder if he really killed himself or if some other drug dealers helped him along the way. It was just too odd that he had supposedly hung himself from a thin tree limb but was kneeling, his weight supported by the earth.

I will never know the answer. But I do know this: He was a good artist. I kept that drawing he gave me for years after, always looking at it with wonder and admiration, wishing I could sketch that way.

I also know that along the way Mike lost his ground, but he gave me a lot to think about, and what I thought about gave me strength. My family moved to the East Coast my first year of high school. My new friends were just beginning to experiment with drugs, and there was tremendous peer pressure for me to go along.

But by now, I felt old and weary when it came to drugs. Been there, done that, seen what they can do. I decided I wanted the chance to know what I was going to be in the future. Mike had given me some firm ground to stand on.

—Diana Chapman
Chicken Soup for the Teenage Soul II

Minutes Like Hours

You walk into the store
and stride down the aisle.
You pick me up and
try to look casual while
you carry me down
to the checkout line.
Pull out your wallet,
you soon will be mine.
Your friends are observing
every move that you make.
The clerk asks for ID—
you show him a fake.
You quickly walk down
to the front of the store.
Your friends are waiting for you
as you step out the door.
You hop in the car
and drive away from the shop.
Then you shut off the ignition,
and pop off my top.
You take a few drinks
and pass me around.
That's when you decide
to take a drive around town.

You turn on your car
and put your foot on the clutch.
I'm sober, you think,
I didn't have very much.
You pull onto the road
with me by your side,
Taking occasional sips
as you enjoy the ride.
Then the brakes on the car
in front of you squeal.
You try hard to stop,
but lose control of the wheel.
You skid off the road,
and you know you have crashed.
The dashboard is shattered,
the windshield is smashed.
Minutes like hours,
You're in treacherous pain,
that washes your senses,
envelops your brain.
The screams all around you
are faint to your ears,
as life flashes before you,
your hopes and your fears.
Minutes like hours,
you plead and you pray,
I'll never touch it again,
just let me live one more day.
Your mind starts to go dark,
it falls apart piece by piece.
And then you slip into blackness,
the pain has finally ceased.

Before you entered that store,
you should have thought twice,
for I am the substance
that cost you your life.

—Vidhya Chandrasekaran
Chicken Soup for the Teenage Soul III

52

So Afraid to Change

was seventeen years old. I had just graduated in the top ten of my high school class. I had a lot of friends. I had a scholarship to attend Johns Hopkins University. I had a girlfriend and a great family.

And when the time came to leave for college, to say goodbye to the place I had always called home, I lost it. I lost it the night before leaving, saying goodbye to my friends. I lost it in the car during the eight-hour drive to Baltimore. And when we actually got to the campus, I lost it completely. There was no way I was going to make it as a college student, not at Hopkins, not anywhere. I needed to go home. I needed to go home now.

My dad disagreed. At first. But eventually, after several hours of discussion back at the hotel room my parents had originally booked only for themselves, it was decided. I would take a leave of absence. The school understood and told me that my acceptance and scholarship would be held for me if I ever wanted them. But I had no intention of ever taking them up on their generous offer. What I wanted to do was go home and be eighteen forever.

My girlfriend was surprised to get the call that I had come back. She seemed more concerned than happy. Probably the right response.

Briefly, everything returned to the way I had remembered. I was back home and nothing had changed. I was still eighteen; I still had a girlfriend; I was still with my family. But then my friends started to leave for their respective colleges. Soon, there weren't as many people around to hang out with, and the phrase "You need to get a job" was being thrown at me from all directions.

On a random drive through my town's shopping plaza, a horseshoe-shaped strip mall, I saw a "Help Wanted" sign in the window of an everything-for-a-dollar store. I stopped in and asked to see the manager. Her name was Jean. She had bangs teased way up above her forehead and popped her gum incessantly. She smelled like a bowling alley.

"You're not going to college?" she asked.

"No."

"That's fine. I never went to college. Just makes you stuck up anyways."

"Yeah."

"So you'll be working five days a week, six hours a day. Your big jobs are mopping the floor and unloading the trucks that come with deliveries."

"I've got the job?"

"Yeah, you got the job, college boy. We'll start you at $4.25 an hour. That's five cents more than what we could legally pay you."

So it was done. Thirty hours a week. $4.25 an hour. Before taxes, a grand total of $127.50 every week. I started the next day.

The first truck arrived at 10:15, fifteen minutes after I had punched in. The second truck came at 1:00. The third truck came at 3:00. By the end of the day I had unloaded almost 12,000 pounds of cut-rate merchandise. I had earned $25.50.

The days wore on. There were many frustrating aspects to my new job, but the one I remember most is how angry I would get when the water in my mop bucket got dirty before I had finished cleaning the floor. One day I just stopped mopping. Jean threatened my job if I didn't return mopping to my daily duties. I made excuses. I hid. I built a small room, deep within the piles of recently delivered boxes. I would read in my little fort. That was where I read *Lolita* and *Catch-22* for the first time.

About a week after our mop confrontation, Jean was fired. Turns out she had been "borrowing" merchandise from the store to furnish her home. About thirty seconds after I'd heard of Jean's dismissal I walked into the storeroom and wheeled my mop and bucket into a closet. I closed the door and never set eyes on them again.

In late October, the regional supervisor made a surprise visit to our store to see how we were doing without the services of a manager. She pulled me aside as her visit was coming to an end. "You're a smart kid, right?" I wasn't sure how to answer so I just nodded. "Well, a smart kid who works hard could really go places here." I wasn't sure if she was joking. "Talk to me in about six months, I might have an assistant manager position opening up in one of our other stores. You could be making one and a half times what you're making now." In six months, I could be making $6.40 an hour. The prospect left me underwhelmed. "Oh," she continued, "and see if you can't find a mop and clean up this floor. It's filthy out here."

On Halloween, my girlfriend broke up with me. She called me after taking her little brother trick-or-treating. She asked me to meet her, that we needed to talk. When I pulled up, she was waiting for me on the curb. She was dressed as a pumpkin. An orange felt globe covered her body from shoulders to thighs. Her head was painted green.

By early November, my posture was noticeably worse. I rarely smiled, and even on those days when I didn't work, my clothes still smelled like cut-rate potpourri. I was down. It seemed like everything I had loved about this town, about being home, had changed. Then one night I got invited to go sledding. I lived outside of Buffalo, where snow in November is not an uncommon occurrence. I snuck onto the local country club grounds, where the best hills were located, with some friends of mine who were enjoying their senior year of high school. Surrounded by the exceptionally clear and chilly night, all they could talk about was college, the people they would meet, the parties they would go to, the chance to finally get out of this "tiny, stifling town." I listened to them for almost an hour. I started thinking about the way Hopkins' campus had looked when we drove up for the first time. I saw the students unloading vans and U-Hauls. A beach volleyball court had been built in front of one of the dorms. Flyers on the trees had announced upcoming parties and concerts. That was all there. And I was here.

And I was jealous.

It shocked me. It was then that I realized I had changed. I had been trying with everything I could muster to hold onto that time of graduations, friends and girlfriends, trying to hold off the future as long as I could, without even realizing that I had been changing the whole time. I'd let some ties drop away, others had come undone. And now I was jealous of my high-school friends. I wanted their future, the same one I had put on hold.

It was time to act.

The next morning, I met my dad in the dining room. "Dad," I said, "you think you could call Hopkins and ask about me heading back there this January?"

He smiled, didn't make a big deal. "I'll see what I can find out," is all he said.

Two months later, my father and I were taking that same route that had proven so problematic in September. The eight-hour drive seemed to take forever, and I'd be lying if I said a little of that old fear, that longing for the past, didn't come back. But every time it did, I thought about that night in the snow. I felt the rush of excitement that came with thoughts of starting a new chapter in my life, with new challenges, and the fear faded away. As we drove through the backwoods of Pennsylvania, we passed by a faded old sign on rusted posts, maybe from the previous fall, maybe from the Great Depression, advertising "jack-o-lanterns next left." I smiled and pulled a map from the glove box. We only had about a hundred more miles to go.

—Chris Sullivan
Chicken Soup for the Teenage Soul IV

53

Have You Ever

Have you ever lived my life?
Spent one minute in my shoes?
If you haven't then tell me why
You judge me as you do.

Have you ever woken up in the morning
Wondering if this was your last day on Earth?
Have you ever left your house
Unsure if you'd return?

Have you ever seen your friend get shot
Outside his favorite store?
Have you ever seen a friend die
From drugs he'd never used before?

Have you ever seen your mom get beat up
By your stepdad messed up on booze?
Have you ever had an unwanted pregnancy
Forcing you to choose?

Have you ever sat beneath the stars
Hoping God will hear?
Have you ever seen your friend drive away
After way too many beers?

Have you ever had a friend
Experiment with weed?
Have you ever covered up guilt
By doing a good deed?

Have you ever considered suicide
As the only way?
Have you ever tried to hide yourself
Behind the things you say?

Have you ever wanted to protect
Your friends and everyone in sight?
Have you ever felt such pain
That you cried yourself to sleep at night?

Have you ever lived my life,
Spent one minute in my shoes?
If you haven't, then tell me why
You judge me as you do.

—Tiffany Blevins
Chicken Soup for the Teenage Soul on Tough Stuff

The Need for Speed

Life is like a coin. You can spend it any way you wish,
but you only spend it once.
—Lillian Dickson

Nobody told me what to expect during my teenage years. But what I was most unprepared for was loss. Not just loss of childhood, but loss of innocence and simplicity, too. I felt like I was standing between two continents, childhood and adulthood, in some in-between, nowhere zone.

So I started doing crazy things that involved speed. Like clinging to the roof of a car while my buddy T. J. gunned the engine and spun in circles in an empty parking lot at night—knowing full well if I were to slip or let go, my life would be over. Or like skiing or biking down steep hills so fast I could barely stay in control—all without a helmet. Was it that the speed made me feel alive? Or was I trying to get away from everything around me?

Although by all accounts I was a normal, soccer-playing, sixteen-year-old suburban kid on the north shore of Chicago, with a B+ average, a doctor for a father and a housewife for a mother, everything seemed to be going haywire around me. I started losing friends in dramatic ways, one after another.

First there was my friend Nick, the basketball team captain, the football quarterback, the guy every guy wanted to be and every girl had a crush on. One sunny suburban day, Nick crashed his motorcycle into a truck. The next day he was paralyzed from the waist down for life. For life? I couldn't fathom the notion. I tried to stay friends with him, but the Nick I knew was gone.

Next was John, the lead guitarist in the coolest band, the guy who would shut his eyes on stage, lean back, bathed in a magenta glow, and let his fingers scatter up the frets, effortlessly, while everyone gawked. He got heavy into drugs, invited his girlfriends to climb the tree outside his window to his bedroom where they'd have sex, and then he'd help them down the tree before dawn. Very Romeo and Juliet, he thought. I'd been friends with John forever and knew that there was something basically good in him that had gotten buried. But whenever I saw him his eyes were glazed over and he could barely walk, and I soon realized there was nothing left between us. He tried suicide a few times in a few different ways, and one frigid January Sunday, his parents had the men in white take him, yelling and screaming, to a psychiatric clinic.

Then my friend Heather, who had always been a great student, suddenly became obsessed over perfecting her homework. She wrote and rewrote term papers, staying up all night, going to sleep just before dawn, walking zombielike through school corridors, lost, often bewildered, always postponing handing in papers so she could make changes. In class, she began plucking hairs from the crown of her head. Her parents sent her away, too.

Those were the dramatic losses. But I felt everyone was pulling away, growing faster, doing more, knowing more, being smarter, moving quicker, getting more grades, girls, glamour. I couldn't get a handle on it. And nobody seemed to be paying any attention to those of us who were left behind.

One day, T. J. asked me to go winter camping about two hours north in Wisconsin. He had the whole thing figured out: We'd snowshoe in with backpacks, a gas stove, sleeping bags and a tent. We'd stay a weekend, then miss a day of school. That was the part that intrigued me: It was a statement to everyone at school that I was different, not interested in the usual stuff, the kind of guy who could take care of himself. "What if there's a freak storm and we freeze?" I asked. He looked at me as if to say, "Danger is what we're after, right?" Against all odds, my parents, after hours of haggling, let me go with him.

So there I was, leaning against the hood of T. J.'s car, strapping on snowshoes. "I never used these," I said. "Just like walking," he replied. But it wasn't. For me, it was more like floating—above the world, above my worries. I liked the slow pace, the tracks I left behind me and the untouched snow ahead.

It wasn't that night, when we made a partial igloo, pitched our tent, melted snow to make water, cooked a pathetic astronautlike meal and fell into deep sleep. Nor was it on the second day, when we melted more snow and fretted about the need for water and the threat of dehydration. But on our last day, it warmed by ten degrees and everything around us started to melt. T. J. was going on about new dangerous stuff we could do back home: laying down on streets so startled drivers would have to stop; climbing up roofs of cheerleaders' houses and tapping on their windows; throwing iceballs at cars as they drove down a lonely ravine, hoping the drivers might chase us... when he spotted an iced-over pond and dared me to touch the center. A voice said, "No." The more he urged me on, the more I had to get away. I began to snowshoe up a ridge, and then I continued until there was no sign of T. J., where the only sounds were my breath and snow falling in clumps off pines.

Suddenly, inexplicably, a surge of sadness seemed to pulse through my feet, up my legs, through my arms and right out my skull. It wasn't like crying, more like an eruption... and it felt good, natural, sane. And when it ceased, some time later, I realized it was just me in the world, but that was a gift, not a curse. My life was mine to make or break. It was my show, my ball game. I couldn't control everything. But I realized I'd lost more than just friends: I'd temporarily lost myself. The speed I'd been seeking by clinging to the top of cars in parking lots hadn't helped me find myself. One-step-at-a-time snowshoes had.

—James D. Barron
Chicken Soup for the Teenage Soul on Love & Friendship

55

Declaration of Humanhood

Dear Chicken Soup Servers,

First of all, I would like to thank you on behalf of all insecure teenagers and young adults. Your books help us understand that we are not alone. I honestly believe that the period from age ten to twenty is the most difficult and loneliest period in life. Your books are teaching us that although we may be different on the outside, inside we're all the same. It's such a hectic time in life that we often forget we're all human. Being human we have certain rights. In order to remind myself that it's okay to be a human (and not a perfect machine), I wrote the "Declaration of Humanhood." I've sent it to you so that, if you choose to make it an ingredient in your next Chicken Soup book, it can remind others that they have the right to be human, too.

Declaration of Humanhood

I hereby declare that I am human.

I am human in my joy and laughter, and I am human in my pain and tears. I am human in my need to love and help others, and in my need to be loved and helped by others. I am human in my dreams and accomplishments, but most of all I am human in my flaws and mistakes.

Being human, I am entitled to the following rights:

1. *I have the right to be imperfect.*

2. *I have the right to make many (sometimes huge) mistakes.*

3. *I have the right to learn from my mistakes and then move on with my life.*

4. *I have the right to forgive myself.*

5. *I have the right to feel what I feel.*

6. *I have the right to laugh until it hurts, and cry until it stops hurting.*

7. *I have the right to live my life as I choose.*

8. *I have the right to happiness.*

9. *I have the right to my own beliefs.*

10. *I have the right to true friends and true love.*

11. *I have the right to be loved by others.*

12. *I have the right to be loved by me.*

Sincerely,
—Michelle Bouchard
Chicken Soup for the Teenage Soul Letters

Chapter
6

Teens Talk
Growing Up

Family Ties

You don't choose your family.
They are God's gift to you, as you are to them.
—Desmond Tutu

A Young Man's Odyssey

The weak can never forgive. Forgiveness is the attribute of the strong.
—Mahatma Gandhi

"Dear Dad," I wrote, "I want to come home." After many minutes of thinking as I sat by the side of a busy highway, I tore the page in half and wadded it into a small ball. I'd started this letter many times, but had never really finished. I wanted to go home—home to my parents and sisters, but...

I had run away from home after finishing high school. My parents had insisted I go to college, but I was tired of school. I hated it. I was determined not to go. And, besides, my father was too strict. I had too many chores to do around the farm. I hated the work!

There had been a quarrel between my father and me. I threw some things into a bag and left angrily, as my father shouted after me, "If you leave, don't come back!" My mother cried openly, and I have seen those tears during a hundred sleepless nights.

The letter had to be written.

Dear Dad,

It's been more than a year now. I've traveled east to west. I've had dozens of jobs. None of them amounted to very much. Always the same questions: "How much education have you got?" It seems they always want college men for the good jobs.

Dad, you and Mother were right about everything. I know now that the work on the farm didn't hurt me, and I'm convinced I need college. I'm also convinced that both of you loved me. That was not easy for me to write, and I couldn't have written it a year ago. I've met some nice people since I've been away, as well as rough and tough people. I thought I could take all kinds, but sometimes it wasn't so easy, especially not having a good home to come to at night, where there was love and security. I wasn't really aware of what a home means until I'd been away for a few months.

Dad, I've learned a lesson. I want to come home. I know you said if I left, that I couldn't come back, but I'm praying you'll change your mind. I know I made you terribly angry that day— and hurt you, too.

I wouldn't blame you if you refused me, but I must ask you. I know I should have written before, but I was afraid you wouldn't want to hear from me.

I want to come home and be a part of the family again. I'd like to go to college and learn how to be a successful farmer, and then, if you'll let me, maybe I could farm with you.

I'm on the road now, so you can't answer me by letter. But in a few days (I don't know what day because I'm hitchhiking), I'll be passing the farm. And, Dad, if you'll let me come home, please leave the porch light on. I'll make it a point to pass at night. If there is no light, I'll just keep on going, and I won't have any hard feelings if the porch is dark. I'll understand.

Give my love to Mother and the girls.

Love,

Your son

As I folded the letter and put it into an envelope, I felt a refreshing relief. It was as if a heavy load had been lifted from my shoulders. I put the letter into my shirt pocket and lugged my beat-up suitcase closer to the side of the road, and held out my thumb to the first passing car. I had a long way to go before I'd know the answer.

Night came and I'd gotten only fifty or sixty miles since noon. I had mailed the letter in a little, insignificant post office. After I dropped the letter into the out-of-town slot, I was a little nervous. Perhaps I shouldn't have mailed it, but it was done, and I had to be on my way.

Sometime the following day, the rides had gotten few and far between. I hadn't any sleep the night before, and I was weary as well as tired. Crossing over the road to a giant oak at the edge of a field, I stretched out on the grass and tried to sleep. But sleep did not come easily. In a nearby field a tractor hummed pleasantly, two dogs chased a rabbit within a few yards of me. From the farmhouse, nestled in a clump of trees on a hill, I could hear small children engaged in play; a rooster crowed and a hen cackled. I imagined I could smell fresh apple pie. Then, with closed eyes, I could vividly see my own home, the one that I had so recklessly left in a moment of anger. I wondered what my little sisters were doing. They could be such pests, but in their eyes, I could do no wrong. And, oh, how my mother could cook, and she was always saying as we sat down to eat, "I fixed this just for you, Son."

I couldn't bear my thoughts any longer. I got to my feet, and with the refreshing smell of fresh-cut hay in my nostrils, I started down the desolate road—the long road home. But was it still my home? My father was fair-minded, but he was strong-willed.

A car picked me up, and it was good to have someone to talk with. The driver was a salesman and very pleasant.

"Where you going, Son?" he asked good-naturedly.

There was a long silence before I said, "Home."

"Where have you been?" he asked.

I knew he wasn't prying. There was something about his face that told me he was interested. "All over," I said.

"Been away from home long?"

I smiled, a little self-conscious, and said, "One year, one month and two days."

He didn't look at me, but he smiled, and I knew he understood. He told me about his family. He had two sons; one was my age and one was older.

As darkness approached, he found a place to eat and insisted that I join him. I was dirty and told him I would shame him, but he wouldn't take no for an answer. He was going to spend the night there, and after we had eaten, he talked me into spending the night, too. He reasoned that I could get cleaned up and get some rest before going on. Somehow, he reminded me of my father. I told him I had very little money, and after he had bought my supper, I couldn't let him spend any more on me.

However, I stayed. The next morning, after breakfast, I tried to thank him, but he said, "You're a fine boy. You see, my older son ran away from home two years ago—two years and fifteen days." He looked away and then said, "I hope somebody will be nice to my son."

I didn't know what to say. He shook my hand and smiled warmly.

"Thank you, sir, for everything," I stammered. "And, I hope..."

"Thank you," he said, "and good luck."

Two days later, I was within fifty miles of home. I hadn't had a ride for hours. Darkness came slowly. I walked, not waiting for anyone to stop. Some inner force was driving me forward—homeward. But the faster I walked, the more doubts I had. Suppose the porch would be dark? What would I do? Where would I go?

A big truck and trailer slowed and stopped. I ran and got in.

"How far you going?" the dark, burly driver asked.

"About forty or fifty miles from here. Are you going that far?" I asked.

"Farther," he muttered.

There was very little conversation. He was not easy to talk to. I pretended to be sleepy and leaned back and closed my eyes.

Thirty minutes later rain began to fall, slowly at first, and then it was coming down in sheets. I dozed, awoke and dozed again.

Then, with the rain pouring, we were nearing my father's farm. I was wide awake. Would there be a light on the porch? I was straining my eyes to see through the darkness and the rain. Suddenly, we were there. I couldn't look. I couldn't bear to look and not see a light. I closed my eyes tightly, and my heart pounded.

The driver chuckled and spoke roughly, "Look at that, would you! That house there, the one we just passed. Must be some kind of nuts! Three or four chairs were settin' on the porch with lighted lamps in every one of them, and an ol' man was out there with a flashlight aimed toward the road—and the porch light was on, too!"

—Calvin Louis Fudge
Chicken Soup for the Father's Soul

57

The Sound of My Father's Voice

have never forgotten the sound of my father's voice as he knelt by my bed with his back hunched, his head craned low and his hands resting on his lap. It's his storytelling voice that I remember—a voice that dropped a note or two but still managed to rise above the murmuring noise of the fans that scattered the hot air in the room. Slow, even and controlled, my father's voice, his presence, filled the room and diffused itself just as the single bulb from the brass lamp cast a dim glow of light over his face.

Growing up, I was always known as the kid with the fun father, the tall dad with the raspy voice and funny African accent who was always willing to throw me on his shoulders or wrestle me to the ground. It was my father who brought my best friend, Chris, and me to car shows, who took us to basketball games, coached our soccer team and, on occasion, took us fishing.

In my father's mind, the future took precedence above all else, which is why he was always there, at every soccer game and outing, tracking and mapping my every move. It was never really a matter of where I was, so much as where I was going. For my father, the purpose of the present was to point the way to what lay next. "What," he asked me nearly every day, "do you want to do when you grow up?" I began following the stock market in second grade as a way of giving him an answer. My father would come home and I would tell him how the market had done. "Up fifty points today, Dad." "Down thirty yesterday." Where the market actually went I never knew, and still don't to this day. I knew though that it went somewhere, and that my knowing mattered significantly to him.

When I entered high school things began to change between my father and me. I suddenly became known as the kid with the mean father: the father who barged into high school parties, disrupting the flow of alcohol in order to pull his son out and take him home. "Not while I'm around," he had always said every time I broke a rule. "Not while I'm here." His presence was almost omniscient, amazing in its ability to trail me around every corner and stand within earshot of every word.

My father and I had what would be the first in a series of small fallouts during those first two years in high school. My friend Chris and I had both suddenly found ourselves thrust into a world where being "cool" meant skipping classes and staying out late at night despite how much work we had to do. When Chris' father left him and his mother our freshman year, I followed him out night after night as he searched for solace or comfort away from home.

My grades began to slip, and my father said he couldn't understand what was happening. When I came home late one weekend after another, he would look at me and say that he didn't know who I was anymore or where I was going. He began to grow angry. I began to grow angry. "I won't wait for you to mess up," he said to me one night. "That won't happen while I'm around." This was tough love for him. This was my father telling me openly, directly and honestly that he would never let go of everything he had raised me to believe, everything he himself believed, if I were to fail myself.

When my best friend, Chris, and I were caught skipping class, I could visibly see the anger in his face for the first time in my life. "Don't you know what it took for me to be here?" he asked me as we walked out of the principal's office. Didn't I know how much my mother and he had sacrificed to come to this country? Didn't I know how much was thrown away in the name of hope to bring me to where I was now? "Everything," he would say, "everything has been for you kids."

By then, though, I no longer feared his presence. We were beyond that now. He seemed distant and far removed from the world I was in. How, I thought, can he possibly understand all that is happening in my life? His words were still there though, as was the voice he had once used to read to me. No longer intimidating, they stood now as the hallmark of our relationship. They reminded me of what we had once had, and what I wanted to have again. I began to look at my face in the mirror every night after I came home, and I knew that my father was right. I didn't recognize the reflection staring back at me.

In the middle of my sophomore year of high school, just before Thanksgiving, Chris ran away from home. His mother came to our house looking for him. She was tired and desperate and on the verge of tears. Before she could finish telling me her story, my father walked into the room with his coat on and his car keys in his hand. He had already heard all that he needed to hear. "We'll find him," he said, as he put his arm around me and walked to the car.

My father and I drove around Chicago for over two hours that night looking for Chris. My father asked me how I was doing, and all I could muster up the courage to say was, "Fine." He asked me what I thought had happened to Chris in the past two years to bring all of this about and all I could say was, "I don't know."

It was below freezing that night, as it is during most Chicago winters, and we both knew that if Chris were here, we probably wouldn't find him, and that even if we did, he probably wouldn't come with us. Truth was, he was out there, and I was with my father, and no amount of pleading or begging would bring us together.

Driving that evening through the nearly deserted streets of the west side of Chicago, I couldn't help but constantly turn my head to stare at my father sitting behind the wheel of the car. I found it strange that he should be driving me again to pick up a friend. I knew then, perhaps clearer and better than ever before, just what he had meant when he had said, "Not while I'm here." I knew then, too, that had he not been there all those years, sitting by my bed or behind the wheel, then I wouldn't have been where I was now, and that he, more than anything else, was the larger-than-life portrait that framed the backdrop through which I viewed the world. I must have thanked him for driving me that evening, for being there, just as I had thanked him a thousand times before for doing just that.

When we returned home that evening, Chris had already found his way back home by himself. His mother called to thank my father. He told her that Chris was like a second son to him, and there was no need for thanks. Years later now, I can see that my father's search for Chris was also a search for me, and that in the end, I also found my way back home that night.

—Dinaw Mengestu
Chicken Soup for the Teenage Soul IV

58

Just Like Always

Dogs' lives are too short. Their only fault, really.
—*Agnes Sligh Turnbull*

For as long as I could remember, Ivan had always been at the door when I came home, wagging his brown tail in greeting. Tonight when I walked in after my classes, he wasn't there.

"Ivan?"

Silence was my only answer.

Then my mother appeared from the kitchen. "Ivan is not feeling well, Lori. He's downstairs in the family room. He's getting old."

"Old? Mom, he's only eleven or twelve."

"Fourteen," Mom corrected. "He's been with us a long time."

"When did he get sick?"

"He hasn't been himself for quite a while. He hasn't had much of an appetite. And he sleeps a lot more."

"But this is the first time he hasn't been at the door to meet me just like, well... always."

"He's made an effort to be up here every night lately because he loves you so much."

"He's going to get better, isn't he?"

Mom avoided my eyes. "I took him to the vet today. The doctor gave me some medicine to keep him comfortable, but nothing else can be done."

I couldn't breathe. A fist grabbed my heart, squeezing tightly. "You... you mean he's... going to die?"

"While you were growing up, honey, he was growing old."

I could have cried. But when you're almost twenty... well...

The phone rang. "Hi." It was my girlfriend Cathy. "What time do you want me to pick you up for the movie?"

"Ivan is sick."

"Ivan? Who's Ivan?"

"Ivan. My dog."

"Oh. I haven't heard you mention him, have I? Anyway, I'm sorry, but what time shall I pick you up?"

"Well, Cath, I... I don't think I can go. I want to stay home with Ivan."

"What? Lori, we've been waiting weeks for this movie to open, and now you're not going on account of a dog?"

"Ivan isn't just any dog, Cath. He's my friend, once-upon-a-time playmate, and—"

"Okay, Lori, I get your drift." I could tell by her voice how upset she was. "Are you going or not?"

"No. I'm staying home with Ivan."

The phone went dead in my hand. Some people just didn't understand.

As I went downstairs, I thought about what Cathy had said. "Who's Ivan?" Had I really never mentioned him? It wasn't that long ago that we went everywhere together. In the last few years, though, my interests had changed. Still, my love for him hadn't. Only how would he know that if I didn't take the time to show him? Ivan seemed happy, so I hadn't thought that much about it.

Ivan's tail wagged weakly as I sat down beside his bed. He tried to raise his head, but I leaned closer so he wouldn't have to, my hand caressing his brown body. "How's my buddy? Not too great, my friend?"

His tail flopped again, his black eyes gazing into mine. Where have you been? they seemed to say. I've been waiting for you.

Tears filled my eyes as I stroked his back. What had Mom said?

I'd grown up while Ivan had grown old. Although I always petted him in passing, I couldn't remember when we'd last done anything together.

I shifted my position and Ivan tried to get up. "No, no," I whispered. "I'm not leaving you. We have a little catching up to do." He settled down again, nuzzling my leg.

"Remember when you were a puppy, Ivan, and how on Mother's Day you brought home a dead mouse and placed it at Mom's feet? Remember how she screamed? You never brought her another one." He was trying to watch me, but he was getting sleepy.

"And remember the time we all went camping and you flushed out that black-and-white kitty that turned out to be a skunk?"

His eyes were closed, but his tail wagged and his feet moved. Maybe he was remembering in his sleep.

Mom tiptoed in with a sleeping bag. "I thought you'd want to spend the night with him."

I nodded. It was like old times—our sleeping side by side—my arm around him.

His tongue licking my ear woke me up the next morning. I hugged him and his tail waved like a feeble flag in the wind. Work didn't seem important, but I knew I'd better go.

"Ivan will be waiting for you when you get home," Mom assured me.

And he was—right at the front door.

"I found him trying to climb the stairs to get up here to meet you," Mom said. "I don't know how he made it as far as he did. I carried him the rest of the way."

"It's like the old days, buddy," I scooped him into my arms and hugged him to my heart. I carried him downstairs and held him until he fell asleep.

He died that night in my arms. I told him over and over what an important part he'd played in my life. And in the end, we were together... just like always.

—Lorena O'Connor
Chicken Soup for the Dog Lover's Soul

New Beginnings

59

My sister and I weren't exactly what you would call close. I was three years younger, and I thought she walked on water. Everything she did was perfect, and I wanted to be just like her when I grew up. If she wore her hair in twin braids with a pink clip one day, the next day I wore mine exactly the same way. I used to follow her and her friends around, begging to be included, but there isn't much room in a thirteen-year-old's life for a pesky ten-year-old sister. As a result, over time, my worship of her became indifference. We were strangers living in the same house, eating together but never communicating.

So when she sat me down last year and told me she'd be going to Israel to study abroad for ten months, I wasn't too concerned. I figured I would get to wear the clothes she left behind and use her CD player. That was the only way I thought her leaving would affect me.

That first night after she left, I sat in my room and tried to do homework. I couldn't shake the feeling that something was wrong, something was missing. The house was too quiet. No Tova's CD player and no Tova's voice giggling on the phone with her friends. Sitting there, I realized just how different it was without her in the house. Even though we didn't always speak, I had felt safe just knowing she was near.

I cried that night. I cried over all the years we had wasted trying to live our own lives and ignoring each other's. I cried that I couldn't even give her a hug before she boarded her plane. But as the night wore on, my tears changed to tears of calm, tears of new beginnings.

I picked up the phone and called her halfway across the world. I waited for her to pick up, my doubts growing with every second.

"Hello?" Her voice sounded as though it came from nearby and not Israel.

"Hey Tova. It's me, Sara. I just called to tell you I love you." My words came out in a rush. I knew that if I stopped in the middle, I wouldn't have the courage to continue. "I know we aren't as close as some sisters, but that doesn't mean I'm not missing you a ton."

For a long time there was only silence on the other end. Finally she spoke. "I've been sitting here, all alone, thinking about you guys back home," she said. "Your voice makes me feel as though I'm right there with you." And before she hung up she said, very quickly just as I had, "I love you, too."

I'm counting down the days until my sister returns home, so I can give her the hug I never gave her when she left and say, "I'm so glad to have you home."

—Sara Ronis
Chicken Soup for the Teenage Soul IV

I Learned the Truth at Thirteen

Big things were happening in my life the summer after I turned thirteen. I had just graduated from junior high, and I'd finally had a chance to dance with John, the boy I'd had a crush on all year. In the fall, I would begin high school. It was all very exciting, but a little scary, too. At least I knew I could always return to the safety of my family if things got rough.

Then, in the middle of summer, my parents shook my entire world and turned it upside down when they told me they were getting a divorce. When my mother said, "We think it's for the best," the words rang hollow in my ears. For the best? How could that be? I was shocked. I couldn't believe that our family was going to break up. Of course, at some level, I always knew my parents weren't very happy. They were rarely affectionate with one another, and they often fought. But I still didn't want anything to change. I wanted my family to stay the same—it was all I had ever known.

My life changed quite radically after the divorce. My mother and I moved into a small apartment across town, while my father and brother, Bill, stayed in our house. I now became a visitor whenever I went to see my dad and Bill on the weekends. I was at an age when I might be expected to start dating, but it was my mother who began going out for dinner and to parties with men she'd met at work or through friends. Then she did the unthinkable—she became engaged! I was immediately suspicious of my soon-to-be stepfather, Dan. I resisted all his attempts to get to know me. I was, in fact, pretty rude to him. Things were definitely bleak.

Even though divorce was not such an uncommon occurrence in the suburb where I lived, all of my friends' parents were still together. My friends couldn't relate to my situation and wondered why I was now quiet all the time. I still got together with them to go out to football games or dances, but I found I wasn't enjoying life the way I used to. I was clearly depressed, especially after Dan and my mother married and I realized that there was no way that things could change back to the way they were.

My salvation came from the last person on earth that I would have expected—Dan, my new stepfather. Even though I wasn't very nice to him, he never gave up on me. Gradually, I began to trust him. I realized that we actually had some things in common, especially when it came to movies and TV shows. We spent a lot of time together hanging out watching TV. That gave us a chance to talk and get to know each other. Then Dan invited me to go running, and I connected with it.

Better still, Dan showed an interest in me that I had never experienced from my own father. Dan was always around when I needed advice on school, friends or boys. I also learned a lot by watching Dan and my mom together. They were often playful and affectionate with each other, so I saw firsthand what a good marriage looks like. Once I began to warm up to Dan, the three of us began spending a lot of time together. We often went out to eat, took short trips, and Dan and I even entered races and ran together. Eventually, I discovered that I finally had the happy family that I had always wanted.

I now realize my parents were right about getting the divorce. Their breakup was the best thing to happen for all of us. My father also found happiness—he remarried and had another child, my half-sister, Michelle.

At thirteen, I learned an important truth—change is not always the worst thing that can happen. Sometimes, it is just what we need the most.

—Carol Ayer
Chicken Soup for the Girl's Soul

61

The Big Tree

was eight when I fell in love with trees. Our family had just moved from Missouri into a brick house in the Sammamish River valley, east of Seattle. Dad and I walked our land, gazing up at cone-shaped red cedars like giant tipis, western hemlocks as graceful as dancers and sky-climbing Douglas firs.

Up on the back hill grew a huge tree, a 700-year-old Douglas fir whose width proved broader than my father's outspread arms. Dad said he was sure it was the biggest tree for twenty miles around. The deep furrows in its bark flowed upwards like great canyons.

My father was an adventurer and a long-time lover of trees, so we weren't surprised when he decided one day to climb the big fir. But standing on the top rung of our long extension ladder and stretching his arms as high as he could, Dad couldn't reach even the lowest limbs.

"Thank goodness," sighed my mother.

Dad winked at me as he climbed down. "Maybe you can figure out a way to get up it in a few years."

I looked up at him, then up farther at the tree. The idea seemed impossible. It rose grandly into the blue northern sky, more of a god than a tree. I wasn't sure when, or how, but I knew right then I would climb it someday.

"You'll see the whole world from up there," Dad said.

I set right in to practice, and scrambled up first smaller and then bigger trees with growing agility. Fifty feet up in the hemlock that grew beside our garage, I was amazed at how our house looked so much smaller and the world so much bigger.

"The higher the tree," Dad said, "the more you'll see. And the more you see, the wiser you'll be."

"Don't encourage him so," my mom complained. "He's already more squirrel than boy. And what happens if he falls?"

"He won't fall. He's a good climber." Dad knew the value of tree climbing, and not just in the sense of boyhood fun and freedom. He wanted me to see the world from a broader perspective.

At twelve, I finally shimmied up between two close-standing trunks and got into the smooth-barked branches of a 125-foot-tall cedar. From the top I looked over the rooftops of the whole neighborhood! I could see the Thorsons having dinner on their porch, Mr. and Mrs. Fluharty talking as they picked beans in their garden, and Mr. Reed trimming the laurel hedge in his driveway, stopping to shoo a dog away.

I felt an omniscience being up there. I could see everything all at once—human things, the wonderful flow of trees and wind and birds and squirrels, and the clouds drifting across the sky.

When I was fourteen, a heart attack took Dad away from us. I climbed even more because it reminded me of Dad; somehow I could feel his strong, gentle presence in the branches.

I hadn't climbed the big tree, though. And I felt bad about that. Dad had wanted me to, and I wanted to. But it was just so huge and the branches so far up.

Years passed, and then in my first year of college, I went mountain climbing with friends and learned something about the use of ropes. My first day back home, I walked up the hill in our backyard with a purpose. I threw a stone attached to some rope over the lowest stub of the big tree. When the rope was secure, I pulled myself up the side of the tree and stood on the broken-off branch. My heart pounding and my body plastered against the rough bark of the fir's trunk, I stretched my arms wide. Carefully, I reached for the next stub and hauled myself up. Before long I was in the limbs and climbing.

The strong, limber branches appeared to welcome me. "Here

you are, at last," the tree seemed to say. The views opened up, wider and wider, and I could hear Dad's voice in my mind: "The higher the tree, the more you'll see... the more you see, the wiser you'll be."

I saw the houses along our lane, then the streets of the whole neighborhood, and then the town on the other side of the river. Thousands of cars and people, all living their lives. As I climbed into the higher branches, my view crested the nearby hills, and I could see out over Lake Sammamish to the Cascade Mountains still capped with snow, and I felt the expanse and lift of the land.

When I gained the top of the tree at last, I caught my breath. Puget Sound shimmered in the west, and across it the peaks of the Olympic range rose into the evening sky. Mt. Rainier, a huge and tranquil presence, rested in the distance. The sun was spinning into the burnished shades of evening when Mom came out the back door and hollered up into the yard, "Ga-arth, dinnertime!"

"I'm up here, Mom!"

Mom glanced up and around, then craned her neck back and finally caught sight of me waving from atop the big tree. She shrieked.

"Don't worry," I yelled. "I'm as safe as I'll ever be anywhere, and I can see the whole world, just like Dad said!"

I ate dinner like usual that night, but no food had ever tasted better. My father was there, too, beside us at the table. I could hear Dad's laugh and see his smile of approval, because I had made it to the top of the tree and seen the whole world—for both of us.

—Garth Gilchrist
Chicken Soup for the Nature Lover's Soul

62

My Amazing Brother

M ark was the most popular boy in his class. He had top grades, was a star athlete and was everyone's friend. His face belonged on the cover of magazines, and he was nicer than ice-cold lemonade on a scorching hot day. He was the classic "all-American boy." Girls chased after him with starry eyes and drooling mouths. Who could blame them? He was absolutely perfect. He also happened to be my little brother.

My brother and I had always been close, yet I had long felt slightly inferior to him. He just seemed to have everything. I, on the other hand, was a shy writer with relatively few close friends. I'm sure 95 percent of the class had no idea I even existed.

High school started, and Mark and I were at the same school; he was a freshman, and I was a senior. We got closer than ever that year. I don't know whether it was the rides to school when we glee-fully sang along to the songs on the radio, the fact that we were both on the swim team and spent three months breathing chlorine fumes together or that we shared the same school gossip with each other. Whatever the reason, our bond grew by the day. We told each other everything. We were each other's confidant.

I helped him with his algebra problems, and he read my papers and assured me they were A+ quality. We listened to CDs every night and danced around the den, laughing. We joked about our parents and their unjust curfew policy. We even hung out with each other at school functions, at the mall and at the movies. He introduced me to everyone he knew—basically the whole school—and I quickly gained more and more friends. People actually started knowing I existed. I was a "somebody."

One night, my brother and I were discussing the upcoming semiformal dance. Mark, of course, already had a date. I didn't have a date and hadn't even planned on going. I never had a date for anything, and I accepted that nothing was likely to change that. When Mark asked who I wanted to go with, I was shocked.

"It doesn't really matter, because I'm not going," was my curt reply.

"What do you mean you're not going? You have to go. It's your senior year!" Mark sincerely didn't understand why I wasn't going.

"Well, you kinda have to have a date to go, and there's not one person who would want to go with me," I told him, using the reasoning I'd repeated to myself over and over.

"You've got to be kidding, Care. There isn't one guy in the whole school who would turn you down. Do you realize how many guys like you?"

"How do you know?" I asked, wondering where my brother was getting such ridiculous ideas.

"Because you're the coolest girl in the world, that's how I know. Everybody thinks so. You're smart, funny, pretty, talented...." Mark counted off on his fingers, as I sat on the edge of my bed in utter amazement. "Any guy who would turn you down has serious problems. I know...."

I didn't hear what else my brother said. My mind was stuck on seven words that had rolled off his tongue: "You're the coolest girl in the world." I ran it through my mind nearly a hundred times before it sunk in. My brother believed any guy would go to the dance with me. My brother, the most popular boy in school, thought I was "the coolest girl in the world."

The rest of the year went by in an exuberant blur. By graduation, I knew nearly everyone at school and had been on many dates. I made new friends and tried new things like coffee, guitar, conversation and karaoke. I was happier than I'd ever been.

Later that summer Mark and I were having our normal nightly chat.

"Mark?" I asked.

"What, Care?" His question was as sweet as his heart.

I thought a minute before saying, "Thanks."

Mark looked puzzled. "Thanks for what?"

Thinking even longer, I replied, "For bringing the 'me' out of me."

Mark smiled and hugged me. "It's always been there, Care. You've always been wonderful you."

I smiled into the darkness as I thought to myself, Yeah, it just took my amazing brother to make me realize it.

—Carrie O'Maley
Chicken Soup for the Teenage Soul IV

Not Just for Girls Anymore!

Carry laughter with you wherever you go.
—Hugh Sidey

"Mom, I'm sick again!" I shouted from the bathroom. My mother appeared in the doorway.

"Did you start this morning, Sweetie?" she asked sympathetically. "Your periods sure are awful for you." She wasn't kidding. It wasn't just the cramps, although those were bad enough. My stomach got so upset that I would throw up for the whole first day, every month. It was completely miserable.

"Why don't you crawl back into bed? It's obvious that you can't go to school today," Mom said. "I'll bring you some Sprite and a piece of toast for your stomach."

I did as she suggested. When she came to my room a few minutes later, she looked distracted. "Honey, the radio just announced that the school district called a fog delay. Tim's bus is going to be coming two hours late, and I have to be at work soon. Can you help him catch the bus?" Tim is my brother, who was six at the time.

"Sure, Mom, I'll make sure he gets to school. Thanks for the toast."

My mother left thirty minutes later. I was responsible for making sure that Tim got on the bus for school. No problem, I thought, until my stomach decided it didn't want the toast I'd eaten. I was resting on the bathroom floor when Tim walked by and asked me why I wasn't at school. He was still wearing his pajamas. "I had to stay home today," I explained. "My stomach is really sick because I have my period." Tim nodded, although he clearly didn't understand.

"It was foggy this morning, so your bus is going to be late. Mom asked me to make sure you get to school. Your bus should be here soon." It was then that we heard the distinct sounds of a school bus horn. Had two whole hours gone by already? I'd been so sick that I'd forgotten to wake Tim up and get him ready for school! My mom was going to kill me!

I racked my brain and decided to call a neighbor and beg her to drive Tim to school. She agreed, and the situation was resolved. I was able to relax with my heating pad for the remainder of the day.

The following week, Tim ate too much sugar and ended up with a stomachache. He was holding his belly when my mom saw him and asked him what was wrong.

"Oh, Mom, my stomach is killing me," he moaned. "I feel awful! I think I have my period!"

Growing up is tough, and sometimes, you have to laugh to keep from crying. The next time you're doubled over with cramps, just think of little Timmy holding his belly, complaining about having his period!

—Diane Sonntag
Chicken Soup for the Girl's Soul

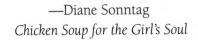

64

The Man My Father Was

Life's problems wouldn't be called "hurdles"
if there wasn't a way to get over them.
—Author Unknown

My parents divorced when I was seven years old. This came as no surprise to everyone around them. My father had been an alcoholic for many years, and it was only a matter of time before it took its toll on their marriage. After the divorce, my mom remarried and my dad moved to a town about thirty minutes away. By the time I was twelve, I felt stable and even happy. I liked having two families.

It was around this time that my dad was fired from his job of nearly ten years. We all knew that it was because of the drinking. We also knew that it would be hard for a nearly fifty-year-old man to find a new job. For a year and a half he remained unemployed, and his situation seemed more and more desperate. He continued to be a big part of my life, though. No longer stuck at work, he attended all of my basketball games and kept our relationship as strong as it ever was.

Finally, he got a job—in the next state. In a few months, my father was settled in his new home and job, while I was left to try and adjust to life without him. He managed to turn his financial situation around, but I was worried about him. He didn't make any new

The Man My Father Was: Family Ties 209

friends and, when he wasn't with me, he was in his apartment alone. He seemed lonely.

When it was my dad's weekend to pick me up, he would drive three hours to get me and we would stay in a hotel. I loved those weekends together, but as time went on my dad seemed to cancel his time with me more and more frequently. He always seemed to get a "stomach flu," and when we did spend the weekend together, he was often in the bathroom vomiting. We all noticed how emaciated he had become; his legs were even thinner than mine. But although he was physically deteriorating, my dad was determined to maintain his relationship with his family. He called his daughter every day.

One night my dad didn't call. I was worried, but my mom calmed me down. We reasoned that he was probably out too late to call and didn't want to wake me. But when he didn't call the next night either, I was really worried.

The next morning, my mom and I decided that we should look into the situation. She told me she would call his office and tried to reassure me on the way to school. I felt strange that day laughing with my friends, like I shouldn't be so happy. I had this weird feeling that something bad had happened.

When I got home, I immediately asked her what his office had told her. As it turned out, they, too, had not heard from him. They got suspicious and went to his apartment to see what was going on. My father never answered the door, so they got someone to break in. They found my dad lying on the bathroom floor in a pool of blood. The police later said that he had died two days before he was found.

After hearing the news, I was in bad shape. I felt like there was no point to life. I took a few days off school and spent them looking at photo albums and going through my dad's old stuff. My father was not a perfect man—sometimes he was insensitive, sometimes unfair, sometimes unforgiving or hurtful or unreliable. My father disappointed me a lot. But when I look back at the man my father was, I am not disappointed. My father was only human. He did teach me how to throw a ball, to wash a car, to appreciate music, to play golf, to love to read, to argue intelligently, to do crossword puzzles, to play the guitar and to be proud of myself. Some children never even get to meet their fathers; I was fortunate enough to know mine for fourteen years.

My father's death is now a part of me, embedded deep within me. I am growing stronger every day. My mother has taught me, rather than forget about my father's problems and struggles, to learn from them. My mother is there whenever I need her; her support has been the anchor that has kept me from drifting away.

As I place the flowers next to my father's ashes, I say a silent prayer and wait there for just a moment. I recall everything about my dad—the good and the bad alike—and I remember the man my father was.

—Kristine Flaherty
Chicken Soup for the Teenage Soul on Tough Stuff

65

Bike Ride

If you don't understand how a woman could
both love her sister dearly and want to wring her neck at the same time,
then you were probably an only child.
—Linda Sunshine

One of my teachers once asked my class what our favorite memory was. I vaguely remember that we were studying self-esteem, and as a discussion prompt, my teacher asked for the moment in which "you felt the best, you felt that you had the world in the palm of your hand." Some described prestigious awards; others described winning a tournament. My answer, however, invited giggles and hesitant smiles. Why? Because I felt the best when I first learned how to ride my bike—at thirteen. I didn't mind my classmate's stares and snickering, because I knew there was more to the story.

My sister and I shared a typical sisterly relationship: we couldn't stand each other. Or, to be honest, she couldn't stand me. I hero-worshipped her. Her taste was the epitome of glamour, her personality the definition of cool. My clothes were mysteriously inclined to look like hers, and even my words tended to mimic those I heard from home. Many times, I even wanted to literally follow my sister, whimpering every time I was barred from attending movies with her. Needless to say, I was a brat and an annoyance to her. Any sort of conversation we had usually degraded to fighting, and try as I might, my sister had an extra six years worth of insulting vocabulary (which meant she usually won). After a while, I stopped trying to impress her and learned to be totally indifferent; perhaps the silent treatment would get more approval. I was wrong. We soon fell into a sad pattern—I avoided her, she ignored me, and deep inside, it hurt. So that's how it was between us. Indifferent or hostile, she was only a sister in name. I truly believed that we would forever be apart, two housemates without conversation, two strangers without warmth. And nothing more.

I still remember the day I learned to ride a bike. I had received the bike that Christmas, which was great, until I realized I had no idea how to ride it. My mom had long since abandoned any attempt to teach me; I had proved to be a panicky, frustrating student. I took it upon myself to learn, a little bit each day, but to no avail; I couldn't ride my bike, and on that fateful day, it was no different. I was coming to the end of my daily one-hour torture, and I was so frustrated that I threw my bike aside and began to cry. I guess that was what caused my sister to come outside. At first I was skeptical and tense, as I thought she would begin to tease me or at least burst out laughing. She did neither. I hunched my shoulders forward and turned my face away, but she gently picked my bike up and motioned me over. That was the beginning. She fearlessly held my hand while the tears dried on my cheeks; she steadily held my bike when my feet faltered. She never once let me fall. And for three hours—three wonderful, blissful hours—we learned to ride my bike. No shouting. No fighting. No arguing.

That day I learned that my sister was human—how else could she have been my teacher? I've seen those TV shows with doting siblings, and I've always longed for that perfect harmony. That was the day, however, I had a taste of what real sisterly intimacy could be like. She saw through my weakness; I saw her compassion. I got off my bike that day empowered, and instead of blind admiration, I now had a newfound respect for my sister and for myself. She was both humbled and exalted before my eyes. My sister walked away quietly that day while I showed off my new skills for my mom, and I did not see her the rest of the day. Perhaps she felt something, too.

The day I learned to ride my bike proved to be my bridge from a snotty, naive little brat to a wiser younger sister. It was a life-changing experience, not a miracle. We still occasionally have our random spats and bitter rivalries, but since that day, it's been easier to get along because we have an unspoken respect for each other. The day she taught me how to ride my bike, she ceased to be a bully and became my sister.

And nothing more.

—Esther Young
Chicken Soup for the Teenage Soul IV

66

My Grandma Told Stories

Grandmother-grandchild relationships are simple.
Grandmas are short on criticism and long on love.
—*Author Unknown*

When I was young, my mother was going to Florida to visit my grandmother. I begged her to take me with her. "I'll take you, but remember," my mother warned me, "Grandma is sick."

I had seen plenty of sick people before, so I figured it wouldn't be a big deal. Besides, by the time we got to Florida, my grandma would probably be okay. Then we would have fun just as we used to. I remembered how important I had felt the summer before when my grandma carried me on her shoulders down the streets of St. Petersburg.

My mother and I took the train to Florida. She brought a bag of cherries along with us. It was a huge bag, but instead of giving me a handful to eat, she gave me the whole bag to hold. After I ate my first handful, I looked at her, but she didn't say anything. Although she sat next to me, she seemed far away, immersed in her own thoughts, as she vaguely looked out the window. I took another handful, and still she didn't say anything. She didn't even notice. My mom let me eat all the cherries I wanted, but when I looked down at my new shirt and discovered cherry stains on it, I was afraid I'd get in trouble. When I told my mom, she said it was okay, and she patiently wiped at the stains with a cold, wet rag.

We took a cab from the train station to my grandma's house. I got more and more excited as we approached. Grandma was a great storyteller and her stories made me feel special whenever she told them.

"Grandma, tell me a story," I'd say, and she would always begin the story, "Once upon a time there was a boy named Billy..." Every story started with a boy named after me. When I arrived at her house, my first words were going to be, "Grandma, tell me a story."

When I got to Grandma's house, she didn't come out to meet me. Even after I ran up the steps, she still didn't come out to meet me. I went into her bedroom. In a moment, I was changed forever, because what I saw in that room wasn't my happy-go-lucky grandmother. It was a crumpled body, thin and drawn.

That night as I lay in bed, I heard my grandma moaning in pain. It had the same effect on me as someone running fingernails across the blackboard. I just wanted it to stop. It continued all night.

The next morning, I asked my mom if I could leave because it hurt too much to see Grandma that sick. She sent me home that afternoon on the plane. A few weeks later, my mother came home and asked me if it was all right if Grandma came to live with us. I said yes, but in reality I never wanted to see my grandmother again.

Although my grandma lived with us for the next few months, I never went into her room. She couldn't get out of bed. I didn't have to see her. Every so often, when I walked past her room, I could see her with her back turned toward me. Sometimes her backside showed from under her nightgown and I saw how wrinkled it looked with her back and bony pelvis showing through her hanging skin. I felt ashamed because I didn't think I should see this side of my grandmother.

One day, my grandma called to me as I walked by her room. I didn't want to go. Her voice struck an intimate and familiar cord inside me. It was a voice I couldn't disappoint. I followed the voice as though in a daze. In her room, I didn't look at her. I just looked at the floor and told myself that this wasn't my grandmother—it just couldn't be.

I was about to run out of the room and leave it forever when she spoke, "Once upon a time there was a boy named Billy..." I followed her words to that place beyond words and crumpled bodies, to that place of recognition and recollection: "...and little Billy loved his grandma very much...." I raised my head and looked at my grandmother. Although her crumpled and dying body hadn't changed, I could now see behind her appearance. I went into her room every day after that until she died, and every day she told me another story about a boy named Billy.

—William Elliott
Chicken Soup for the Teenage Soul on Tough Stuff

67

Chicken Soup
for the Soul

The Doctor's Son

I grew up in a small town in northern Vermont. I suppose it's a typical small town—a few houses, lots of trees and a business district consisting of a dozen stores, two restaurants, three service stations and a doctor's office. Like most villages in rural Vermont, Enosburg is a community where neighbors greet each other by name. Even now, although I've lived elsewhere for nearly twenty years, the residents of Enosburg still welcome me with a smile. "Doctor Eppley's son is back," they say.

My parents moved to Vermont when I was still an infant. A soft-spoken man, my father settled quietly into his medical practice. Within a few months the people of Enosburg accepted him as one of their own. Word passes quickly in small Vermont towns. They know good people when they meet them. Around town the neighbors greeted my father as "Doc Eppley." And I soon learned that as long as I lived in Enosburg I would always be known as "Doctor Eppley's son."

On the first day of school, my classmates crowded around me because I was the doctor's son. "If you're anything like your father, you'll be a smart boy," my first grade teacher said. I couldn't stop beaming.

Throughout the first years of my life, I never tired of letting others know that my father was one of the town's most respected citizens. Somewhere in the midst of my teenage years, however, something changed. I was sixteen years old and the neighbors still called me "Doctor Eppley's son." They said that I was growing up to be an honorable and industrious young man, living an honest life just like my father. I groaned whenever I heard their compliments.

I wondered how I would ever fit in with my teenage friends. Having a popular father worked to my advantage when I was younger, but now that I was in high school my father's good name seemed like an ugly shadow that followed me wherever I went. And so when strangers asked me if I was Doctor Eppley's son, I replied emphatically, "My name is Harold. And I can manage quite well on my own." As an act of rebellion, I began to call my father by his first name, Sam.

"Why are you acting so stubborn lately?" my father asked me one day in the midst of an argument.

"Well, Sam," I replied, "I suppose that bothers you."

"You know it hurts me when you call me Sam," my father shouted.

"Well, it hurts me when everybody expects me to be just like you. I don't want to be perfect. I want to be myself."

I survived my last years of high school until finally I turned eighteen. The next fall I enrolled in college. I chose to attend a school far from Enosburg, a place where nobody called me "Doctor Eppley's son" because nobody knew my father.

One night at college I sat with a group of students in the dormitory as we shared stories about our lives. We began to talk about the things we hated most about our childhoods. "That's easy," I said. "I couldn't stand growing up in a town where everybody always compared me to my father. Just once, I'd like to be known as someone other than 'Doctor Eppley's son.'"

The woman sitting next to me frowned. "I don't understand," she said. "I'd be proud to have a father who's so well respected." Her eyes filled with tears as she continued, "I'd give anything to be called my father's child. But I don't know where he is. He left my mother when I was four years old."

There was an awkward silence, and then I changed the subject. I wasn't ready to hear that woman's words.

I returned home for winter break that year feeling proud of myself. In four months at college, I had made a number of new friends. I had become popular in my own right, without my father's help. My parents marveled at how much I had changed.

For two weeks I enjoyed being back in Enosburg. The main topic of interest at home was my father's new car.

"Let me take it out for a drive," I said.

My father agreed, but not without his usual warning, "Be careful."

I glared at my father. "Sam, I'm sick of being treated like a child. I'm in college now. Don't you think I know how to drive a car?"

I could see the hurt in my father's face, and I remembered how much he hated it whenever I called him "Sam."

"All right then," he replied. "The keys are in the kitchen."

I hopped into the car and headed down the road, savoring the beauty of the Vermont countryside. I drove a few miles and then stopped at a busy intersection in a nearby town. As I stepped on the accelerator my mind was wandering, and I failed to hear the screech of brakes in front of me. I only heard a thud as I reacted too late.

The woman in the car I had struck jumped out of her vehicle unhurt. "You idiot!" she screamed. "Why didn't you look where you were going?"

I peered through the windshield and surveyed the damage. Both cars had sustained serious dents.

I sat there like a guilty child as the woman continued with her barrage of insults. "It's your fault," she shouted. I couldn't protest. My knees began to shake. I choked back my tears. The woman's words came so quickly that I didn't know what to do. "Do you have insurance? Can you pay for this? Who are you?" she kept asking. "Who are you?"

I panicked, and without thinking, shouted, "I'm Doctor Eppley's son."

I sat there stunned. I couldn't believe what I had just said. Almost immediately, the woman's frown became a smile of recognition. "I'm sorry," she replied, "I didn't realize who you were."

An hour later, I drove my father's battered new car back home. With my head down and my knees still shaking, I trudged into the house and handed the keys to my father. I explained what had happened.

"Are you hurt?" he asked.

"No," I replied solemnly.

"Good," he answered. Then he turned and headed toward the door. "Harold," he said as he was leaving, "Hold your head up. There's no need for you to slouch."

That night was New Year's Eve, and my family attended a small party with friends to celebrate the beginning of another year. When midnight arrived, people cheered and greeted each other with laughter. Across the room I saw my father. I stepped toward him. My father and I rarely hug. But recalling the day's events, I wrapped my arms around his shoulders. And I spoke his real name for the first time in years. I said, "Thank you, Dad. Happy New Year."

—Harold Eppley with Rochelle Melander
Chicken Soup for the Teenage Soul IV

Chapter
7

Teens Talk Growing Up

Special Memories

No one can pass through life, any more than he can pass through a bit of country without leaving tracks behind, and those tracks may often be helpful to those coming after him in finding their way.
—Sir Robert Baden-Powell

Second Kind of Mind

Attitude is a little thing that makes a big difference.
—*Winston Churchill*

Thoughts don't have to be "real" or "true" to create failure or success in our lives. They just have to be believed.

My family members were great conversationalists around the dinner table. Certain subjects came up with regularity. One in particular was that some members of my family, yours truly included, were dumb in math. I always heard my name at the end of the family list of the mathematically impaired. After fourteen years of this, I began to accept it as an indisputable and unchangeable fact.

In high school, I failed algebra three times. Eventually, I passed and was accepted to a college in Wisconsin, where I applied for a psychology degree. One small problem stood between me and my degree—statistics. It was a four-hour lab that had to be taken in my junior year. After hearing all the horror stories circulating about statistics, I mentally went into the fetal position. The panic was overwhelming.

One day I was called into my professor's office. Professor Fine, a short, stout man with thinning hair and a perpetual smile, sat on the front of his desk with his feet dangling over the floor. He read my transcript and held up his hands over his head.

"My son, this is your lucky day." I looked up. He repeated, "This is indeed your lucky day. This is where all of your tenacity pays off. You're going to be great in stats." He had a huge smile on his face.

"How's that, Doc?" I asked.

He shrugged. "You have the second kind of mind. Listen. First kind of minds are the kids who do well in algebra but don't get stats. They struggle like crazy in stats. It's a different kind of math that takes a different kind of mind. Second kind of mind is like yours." He held up my grades.

"Didn't have a clue about algebra, but you'll probably get an A in stats. Kids who get algebra don't get stats. Kids who don't get algebra understand statistics with no problem. If you failed algebra once, I'd guess you'd get an A or a B in stats. Think about it, son. You flunked three times. You're gonna be a genius." He raised his hands over his head again. Eureka!

"Really?" I asked, confused.

He jumped to the floor and held my face with his free hand and looked me square in the eyes. "Really, and I'm happy for you. You never gave up, and now it's going to pay off."

I was ecstatic with the news. He tossed my transcript on the floor near the trash can, shook my hand and slapped my back with great enthusiasm.

As I left the old ivy-covered brick building and started across the campus, I looked up to the second-floor window. Professor Fine was smiling, holding up two fingers for "second kind of mind." I smiled back and held up three fingers for "flunked three times." This scene was repeated a thousand times until I reached my junior year. Each and every time, there was a smile of approval on his face, a firm and enthusiastic handshake, perhaps an introduction to another professor during which glowing expectations were repeated.

Eventually, I began to tell my friends how well I expected to do in statistics. This singular change in attitude affected all my grades. With the awareness of my new "second kind of mind," I received the best grades of my life in college. I never believed I would do that well and probably wouldn't have if it had not been for Professor Fine's intercession.

For two years, I looked forward to taking statistics. When the time finally arrived, I did something that I had never done in any other math class—fought for a front-row seat. I asked so many questions I was often called a pest. My statistics book was never very far from me that semester. Also, there was little time for friends and hanging out. I set priorities and stuck to them.

Despite what the professor had said, it was hard work and took concentration and an occasional tutor. It paid off. I received one of only a handful of As that year. Shortly after, I ran into one of the professor's former aides, who said, "Congratulations. Professor Fine tells his really slow students that 'second kind of mind' story." And then he looked at me and said, "You'd be surprised how often it works. The mind is amazing, isn't it?"

—JeVon Thompson
Chicken Soup for the College Soul

69

No More What Ifs

You may be disappointed if you fail, but you are doomed if you don't try.
—Beverly Sills

It was my dad's fifty-third birthday, but something else about that day was also very special. I called my dad up to see if he would like to have lunch together for his birthday. He agreed, and half an hour later I arrived at his school. (He's an elementary principal.) He ordered us BLTs at a nearby restaurant.

We walked together to the small fast-food restaurant. As we neared the door, two young girls walked in: two beautiful goddesses. They recognized my father, and approached us. "Hey Mr. Margheim," they happily chimed.

My dad had been their elementary school principal, so he introduced us. "Chance, this is Stephanie."

"Uh, hi," I said. I didn't catch her friend's name. I was under the assumption that they were both college students. My dad must have read my mind because he asked them their ages. Embarrassed, I rubbed my hands over my face, paranoid. Do they know that I'm interested; am I obvious?

"Juniors," they said in unison. Perfect, I thought. I am a senior.

The conversation pretty much ended there, unfortunately. They were both working, so I figured that it would be best not to talk to them too much. My dad and I sat down. He ate, I couldn't. My stomach was doing flips; I was secretly waiting for Stephanie to approach me, hair blowing, eyes sparkling...

I guess we waited for some time before my dad gave me the old nudge. "Gotta get back to work," he whispered.

As we left, Stephanie gave me the usual, "Bye, nice to have met you."

"You, too," I crooned, lowering my voice.

The car ride back was silent. I am usually the conversation starter, but I was too deep in thought. I stared out the car window, thinking. I thought to myself as I got out of the car and walked into my father's office. After much contemplation, I decided, I was going to ask this girl out! I gave my father a hug, wished him a happy birthday and left.

My mind was asking a million questions. No more what ifs, I said to myself. I am tired of what ifs.

I pulled into the parking lot of the fast-food restaurant, and sat in my car for a good half hour, contemplating my move. I was nervous, very nervous, heart-popping-out-of-my-chest nervous. I literally felt like I was having a heart attack! I took a deep breath, prayed and walked into the restaurant. She was talking to someone, so I waited by the counter. Her eyes met mine, and she walked over to me. After what seemed like an hour of staring at her, I opened my mouth and let the words fall out.

"Umm, I know this is gonna sound crazy, but would you like to go out sometime?"

What a relief! I finally asked someone out! I studied her face, reading her reaction.

"Awww, that's nice, but I am serious with someone right now."

"Oh, yeah, okay, don't worry about it," I said, "that's fine."

"It was a good try though, right?" We both laughed. Our chat ended with a friendly handshake, and a "see you later."

Surprisingly enough, I wasn't disappointed. True, I would have loved to come home that night telling everyone that I finally had a date; and yet, I felt great! I had finally faced my fear and bit the bullet. I was prouder of myself at that moment than I had ever been in my life.

For the first time in seventeen years, I had faced my fear. I went home that day, and for once, I didn't have to ask myself, what if?

—Chance Margheim
Chicken Soup for the Teenage Soul III

70

My Fundillo
(All the Wrong Places)

here I was, sitting in a top floor tenement walk-up in the Bronx, waiting for the '80s to be over. You remember the '80s? Bad clothes. Bad hair. For me, it was high school. Or more specifically, tenth grade, where my best friend, Joanie Boom-Boom, vogued through the girls' locker room in her new black lace bra like it was a trophy.

Believe it or not, I wasn't jealous. I know that for most people, the female rite of passage is getting your boobs, but for Latinas our body part of choice is the buttocks. This is the cheeky skeleton in the Latina closet, the five happy words to describe one's bottom: culito, nalgas, fundillo, cheecho and delicioso!

Now you might say everyone has a bottom, and of course they do. It's just not the perfect Latina bottom: not too wide in the hips, yet full and meaty across the beam. Not as high as a bubble butt, but completely lifted off the back of the thighs. Picture two teardrop-shaped globes of firm, pliant, undimpled muscle, with built-in rack-and-pinion steering that allows each cheek to undulate separately from the other even when its proud owner stands completely still. There was no escaping this perfect posterior in my house. Every salsa album cover had one, and every merengue album had two. Every novia on every novela on Channel 47 had one. My sixty-year-old abuela had one. My thirteen-year-old cousin, Evie, had one. Every Latin woman in NYC had one. Except me.

I was a normal teenager otherwise. I just had this one problem. I didn't have a butt! And to the women in my family, this was a disaster that needed to be prevented, a catastrophe that needed to be averted, a disease that needed to be cured.

My titi Carmen said, "Pray for her." My titi Ophelia said, "Stop feeding her," and after I walked by, "Ay no, hide her till she's twenty-one." And then my mom said, "Listen to me, all of you. No daughter of mine is going to be a gordita."

My mom, Lucy, was the Jackie O. of East 103rd Street. She never raised her voice, never cursed, and was never seen in public without full makeup, high heels and stockings. After twenty years of marriage and two babies, she still weighed exactly the same as the day she got married: ninety-eight pounds—seventy pounds of which was butt. And she was convinced that with the right makeup, diet and foundation garments, her little gordiflona would be transformed into una gran mamichula.

Now I wasn't really fat, they just thought I was because I didn't have a shape. Their shape. Pear shape. So I tried it my mom's way. I ate plain boiled chicken with no rice or beans. I let her buy me control-top panties. And still, no butt. I was sure there was something else wrong with me. Maybe I was adopted. Maybe I should go talk to someone who really knew about such things. And so I went to see my best friend, Joanie Boom-Boom.

Safe in the teenage sanctuary of Joanie's room, I spilled my guts about my lack of development. "You're just a child," she said. "You'll grow... someday." Then she started admiring herself in the mirror. I went into the bathroom, checked out my butt in the mirror and cried. No matter how far I twisted around, all I could see was... nothing. Joanie was right. I would be at least thirty before I looked like a woman, and by then I would be too old to enjoy it. I went back to her room to say goodbye and there she was, still enraptured by her reflection in the mirror, but now stuffing wad after wad of tissue paper into each cup of that black lace bra. Instead of being angry that she was cheating, I realized something about being a woman. If she could stuff her bra, why couldn't I stuff my bottom? Her secret would be safe with me.

I laughed, and Joanie turned around.

"How long have you been standing there?" she asked.

"Uh, I just got here," I lied. "Let's go get pizza."

For the rest of the weekend, I finally had something behind me I could be proud of. Sort of. It shifted around a lot, and I couldn't really sit down or it would flatten out, so I walked around the house as if I were holding a dime between my cheeks, just like my mom said a real mujer walked. But my family—who could spot unplucked eyebrows at thirty paces—didn't notice a thing, even when I shimmied it right in front of them. I couldn't believe they couldn't see the total and complete transformation of my body. But that was okay, because the next day at school, I was sure all my friends would.

Everything was fine until gym class, when I realized I would have to get undressed. I tried to hide in a corner, but of course Joanie saw me and came over. I turned around with my back toward the lockers and Joanie said, "Hey, Michele, you got something weird hanging out of your..." And she pulled a ten-foot-long trail of Charmin out of the back of my underwear and into the cold fluorescent light of the locker room.

"Oh, my God!" she shrieked. "Michele stuffs her butt! Michele stuffs her butt!"

Everyone in the locker room froze. I knew my life was over, and there was only one thing left to do. I pushed Joanie over a bench, and as she fell, her black lace bra popped open and out flew enough pink Kleenex for every Ortiz funeral parlor in the Bronx and half of Brooklyn. As the entire locker room howled, Joanie leaped on me. She pulled my hair, and I tried to strangle her with what was left of my toilet-paper tail. Finally, a teacher pulled us apart. We were both suspended for three days.

My family didn't take it very well. Titi Carmen said, "Take her to church." Titi Ophelia said, "Take her to jail." My mom just said, "How could you?"

I wasn't sure if she meant the stuffing or the fight.

And while everyone around me argued, I grew. Almost five inches in two years. The extra ten pounds around my middle somehow migrated just the right distance, and if I may say so, produced some of the finest nalgas in my entire familia!

—Michele Carlo
Chicken Soup for the Latino Soul

71

Coffee Shop Kindness

Treat everyone with politeness, even those who are rude to you –
not because they are nice, but because you are.
—Author Unknown

My senior year of high school was an extremely hectic one, to say the least. If I wasn't studying and worrying about my grades, I was juggling multiple extracurricular activities or attempting to make sense of my plans for college. It seemed as if my life had turned into one crazy cloud of confusion, and I was stumbling around blindly, hoping to find some sort of direction.

Finally, as senior year began to wind down, I got a part-time job working at the local coffee shop. I had figured that the job would be easy and, for the most part, stress free. I pictured myself pouring the best gourmet coffees, making delicious doughnuts and becoming close friends with the regular customers.

What I hadn't counted on were the people with enormous orders who chose to use the drive-thru window, or the women who felt that the coffee was much too creamy, or the men who wanted their iced coffees remade again and again until they reached a certain level of perfection. There were moments when I was exasperated with the human race as a whole, simply because I couldn't seem to please anyone. There was always too much sugar, too little ice and not enough skim milk. Nevertheless, I kept at it.

One miserable rainy day, one of my regular customers came in looking depressed and defeated. My coworker and I asked what the problem was and if we could help, but the customer wouldn't reveal any details. He just said he felt like crawling into bed, pulling the sheets up over his head and staying there for a few years. I knew exactly how he felt.

Before he left, I handed him a bag along with his iced coffee. He looked at me questioningly because he hadn't ordered anything but the coffee. He opened the bag and saw that I had given him his favorite type of doughnut.

"It's on me," I told him. "Have a nice day."

He smiled and thanked me before turning around and heading back out into the rain.

The next day was miserable as well, rain spilling from the sky. Everyone in town seemed to be using the drive-thru window because no one wanted to brave the black skies or the thunder and lightning.

I spent my afternoon hanging out the window, handing people their orders and waiting as they slowly counted their pennies. I tried to smile as the customers complained about the weather, but it was difficult to smile as they sat in their temperature-controlled cars with the windows rolled up, while I dealt with huge droplets of water hanging from my visor, a shirt that was thoroughly soaked around the collar and an air conditioner that blasted out cold air despite sixty-seven-degree weather. On top of that, no one was tipping. Every time I looked into our nearly empty tip jar, I grew more depressed.

Around seven o'clock that evening, I was in the middle of making another pot of vanilla hazelnut decaf when the customer from the day before drove up to the window. But instead of ordering anything, he handed me a single pink rose and a little note. He said that not too many people take the time to care about others, and he was glad there were still people like me in the world. I was speechless and very touched; I nearly forgot yesterday's deed. After a moment, I happily thanked him. He told me I was welcome and, with a friendly wave, drove away.

I waited until I saw his Jeep exit the parking lot, then I ran to the back of the shop and read the note. It read:

Christine,

Thanks for being so sweet, kind and thoughtful yesterday. I was sincerely touched by you. It is so nice to meet someone who's genuinely nice, warm, and sensitive and unselfish. Please don't change your ways because I truly believe that you will excel. Have a great day!

Hank

As the day passed, I had plenty of complaining customers, but anytime I felt depressed or frustrated, I thought of Hank and his kindness. I would smile, hold my head up high, clear my throat and politely ask, "How can I help you?"

—Christine Walsh
Chicken Soup for the Teenage Soul III

72

Going Home on the D Train

I've lived in New York City for all of my seventeen years and can't imagine living anywhere else. It's an amazing city full of sights and smells and sounds unlike anywhere else on Earth. Being a city with a population of more than eight million adds to its excitement, as well as to the mistaken belief that it's filled with cold, aloof and uncaring people. Taken as a total number, it's hard to imagine connecting with all its citizens, but when you deal with one person at a time something different happens.

It was a cold November day, and New York City was still reeling from the devastation of September 11. All the members of my soccer team were glad to have an excuse to get out of school. It was the first game of the year, and we had suffered a horrible defeat; still, we were just excited to be starting the new season. We were twenty high school girls walking and laughing through the streets of the Bronx, ignoring the occasional whistles from the men we passed. We got to the subway station just as our train was coming in. Piling onto the D train, we glanced around the car, finding it full of blank stares and vacuous expressions. As the train started moving, twenty boisterous voices erupted at once, discussing everything from the attitudes of the girls on the opposing team to our plans for later that night.

All of us lived in Manhattan. Even though Manhattan and the Bronx are both boroughs of New York City, they're pretty far apart, so we had at least an hour-long train ride ahead of us. To amuse ourselves and pass the time, we began to sing. Various genres of music filled the train's car, from Bob Dylan to Christina Aguilera. Even though only one of us could really sing, we all sang along as loudly as possible; what we lacked in musical talent we made up for in volume and enthusiasm. I wish I could freeze that moment: being with my friends, feeling happy and not thinking about anything else. It was an amazing feeling that got even better as the train moved on.

Our fellow riders had different feelings. A few smiled in our direction, but most shot us disgruntled looks (was it our obvious lack of musical talent?), and some were downright hostile.

All our voices stopped almost simultaneously as an old man entered the car from the subway platform. His clothes were tattered, and his face was covered with a stubbly beard. In his hand he held a Styrofoam coffee cup emblazoned with "I Love NY." Despite his shabby appearance, he carried himself with dignity. He spoke softly, but his voice projected through the car: "Hello, ladies and gentlemen. I hope everyone is staying warm and healthy this winter. I am going to sing a couple of my favorite old songs for you during your trip. Please listen, and I hope you enjoy."

No one on the train looked up. Most people slid down behind their newspapers or feigned sleep, but we girls watched him carefully. As his lips parted and he began to sing "Joy to the World," we were so carried away by his eloquent voice and presence that we found ourselves chiming right in. After we had finished, we heard clapping and looked around to see that the people who had been in their own worlds a few moments before had now crossed over to ours to listen and marvel at this rare moment. His exquisite voice leading ours made it all sound so beautiful. The singing continued for a few more songs, then the old man sang a song he introduced as his own. When he was finished, he was lauded just as before when we had sung along with him.

For his final song, he chose something that was sure to move everyone: "God Bless America." With this song, not only did the twenty of us join him, but so did everyone else in the car. The stirring strains of "God Bless America" rang through the subway train and out into the station where we stopped. Many people left their own cars to come and see what was happening in ours—and to join us. This impromptu chorus on the D train, this medley of voices and unity of spirit, was real and marvelous. Its significance became clearest to me when I noticed a woman holding a baby in her arms, singing through the tears that were streaming down her cheeks.

The power of this moment will be with me forever. A moment when a group of strangers, all New Yorkers, tough and jaded, connected with a group of high school girls and a ragtag homeless person, and allowed their voices—and their hearts—to be as one.

—Simone McLaughlin
Chicken Soup for the Soul: Stories for a Better World

I Could Be Hauling Water

I had the blues because I had no shoes until upon the street,
I met a man who had no feet.
—Ancient Persian Saying

Like many schools in the United States, mine offered a variety of after-school activities. It didn't matter if you were athletic, studious or dramatic—a club or program existed for just about every interest. Yet I wasn't satisfied.

My school offered girls' soccer, but I wanted to play lacrosse. The drama department was doing a serious play, but I wanted to perform in musical theater. I could sign up for the chess club. Instead I complained because there was no debate club. For each after-school activity, teachers gave their time to help students. Clean classrooms and supplies were always available. Buses took students to other schools for competitions or enrichment programs. I took all of this for granted until I got a different perspective on after-school activities.

In the winter of 2001, I had the opportunity to go to Kenya and Uganda. My family and I visited a school where the students studied on hard wooden benches, walked over dirt floors in bare feet and had no after-school activities at all. Who had time for fun and enrichment? Many kids walked five miles just to get to and from school. The students living in orphanages went to their group home to do chores, like walking three miles to fill buckets of water. Without running water or electricity, teachers were challenged just to teach lessons, let alone plan arts and crafts or sports activities. If the students were lucky enough to have a few free minutes after school, they jumped rope or played the bongo drum—sharing two jump ropes and one drum between 230 students.

The schools in Kenya and Uganda were so poor that students shared pencils and paper. They didn't have white boards, so teachers used big slabs of slate as blackboards. The rough texture of the rock made it hard to write with their precious pieces of chalk. These students had few books, no computers, no colorful posters and definitely no creative after-school programs.

One day after school my family and I ran an after-school craft program to teach the kids how to make paper bag puppets. We passed out glue and markers and told the kids they could start working. They just sat there and looked at us with big eyes. They understood English, so I couldn't figure out why they hadn't started decorating their paper bags. We suddenly realized they had never seen markers and didn't know how to remove the caps. I demonstrated pulling the cap off. The kids laughed and got excited when they saw how the markers made colorful designs on their bags. They had never seen glue either, so they figured you pulled the cap off the glue, just like the markers. It got a little messy, especially when the kids pulled the orange caps off the glue bottles!

It struck me that these kids, many my own age, had never watched television or worn uniforms on a sports team. Uniforms? They didn't even own a basketball! Throughout my visit, I never heard any students complain. They didn't moan and groan about walking over hot dirt to carry heavy water containers. They gladly shared the markers we gave them and treasured their simple paper bag puppets. And they never complained about being bored.

Looking back on the lives of the students I met in Africa, I returned to school with a new outlook on activities. I stopped complaining about after-school programs and joined the soccer team without another complaint about the lack of a lacrosse team.

—Sondra Clark
Chicken Soup for the Teenage Soul: The Real Deal School

Bloopers from College

Admission Essays

Caught up in the hurly-burly, helter-skelter and hugger-mugger of college applications, a student aspiring to enter Bates College once wrote, "I am in the mist of choosing colleges." The admissions departments at Bates and Vassar Colleges have compiled a list of bloopers from their admissions essays:

- If there was a single word to describe me, that word would have to be "profectionist."

- I was abducted into the national honor society.

- In my senior year, I am serving as writting editor of the yearbook.

- I want to be bilingual in three or more languages.

- I have made the horror role every semester.

- I want a small liberal in the northeast part of the country.

- Bates is a college I can excell in.

- I am writing to tell you that I was very discouraged when I found out that I had been differed from Bates.

- I am thinking of possibly transferring to your college. I applied as an undergraduate but was weight listed.

- I first was exposed through a friend who attends Vassar.

- I would love to attend a college where the foundation was built upon women.

- My mother worked hard to provide me with whatever I needed in my life, a good home, a stale family and a wonderful education.

- Playing the saxophone lets me develop technique and skill which will help me in the future, since I would like to become a doctor.

- Such things as divorces, separations and annulments greatly reduce the need for adultery to be committed.

- I am proud to be able to say that I have sustained from the use of drugs, alcohol and tobacco products.

- I've been a strong advocate of the abomination of drunk driving.

- Activities: Cook and serve homeless.

- Another activity I take personally is my church Youth Group.

- He was a modest man with an unbelievable ego.

- The worst experience that I have probably ever had to go through emotionally was when other members of PETA (People for the Ethical Treatment of Animals) and I went to Pennsylvania for their annual pigeon shooting.

Now it is clear why one candidate wrote in his or her admissions essay, "I would like to see my own ignorance wither into enlightenment."

—Richard Lederer
Chicken Soup for the College Soul

Chapter 8

Teens Talk
Growing Up

Overcoming Obstacles

*If you don't like something change it; if you can't change it,
change the way you think about it.*
—Mary Engelbreit

Struggle of a Preteen Couch Potato

In fifth grade, I weighed, well, a lot. I was short and, as much as I hate to admit it, fat. As an inactive couch potato, I didn't fit in. My parents were constantly trying to limit what I ate, control what I did and send me out into the backyard to run around. In general, I was an unhealthy kid who ate junk food, and needed a growth spurt and a lot of exercise.

One summer, in a last-ditch effort to get me to lose weight, my parents cut out all snacks and made me run a mile each day around our backyard. (Twenty laps. It was like running around in a tiny circle.) The only things that gave me motivation were the fifty cents a day my parents promised me for running and a need to have more money than my little brother.

Throughout that year, my parents continued to fuss about my weight. I had lost a few pounds, but I was far from the "ideal standard" set by most people. But the school year went by much better than the last, and so that spring I decided to try out for the varsity swim team the following year. I joined a local club team to train with over the summer and started out swimming with kids who were eight years old to my twelve. I felt slow, old and, in general, weak. But I grew hopeful as fall approached, until I saw the fitness test that middle schoolers had to pass to make the team. I couldn't do anything that was on the test.

Instead of giving up or waiting until I was a freshman, I spent my seventh-grade year swimming off-season, still working toward varsity. I quickly moved up to where I was swimming with kids who were mostly my age, although not very fast. Soon I was first in my lane, set after set. I worked with that same group from September to Christmas, struggling as my unathletic body learned what working out actually meant.

When my coach, Katie, left, I switched to a group where I knew no one and everyone looked down on me. Some thought that I wasn't worthy of swimming with them, but that changed quickly as I worked my way up the lane. As people left the club, others moved up, and I got faster. Within a few months I was invited to advance into a highly competitive group that met five days a week for two hours.

The next summer I once again put my name on the sign-up list for the varsity team. By this point, I was truly in shape. My whole life had changed.

But I still had to pass the physical fitness test, and that was a challenge. I did the forty-four sit-ups in a minute on my first try—that was the easiest part for me. I ran my mile and a half in the allotted fifteen minutes my first time out. (Thank goodness! I don't think I would have wanted to do that twice!) I cleared my long jump with ease, leaving only one challenge to go: holding my chin above a bar for fifteen seconds. That day I tried it and missed by a second and a half. My heart was broken, but a week or two later, I came back to do better. Once again I failed. On my third try, I filled my mind with determination and made it with a second to spare! My hopes soared as I was cleared to be on the team.

I'll admit it: The first day I was scared to death. Do they make cuts? Am I going to be the slowest one? Will I just be humiliating myself? What if I can't finish the practice? The only thing that kept me sane was my friend Caitlin, who was a year older and helped me through the first few days.

After filling out some paperwork and talking, Bob, the coach, told us to get in the water, new people in lane one, returnees in the other lanes. Caitlin told me to come over to lane six with her, and I was skeptical. Although I protested, Caitlin finally convinced me. I began leading the lane, and then found myself moved up, lane after lane. I figured it was just because all these girls were out of shape, and soon I'd be back in lane six, going last and hopelessly behind everyone.

Surprisingly, I never got moved down. I stayed in one of the fastest lanes for a few days, and the coach told me that in the first meet I was going to swim distance—the dreaded 500-meter freestyle. I fought. Maybe he thought I could swim a seven-minute race, but my best time was eight minutes. He didn't care, and a few weeks later I found myself facing my first varsity event, the 500-meter freestyle, with a stomach full of butterflies.

I stepped up on the block, strapped on my goggles and took a deep breath. I sucked up my fear and got ready to race. I started out last, then caught up to one girl and passed her. With every breath, I could see my entire team lining the side, cheering me on. My adrenaline ran high as I raced against another girl close to me. I caught up to her, and although my sprinting has always been horrible, I edged her out in the end, finishing fourth in my first varsity meet ever. I pulled myself out of the pool, exhausted, and my whole team congratulated me. I was on cloud nine when I found out I'd swum the race in a personal record: 6:52! Coach Bob was right. I was a distance person.

After the race, my coach told me something I'll never forget. "We never expected you to beat anyone! Good job!" he said. And in some ways, he was right. Who would have expected the overweight couch potato to beat varsity swimmers in the longest race known to high school swimmers? No one, that's who. I'm still amazed that I did it.

Sometimes I feel like I'm in a dream, and I picture myself back in lane six, in the very back, struggling to keep up. But then I wake up and remember how far I've come, and I know there's no going back.

—Katelynn M. Wilton
Chicken Soup for the Teenage Soul: The Real Deal School

76

Out

The moment I entered the high school for the first time, I knew that things were going to be rough. Everyone seemed very similar, which as you know, is horrifying. I felt like every color and difference in this new world had been blurred together by a giant smudging eraser. I felt alone and unimportant, feeling my heart thumping in my ears at the thought of being the one student all the other kids took turns beating up after school.

The first quarter of freshman year was where the real learning took place. I began to notice things about the students, how they acted, how rumors spread and what kind of people were absolutely hated. One of the loudest statements that the mob of three thousand teenagers made was, "We hate gays." Although it seems to be a trend to call things that you despise "gay," the kids around me weren't just calling objects and subjects and ideas "gay." They would talk about the gay kids in our school, literally torturing them each and every day with their words.

Being gay, I was horrified. It was "their" domain, a place that I obviously didn't belong. I knew one "out" gay person at school, a senior. Later I would learn that on Senior Awards Night at the end of the year, he was nominated as "the most stereotypical." That was when he dropped off the face of the Earth and left me alone, like a snowflake floating in the middle of a hailstorm. Early in the year he had been a bright shining beacon of "If you do not like who I am, I couldn't really care less." I envied him, and yet I walked wordlessly through the crowded halls inches behind him, a shadow to his flame.

Our school had started a gay-straight alliance, which I joined as soon as I could. I knew that the club would be small, but at least it was somewhere that I could go to complain about the daily strife of high school teenage life. The teacher monitoring us really supported me and kept everything that we said in that room completely confidential. Finally I was surrounded by people like me, gay and hiding, afraid of our peers and teachers in high school.

Well, we weren't hiding for long. Kids ridiculed us and mocked our club, mocked our ideas, and further harassed our dying gay-student community (as tiny and fragile as it was). We were the lowest of the low at that point, and it left me no other choice than to finally come out of the closet, be proud and let everyone know they couldn't keep me in the dark anymore.

I stood up one day in front of my English class and read my persuasive essay, all about the discrimination and hate of gays that our school, city and country contained. I was nervous enough to be shaking, wondering if I would be murdered after school, my body never found. I knew it was a good essay, and even though it was about discrimination and hate and becoming tolerant, it was really my own secret revenge. On that day and in that class, I came out to each and every one of them. I let them know how proud I was without ever wearing a rainbow-colored ribbon, and I let them know that they couldn't force me back into the shadows without me ever firing a gun. I finished reading my essay with steel in my voice, staring into their eyes rather than hovering behind my paper. For a few seconds there was nothing, as if I had put them all in comas of shock. But then the clapping began. And one by one, students stood up. I had to catch my breath, my spine tingling. I was getting a standing ovation. I knew then that a new revolution had begun, one that I would single-handedly control.

Over the course of the year, I grew to be like that senior who I had worshipped. I wore rainbow key chains on my lanyard and my buttons from Gay Pride 2004. When I had first come into the high school, I believed that the out and proud students were the ones who got bashed and harassed. Sure, it is hard some days, and there were a few cruel words here and there, but I have never been tied to the flagpole and burnt after a gay-straight alliance meeting.

The gay students who are most picked on are those who are still in the shadows, as I used to be. I think that my peers are afraid of me, afraid of how I stand up for my rights and how I don't keep my mouth shut. But they have no reason to be afraid of the poor kids still in hiding, so the mute ones get the brute force of their attacks. I can only hope that someday teenagers will stop being so afraid to come out because it will definitely be the best thing they ever do for themselves.

Today I saw a small freshman hovering behind me in the crowded halls of Harold High School. I made sure that my flame burned bright and my spirits soared, so that someday I will light his match.

—Aubrey Restifo
Chicken Soup for the Teenage Soul: The Real Deal School

Applying Myself

Those who dream by day are cognizant of many things which those who dream only by night may miss.
—*Edgar Allen Poe*

At thirteen years old, I was like any other kid my age. I liked computer and Nintendo games. I complained about too much homework, and I hated when my little brother ate the last Fruit Roll-Up in the box. I guess I looked like any other kid my age, too. I wore baggy pants and oversize T-shirts—you know, the typical middle school prison garb. However, inside I harbored a secret that made me feel different and weird.

You see, I was diagnosed with ADD. This is the hip term for attention deficit disorder. I couldn't even get the cool-kid type where you're hyper. I had to get the dreamier, "space-cadet" type. I can look straight into your eyes and not hear a word you're saying. It's sort of like in the Charlie Brown TV specials. All the adults' voices in the cartoon sound like endless droning. "Mwop, mwop, mwop, mwop." I appear to be listening while all the while my mind is somewhere miles away.

After extensive and boring tests, the doctor explained to my mom that I was what they called "dual exceptional." It sounds pretty cool, doesn't it? No, it doesn't mean that I have any special dueling abilities like the swordsmen in The Three Musketeers. It also doesn't mean that I have a major psychiatric disorder like multiple personalities.

That might be kind of cool in a weird sort of way. What "dual exceptional" means is that I am what they call "gifted." This means I'm pretty bright, and yet I'm also learning disabled. This makes school challenging for me.

Yes, you can be gifted and learning disabled at the same time. The two words are not a contradiction in terms. I once heard a comedian refer to the words "jumbo shrimp" as one of these conflicted phrases.

I've learned to accept the fact that I'm an enigma to some. Still, it is a bummer to be misunderstood. The whole syndrome can sometimes make me feel like I am on the outside looking in. Everyone else seems to be getting it, and I'm not.

What really burns me up, though, is when teachers don't get it. In middle school, I took Language Arts with Mrs. Smith. She had piercing brown eyes that made you feel like you had done something wrong. Her no-nonsense, rigid posture made her look as though she'd forgotten to take the wire coat hanger out of her dress. Her face was angular, stiff and white, like a freshly starched and laundered hanky. A smile rarely creased her well-powdered complexion. I could imagine only an intermittent smirk grazing those thin red lips as she X'd her way through someone's failing test paper with her glorious red marker.

I was enrolled in Mrs. Smith's gifted section. That first day, she not only set down the rules of her cellblock, but she handed out copies of them for us to memorize and be tested on the following day. I knew right away that I had better "advocate" for myself. This is just some big, fancy-shmancy term that means to stand up for yourself. In my case, trying to explain, for the umpteenth time, about my learning disabilities. Basically, I have lousy reading comprehension and my handwriting is the pits. So I told her that I have ADD and that I might need to take home some reading assignments because my concentration is better when I am in a quiet setting. I went on to explain to her about my "fine motor skill" problems, which make my handwriting look like chicken scratch. I asked her if I might be able to use my word processor at home to do written assignments.

As I explained all this to Mrs. Smith, she gave me a squinty-eyed look down her bespectacled nose and said, "You are no different from anyone else, young man. If I do for you, I have to do for all the others." She snorted once and then added, "I will not give you an unfair advantage over your peers!" And with that, the bell rang and a herd of students swept me away to my next period.

The comprehension packets were rough. You had to read them, digest them and write an essay on them, all within the forty-five-minute allotted time. Not only couldn't I finish the reading, I couldn't write my essay fast enough or neatly enough to be legible. The result was that each paper came back decorated by Mrs. Smith's flaming red pen. She was like the mad Zorro of red X's.

One day, after she had handed me back my fifth X'd-out paper of the term, I approached her desk for the second time.

"Would you mind very much if I completed the next packet at home, Mrs. Smith? I think I might do better where there is less distraction." Then I backed away from her desk as though I were within firing range of her loaded mouth.

Mrs. Smith bit her thin red lips as her trademark smirk spread across them. "It's against school policy, young man. No unfair advantages. I have treated all students the same in the thirty years I have taught here." Then she flared her nose, clicked her heels and turned away from me, in more ways than one.

So I did what any other kid would do in my situation: I smuggled the packet out of the classroom. I felt like I was doing something illegal, and yet my motives were pure. I had to prove to her, or rather prove to myself, that I could do the work under the right conditions.

I secretly unfolded the contraband on my bed that night. The story, which had seemed so confusing in class, became quite clear to me in the still of my room. I not only got it, I could even relate to it. It was the true story of Louis Braille. He lived in the 1800s and was blinded by a childhood accident. During this time, society shut off the blind from having much of an education. Many were left with the bleak future of becoming homeless beggars. Despite much misunderstanding of his disability, Louis Braille "advocated" for himself.

He developed a reading system of raised dots for the blind, which enabled him to read on a par with his peers. A world of books and knowledge opened up to him that he and others like him were literally blind to before. I was like Louis in my classroom setting. I was being made to learn like the other students who were sighted in a way I wasn't.

That night I sat down at my word processor. My thoughts spilled out so fast that my fingers danced across the keyboard, straining to keep up. I explained myself in terms of Louis, in hopes that Mrs. Smith would finally understand me. Funny thing is, somewhere along the line I began to understand myself in a way I never had before.

I cited many other famous people who were in some way different in their learning styles and abilities throughout history. Hans Christian Andersen was said to have been learning disabled, and yet he wrote some of the best fairy tales of our time. I summed it all up by asking, "If I were a student with a vision impairment, would I be seated in the back of the room?" I questioned, "Would I have my glasses taken away from me so that I would not have an unfair advantage over other, glassless students?"

Mrs. Smith never looked at me as she handed my paper back facedown on my desk that day. She never even commented that my work was done on the word processor. As my eyes focused in on the white page, I found an A decorating the margin instead of her customary X. Underneath were her neatly red-penned words: "See what you can do when you apply yourself?"

I took the paper, tucked it away in my folder and shook my head. I guess some people will never get it!

—C. S. Dweck
Chicken Soup for the Teenage Soul on Tough Stuff

78

Andy

I f you watch television or movies, you've heard a gunshot before. That loud fiery blast that rings from the screen and bounces around in your ears. It's unmistakable. War films, mob movies, cop dramas—they're all wrought with them. Gunshots. You think you know what one sounds like.

I didn't, no matter how many of the fake kind I heard in my childhood.

When I was still in fifth grade my best friend, Andy, was shot. Right through the head. It was a freak accident. I saw it, but more importantly, I heard it. There was no bang. No fiery blast. The shot came from an air rifle; it was just a soft crack and a hiss—and Andy fell down. Sounds and images that I will never, ever forget.

The doctors didn't expect him to live. The pellet had gone through his temple and lodged in his brain. Fluid built up around it, and he went into a coma. His family and friends were in shock. People hoped, they prayed, they cried, anything they felt they could do to bring Andy back, but the outlook was grim. There was no one to blame, but still we searched for answers that weren't there. I, for one, tormented myself with the thought of, Why not me? I was torn between feelings of guilt that it wasn't me in his place... and undeniable relief... that it wasn't me in his place. There were too many feelings and I tried to figure out what feeling was "correct."

Then came the day when Andy woke up. He opened his eyes, and later he sat up in his bed. I went to the clinic and played catch with him with a foam ball. It was all he could do, really. He couldn't even speak. He had to essentially relearn everything, and they said he would never walk again. But then they had said he wouldn't pull through either. It didn't take long before Andy was in therapy, tirelessly working his way from the bed, to crutches, to his own two legs and feet.

Throughout high school, Andy and I were, as always, the best of friends. He was still handicapped from the accident and couldn't use his left arm, but he worked it seamlessly into his daily life. He could shoot a basketball as well as ever. He taught himself how to play even the most complicated video games with one hand on the control. But even more impressive and inspiring to those of us who love Andy was that he just went back to being a kid. He went to school every day, did his homework, played sports, was active with his church and had a girlfriend he was crazy about. He was always aware of his injury and accepted it as part of who he was, but it didn't consume him. And so it was for the rest of us.

Andy taught me what it means to be a friend. To be genuinely happy when they achieve, to feel real pain when they hurt, to smile when they smile. To find hope and strength in the gravest situations. Whether you believe in miracles or not, Andy's recovery was something truly special. Andy used to thank me on occasion, telling me things like, "I couldn't have gotten through it without you." The ironic thing is that I couldn't have gotten through it without him.

—Scott T. Barsotti
Chicken Soup for the Teenage Soul IV

79

A Challenge
That I Overcame

I was nervous as I sat waiting in the hospital room, unsure of what Dr. Waites, the pioneer of diagnosing developmental dyslexia, was telling my parents about the test results.

It all began when I moved to Dallas in the fourth grade, and I noticed that I was behind in my reading at Saint Michael's School. Reading out loud, I had difficulty with half the sentences. My teacher, Mrs. Agnew, said my reading comprehension and ability to pronounce words was at a lower lever than other fourth graders. I was scared every time she called on me to read aloud because, although I would try my hardest, she would always have to help me with the words. Mrs. Agnew suggested that I be tested for dyslexia.

At first I was confused about why I was being tested; I had been in all honors classes at the public school I had previously attended. The test made me feel uncomfortable, and I was scared to answer the questions, in fear of facing failure.

The test results showed that I had developmental dyslexia. At first I felt discouraged by this diagnosis, but eventually, I became determined to master my disability. I got tutors and speech therapy. I even tried to conquer the disability myself. I would read difficult books, hoping to increase the confidence I had in myself. I began to read and comprehend the readings better. I even began to love reading, which is kind of ironic since I had once detested it so much.

I had finally overcome my learning disability. Dr. Waites confirmed this when I was tested again. He said that my dyslexia was at a minimum. I was overjoyed. But even though I had conquered one of the biggest challenges in my life, I still felt like something was missing.

The missing link was filled when I put on my candy-striped uniform for the first time and walked down the halls of the hospital as a volunteer, the same hospital where I had once sat, nervous and confused. Because I felt so lucky to have had access to this facility that had helped me so much, I wanted to give back by being a volunteer.

One day a little girl in a wheelchair asked me to read a book to her. I read the book very slowly so that she could understand the story and the words. When it became time for me to leave, the girl thanked me for reading to her. I walked out of her room with a huge smile on my face. Eight years ago I would have hesitated in reading a book to this little girl, but now I was confident. I had overcome my disability and was helping others to overcome theirs. I am determined to succeed in life, and in the process, help others face and conquer the challenges that I have overcome.

—Arundel Hartman Bell
Chicken Soup for the Teenage Soul II

Numb

The sharp edge of the razor cuts my skin easily.
I'm numb to the pain,
Numb to the blood,
Too numb to realize what's happening,
To realize what I'm doing.
One cut follows another,
And another,
Till I can't stop.
The razor falls from my hand,
Blood drips down my arm,
Tears roll down my cheeks.
What have I done?

—Jessica Dubose
Chicken Soup for the Teenage Soul on Tough Stuff

81

Oxygen Is a Crutch

You have powers you never dreamed of.
You can do things you never thought you could do. There are no limitations
in what you can do except the limitations of your own mind.
—Darwin P. Kingsley

I step onto the starting block—head down, hands down—and explode at the pistol's crack, body arcing up into the air and down. I slice through the water, pull hard, kick hard, strain, set my teeth and force more strength from loudly protesting muscles. I gulp in oxygen when I turn my head for a precious breath. But mostly I just keep my head down and swim like there's no tomorrow.

By all rights, I shouldn't have even been there. By all rights, I should have been on the sidelines at the Blossom Valley Athletic League Championships, watching my teammates fight to maintain Evergreen Valley High's 200-medley relay winning streak. I should have been cursing the bodily limits that kept me from doing what I wanted to do. I should have been sulking in a corner, spirits crushed, hopes asunder, dreams damned.

But instead, only months after a near-fatal asthma attack, here I was in the water again, anchoring the relay team.

Asthma has been my constant companion since I turned five years old. An inhaler has always sat in my back pocket, a medical bracelet on my left wrist, and medicines and breathing devices on my bedroom dresser. But none of that ever meant that I couldn't torpedo through the water as well as the kid in the next lane. None of that ever weighed on my mind much, because I knew that I (whoever that was, because I was still in the process of figuring that out) was surely much bigger and much stronger than some puny medical condition.

Swimming became my refuge, my passion, my reason for living strong. I didn't love it because of any natural talent or biological blessing. I think the challenges of being a severe asthmatic made me embrace athletics more because I have to push myself for each race, each game, each meet. Because competition is a constant challenge. Because when I lose and flail and fall, I get up and do it all over again. And so I do not fail, because I do not give up.

When an intense practice sent me spiraling into unconsciousness and a near comatose state last year, my doctor and parents were leery of ever letting me anywhere near sports again. But I wasn't about to be deterred. I wasn't about to turn my back on the love of my life. I wasn't about to quit—no way, no how.

I like to think this is akin to the sort of character that drives Olympic athletes, that if I can't yet equal my idols in speed or strength or stamina, I might look them eye to eye in terms of pure grit.

And so, with a pack of epinephrine syringes, a stethoscope and a whole army of inhalers in my duffel bag, I marched back toward the pool. Ready to get back into fighting trim, train until I puked, rebuild myself.

Ready to race and begin again.

—Julia Lam
Chicken Soup for the Teenage Soul: The Real Deal School

82

Pay Attention

The most important thing in communication is to hear what isn't being said.
—Peter F. Drucker

Jason came from a good family with two loving parents, two brothers and a sister. They were all successful academically and socially. They lived in a posh neighborhood. Jason had everything a boy could desire. But he was always into some kind of mischief. He wasn't a bad kid who caused trouble, but he always wound up in the thick of things.

In first grade, Jason was labeled Special Ed. They tried to keep him out of the regular classes. In middle school, he was the "misfit troublemaker." In high school, although never officially tested, Jason was tagged with having attention deficit disorder (ADD). More often than not, his teachers kicked him out of class. His first report card had one C and the rest Ds.

One Sunday, the family was enjoying brunch at the country club when a teacher stopped and said, "Jason is doing so well these days. We're pleased and delighted."

"You must be mixing us up with another family," said the father. "Our Jason is worthless. He is always in trouble. We are so embarrassed and just can't figure out why."

As the teacher walked away, the mother remarked, "You know, honey, come to think of it, Jason hasn't been in trouble for a month.

He's even been going to school early and staying late. I wonder what's up?"

The second nine-week grading period was finally up. As usual, Jason's mom and dad expected low grades and unsatisfactory marks in behavior. Instead, he achieved four As and three Bs and honors in citizenship. His parents were baffled.

"Who did you sit by to get these grades?" the dad asked sarcastically.

"I did it all myself," Jason humbly answered.

Perplexed and still not satisfied, the parents took Jason back to school to meet with the principal. He assured them that Jason was doing very well.

"We have a new guidance counselor and she seems to have touched your son in a special way," he said. "His self-esteem is much better and he's doing great this term. I think you should meet her."

When the trio approached, the woman had her head down. It took a moment for her to notice she had visitors. When she did, she leaped to her feet and began gesturing with her hands.

"What's this?" asked Jason's father indignantly. "Sign language? Why, she can't even hear."

"That's why she's so great," said Jason, jumping in between them. "She does more than hear, Dad. She listens!"

—Dan Clark
Chicken Soup for the Teenage Soul II

83

When I Get Out

To the Authors of *Chicken Soup for the Teenage Soul*,

I am a fifteen-year-old girl serving time in a juvenile detention facility in Washington. I have seen a lot for my young age. I started doing drugs heavily in seventh grade. In eighth grade, I started throwing up my food, starving myself, popping diet pills and speed, snorting lines of crank and crystal meth, and cutting myself. I was five feet, seven inches tall and eighty-five pounds when I was admitted to the psychiatric unit of the hospital.

I didn't really learn anything even after I was discharged because I ran with gangs and continued taking drugs. Life was a party. The gangs I knew were my family. I was both physically and verbally abusive to my mom, who loved me the most. One night I needed a place to stay so some guys picked up me and my friends, and we broke into a house and had a big party. We found a gun while everyone was getting drunk, and we played with it. The cops came the next day and, though we had thought of stealing the gun, we didn't—but someone else did.

Now I am stuck here, charged with first-degree burglary of a firearm, even though I never took the gun. I will have the record forever. I face the chance of being sent to adult prison for five years. I do take full responsibility for the events that led up to the gun being stolen. I know that no one could have saved me, but myself—and I failed.

While I do my time, I read, and my mom bought me your book, *Chicken Soup for the Teenage Soul*. It's such a good book to have in this place, and something I really needed. I especially liked the story "Unconditional Mom." I have laughed and cried while reading this book. It has made me rethink what I want my life to be when I get out. I do know I want to change. I'm a smart person who made stupid choices and lots of mistakes. I am grateful I'll be given a second chance.

Thanks for this book and thanks for listening.

Sincerely,
—Lisa McKinney
Chicken Soup for the Teenage Soul Letters

Chapter
9

Teens Talk
Growing Up

Reaching for the Stars

If you don't go after what you want, you'll never have it.
If you don't ask, the answer is always no.
If you don't step forward, you're always in the same place.
—Nora Roberts

Head Butting the Wall

Always be a first-rate version of yourself, instead of a second-rate version of somebody else.
—Judy Garland

I grew up in a small town in New Jersey where I felt bored and trapped. My family life was all about, "Mom works, Dad works and kids are expected to go to school." My parents didn't have the money to buy me stuff I got interested in, and we didn't have any time to spend together except during meals. That didn't cost anything or take up any extra time.

I was angry and frustrated most of the time—it seemed that no matter what I did or said, I felt like I was head butting the wall and getting nowhere. No one could get through—not my parents, my teachers or my guidance counselor. No one could help me.

Then I started high school, and a lot of the people I knew began using drugs and alcohol. Because I wasn't interested in that, I found myself on the outside of my peer group. I was totally alone and I hated the world.

I started roaming the streets looking for trouble. I fought older, tougher guys around town and gained a reputation for being crazy. I'd take any dare. If someone said to me, "Smash your head on this rock for five bucks!" I would.

I was well on my way to prison or the morgue when I stumbled on punk rock music. The whole idea of a punk lifestyle sounded cool.

So, I spiked my hair and took on a whole new identity until, one day, some real punkers came up to me in the hall at school.

"Hey, man, are you punk?"

"Yeah, yeah, man, I'm punk," I fumbled.

"Oh, yeah? What bands do you like?"

I didn't know any bands—none.

"Who do you listen to?" I didn't know one band from the other. Then my eyes landed on their band-logo T-shirts.

"Dead Kennedys, Black Flag, The Misfits..." I thought I had them fooled. But I was pretty much busted.

"Stop looking at our shirts. You don't really know any punk bands, do you?"

Totally busted. Where do I go with this? I thought to myself. Before I could come up with a strategy, one of them dared me to come home with them to his house. We went down into his basement and they shaved my spikes off. Then they said I was really punk. The next thing I knew, I was meeting up with them after school and hanging out.

Some of my new friends would occasionally get hold of a skateboarding magazine, and they'd show me pictures of some decks. When I saw the boards, I connected. I became obsessed. I wanted to get my hands on a board and more of those magazines. One kid, the younger brother of one of my friends, had a stash. I cruised over to his house and knocked on the door.

"Hey, man, can I take a look at some of your skateboard magazines?" I asked.

This guy was hardcore. He wasn't about to let me touch his prized possessions, but he let me stand on his back porch and look at them through his screen door as he turned the pages, one by one. That's when I saw an article about street skating and a photo of a guy jumping off a car.

"I can do that! I can totally do that," I tried to convince him. He looked at me, doubting every word, but he got his board out and challenged me right then and there. I took the dare, grabbed the board and got up on his grandpa's car. Slam! I hit the ground. I got back up. I went through the same thing over and over—biting dust every time. Then finally... I landed it!

He screamed, "You did it! You're a skateboarder!"

I was hooked, rushing on adrenaline. I wanted to experience it again and again.

I began to follow a group of guys in my neighborhood that had boards. I'd beg them to let me skate. They treated me like dirt, but because they had boards, I took it.

I had to figure out how I could get my own board. I finally conned my mom into giving me money for a board by promising her that it would be my one and only Christmas present. I ordered a board and when it arrived, I was totally stoked. Then my mom made me hand it over. Her words, "Sorry. You can't have it until Christmas, Mike," were torture.

Weeks later, Christmas came and finally I got my board. I skated every spare second I could. I went from skating a few minutes a day to hours a day. I'd skate to and from school, after school, after dinner and after homework. When I started trying to skate the half pipe, I'd get nothing but grief about my style. I was doing everything I could just to gain the speed needed to get up the other side of the ramp. I'd flap my arms to get momentum. "Look at the chicken-man," guys would taunt. I didn't care—whatever it took, I'd try it. I lived and breathed skateboarding. It was my sanctuary and my salvation; it was my "thing."

I easily navigated the traps and pitfalls of high school and adolescence by just getting on my board and riding. But it wasn't just the physical act of skateboarding that made an immediate and lasting impact on me; it was the entire subculture of doing your own thing. Instead of following the crowd, I had discovered my individuality. My small town that once felt full of dead end streets suddenly opened up. I found a wide open country of possibilities. At fourteen, that's some vital stuff.

I truly believe everyone needs to find something to help them discover their identity and give them a sense of purpose, meaning and direction. For me... it just happened to be skateboarding.

Skateboarding saved my life. It gave me the ability to express myself, connect to a passion and offer something unique back to the world. Now, as a professional, I travel the world, skateboarding and sharing my life story.

I'm still head butting the wall, the difference is that now I'm fighting to keep the sport of skateboarding open to everyone and anyone—regardless of how good they are, what they look like or where they live. I want everyone to know that if they just believe in themselves and have a passion for the sport, anything is possible.

—Mike Vallely
Chicken Soup for the Preteen Soul 2

85

Girl Power

As Olympus was heaven to the gods, this was heaven to me: the orange court with its three-point line, free-throw line and boundaries. This was where I wanted to be—the basketball court. It was my life, my destiny, my future.

The noisy gym held a bunch of students talking, rapping, eating or just staring into space. Our gym teacher stepped in front of us. "If you want to play basketball, get on the court," he blurted.

As usual, most of the prissy girls were scared that their makeup would smudge or their hair would get ruined, so they went to sit in the bleachers and flirt with the boys. But I jumped right onto the basketball court. Unfortunately, I was the only girl. Man, should I sit down? Or should I show my moves to these boys? But what if the boys are WAY better than me? I would look like a high school basketball player going up against Kobe Bryant. Oh well, I'll look like a chicken if I sit down now. With these things in mind, I took my spot on the court.

The game was about to begin. All the teams had been selected, and I was one of the first picks on the blue team. I was thrilled! Then I heard a group of girls snicker, and one said, "The only reason you got picked is because you're the only girl and they felt sorry for you."

That can't be the reason. They chose me to play against the best boys... or did they just want to embarrass me?

Resolutely, I strolled to my position when a boy in the bleachers yelled, "Girl, get off that court. Basketball isn't your game." His words ground into me like I was a piece of dust on the gym floor.

The coach blew his whistle, and the game began. Here I go, I thought. I should show these boys my skills and make them EAT my dust.

I tried blocking passes, but the guys just shot over my diminutive body and swooshed the ball in. I tried to guard them, but they pulled some tricky moves and I felt stupid as I spun around looking for the ball. One boy crossed over me, bounced the ball between my legs and shot a three-pointer. Then another did a fake pump, acting like he was going to shoot the ball, and when I jumped up to block it, he dribbled around me and slam-dunked it. Yet another boy held the ball in the palm of his hand and kept fake passing it to other players. You name it, they did it.

Finally, I stole the ball. I was shocked to see the orange sphere in my hands. I was so excited that I didn't even move until everybody shouted, "Run! Run!" The ball was mine. It was my chance to shine, my opportunity to make the people who doubted me look dumb. I knew that witnessing my skills would silence the teasing, but I had to do this right.

I ran across that basketball court like a tornado destroying a city, and BAM, I tripped. I couldn't believe it. How had it happened? I couldn't even hear myself think because there was so much laughter coming from the bleachers. It was then that I realized that my Nikes were untied. Oh my goodness, I thought. Here I was trying to make myself shine, but I made a fool of myself instead. The same boy from the bleachers chuckled, "Ha, you silly girl! Now you know you can't play, so get off the court."

Had the team lost? I wasn't even paying attention because I was so busy trying to hide from the crowd. I looked down to see the basketball court beneath my feet. Oops! I was still on the waxy court, and the other team had already started to shoot. So I tied my shoelaces and hopped off to the side. I planted my bottom on the first row of the bleachers, even though I wanted to crawl under them so that no one could see me. The prissy girls, obnoxious boy and even the coaches were smirking and laughing at me. How was I going to get through this humiliation?

An hour later, the laughter had slowed down, but I knew that it was still in their memories. If I didn't do anything, by the end of the day the whole school would know about my little incident. No one would know what really happened because people were bound to exaggerate the story to make it funnier. I knew I had to do something to prove I was competent.

"Coach, can you put me in the next round?" I asked.

"You want to go in the game? Come on, Araz," he said.

"I want to play," I countered.

"You'll hurt yourself. Just let the boys finish off what they started."

"No, I want to do this." I stood firm.

"All right, then. It's your decision, but don't come whining to me if you get hurt," he mumbled.

So I went back in. This time I played for the red team. The spectators' eyes rested on me. I felt the pressure to show them everything I could do. The game started with a tip-off. I got the ball, dribbled it down the court, crossed a boy over, and made a layup. "Ohh," the crowd cheered. I did the same thing when I got the ball again, except this time I did a reverse lay-up. Again I heard the crowd roar.

I felt like I was in control of a ball of fire. This was the attention I craved. I wanted people to notice me for my talents, not my mistakes. I was doing all different types of moves on these boys. You name it and I did it. The roles had switched. Maybe Michael Jordan had entered my body. By the end of the game, I had beaten just about every boy on that court, and people were coming up to me and complimenting me on my playing.

I had done it. I had done what had seemed like the impossible. Even though I felt like hiding in the bathroom and never getting on the basketball court again, I dusted myself off and tried again. Something told me to get back on that court and prove everybody wrong. Just like the basketball, people tried to knock me down, but I bounced right back up.

The best part of that day was when a certain boy, that same one who had made fun of me, came up to me and said, "Nice game! You played great. Most girls would've given up as soon as I teased them. You got back on that court and played like Jordan. It sure is hard to break you down. Next time, I want to play you one-on-one." That put a smug smile on my face for the rest of the day. I felt like a true achiever.

—Araz Garakanian
Chicken Soup for the Teenage Soul: The Real Deal School

86

Never Say Quit

The highest reward for a man's toil is not what he gets for it, but what he becomes by it.
—*John Ruskin*

I was fresh out of college and had just started my teaching and coaching career at St. Bernard's, the same high school I had attended. Compared to the schools that surrounded us, we were rather small, with two to three thousand students. My first year I served as an assistant coach with our football and basketball teams; during the spring, I was in charge of the track program.

We had a phenomenal year. Our football team won ten games, finishing the season undefeated. Our basketball team won twenty-one games, losing only five. We emerged as conference champions in both sports.

Being young and naïve, I didn't recognize what extraordinary athletes we had that year. By the next fall, fourteen of our former students would be playing college football—four with major scholarships. Two others would be running track for Division I universities. In twenty-five years of coaching after that, I never encountered a more gifted group.

Yet the student who made the greatest impression on all of us wasn't one of these promising young men. Physically he was as different from them as a donkey from a thoroughbred. His name was Bobby Colson, and his impact will last the rest of my life.

Bobby was the freshman brother of our star two-mile runner, Mark Colson. Early in the season, Bobby stopped me in the school hallway. At five-three and 175 pounds, he looked like the model for the Pillsbury Dough Boy. He told me that he'd been doing some serious thinking about joining our track team and believed he could make an important contribution. He added that he didn't know in what events he could help us, but felt confident that he had something to offer. I was impressed by his presentation and self-confidence.

Given his physique, the logical role for Bobby was that of a "weight man"—an athlete who specializes in shot-put and discus throwing. We quickly encountered a setback, however: Even though Bobby's 175 pounds were a lot of weight for a freshman, he didn't have an ounce of visible muscle. Not only was he unable to put (throw) the shot, he could barely pick it up.

Undaunted, Bobby proceeded with me to the discus area. A discus is considerably lighter than a shot, so immediately we were off to a good start. I coached him in the proper grip, delivery and release. Things seemed to be going fairly well. On command, Bobby would assume a wide stance, bend his knees, spread his fingers, bring his arm back and forth three times, and let fly.

That is, most of the time he'd let fly. Every few tries, though, he'd forget to let go, or he'd start to run right out of the circle, holding the discus in front of him in his pudgy little mitt. Whenever he actually released the discus, he would quickly spread out the measuring tape to see if his throw challenged the freshman-sophomore school record of 131 feet. Finding he had more than 110 feet to go didn't seem to faze him.

We decided that Bobby might see greater results by adding the spinning technique to his discus endeavors. We stayed after the official close of practice to review the required footwork dozens of times. I even drew footprints on the circle to show him exactly where to step. Bobby was incredibly persistent and extremely coachable. I began to wish that all my athletes shared his attitude.

The moment came to give the new technique a try. It was a sight to behold. Once Bobby got to spinning, he resembled a human centrifuge about to explode. He was still twirling when the discus flew out of his hand and landed twenty-seven feet in the opposite direction from where we'd intended. After I got Bobby to stop turning, he staggered around like a wounded water buffalo for a few minutes, looking as if he might throw up. Then he rushed to measure his latest effort—that's how I know it was exactly twenty-seven feet.

Bobby felt very encouraged by this outcome, but I didn't think the season was long enough to get his technique to the point where we weren't endangering lives—his own included. After a bit of smooth talking on my part, Bobby agreed that we should investigate another event. The long jump seemed like a possibility; the only problem was, Bobby couldn't make it to the landing pit from the takeoff board. We quickly eliminated the pole vault, high jump, hurdles and triple jump. Bobby wasn't blessed with a lot of foot speed, so sprints and relays also went by the wayside. When we ended the session, I was at a loss what to suggest for the following day's practice.

As it turned out, Bobby made his decision without me. The next morning he informed me that he was going to be a two-miler like his brother, Mark. I knew Bobby idolized Mark, who not only was an outstanding two-miler but also an outstanding person and team leader.

I admired Bobby's enthusiasm, but to myself I questioned whether the two-mile race was a good choice. Yet Bobby was determined, and for the next two weeks, he painfully but gamely struggled through his workouts.

Our first meet was a "triangular" between St. Basil's, Notre Dame and ourselves. In those days, the two-mile race was the first running event at each meet. Because of the length of the event, both the frosh-soph and varsity teams ran at the same time; the younger runners wore their shirts inside out to identify their level. Field events all started at the same time as well.

So here we were, with the two-mile well underway. At the varsity level we were set to finish first and third. Mark Colson launched another memorable season by setting a new conference record.

Then there was Bobby. Every team has one or two very slow

frosh-soph runners, but next to Bobby, they all looked like sprinters. When all the other runners had finished, Bobby still had three laps to go. The host team started putting hurdles on the track for the next event. I yelled at them to leave lane one open, so Bobby could finish the race.

As Bobby completed his first of his remaining laps, I could see tears on his cheeks. I didn't realize it, but several boys from the other squads had started calling him names and making fun of him. Only our high jumper, Pat Linden, knew what was happening. He left the high-jump area and stationed himself at the far curve to shout words of encouragement to Bobby.

Meanwhile, other athletes continued to ridicule Bobby, shouting at him to get off the track. Bobby was crying more noticeably now, but he kept going. A few more of our varsity team members noticed Pat's absence and went to join him in urging Bobby on.

During my many years of coaching since then, I've seen top athletes walk off the track when they knew they weren't going to win a race. Usually they developed a pulled hamstring or something of that nature—though often I thought the injury was more to the spirit than to the body. Bobby, in contrast, never once considered leaving that two-mile race, grueling as it plainly was for him. Once he started, quitting was not an option.

After he finished the race, Bobby went from event to event encouraging his teammates. When one of our athletes took a first place, Bobby got more excited than the winner.

A few days later, we had our second triangular meet, with Holy Cross and St. Patrick's. The scenario in the two-mile was much the same as before, except this time all our athletes left their respective areas to urge Bobby on. Imagine: Our whole team lined up around the track, clapping and cheering for Bobby as tears coursed down his face. It was really a moving sight to see.

By our third triangular meet, at Bergon High School, word had spread about Bobby. This time our team members weren't the only ones rooting for him—all the other teams were there, too, filling the straightaways as well as the curves.

At the end of the season, the varsity team purchased a large trophy for Bobby and had it inscribed: To Bobby Colson—Our Most Courageous Athlete, St. Bernard's Track Team 1968.

Bobby had been right when he told me that he felt he could make a significant contribution to our track efforts. He had joined a good team and made it into a great family. His example helped us all to understand that talent is God given, and we should be thankful, but conceit is self-given, and we should be careful.

We didn't find out until late that summer, but Bobby Colson had a rare form of leukemia. He died the following fall.

—Bob Hoppenstedt
Chicken Soup for the Unsinkable Soul

Something Unbelievable

Nothing splendid has ever been achieved except by those who dared believe that something inside them was superior to circumstances.
—Bruce Barton

When I turned sixteen, my Ghanian parents decided to make the ultimate sacrifice. They sold all of our earthly possessions and bought me a plane ticket back to America where we'd lived years earlier. I would have a better life than those before me.

When I returned to the States, I had fire in my blood. I was ready to take on the world. I was unstoppable. I arrived at Charlotte International Airport in North Carolina, and then traveled south to Florence, South Carolina, where I would finish high school. In those early hours, North Carolina seemed like Las Vegas to me, with all the lights, billboards, neon cowboys on taverns, twitching crucifixes on small Southern churches, and streets with names like Avalon and Magnolia. I was mesmerized, amazed, inspired. In one of the first letters I wrote to my family, I called it a sight to behold.

On the first day of school, I sat in the front row of my English class just as I had done so many times back home. The teacher was an aging Southern belle named Ms. Smith with leathery skin and blue eyes turning gray with age. Her voice was pleasant and her twang delectable. I remember her well, but not just for the accent.

With about six minutes of the first class remaining, Ms. Smith announced that an African was amongst us. The students looked around for a real-life National Geographic experience. I honestly didn't know she was talking about me. After all, I'd never been called "the African."

"Come on now! Introduce yourself to the class and tell them what your name means!" Ms. Smith insisted.

She walked over to my desk and told me to stand up. Everyone stared. I was mortified. I knew they were looking for tribal marks, some proof of my ethnicity.

"Good day," I said proudly, after a moment's hesitation. "I bring greetings to you all from Ghana. I am Mary Akua Spio."

My words fell like laughing gas bombs. With each syllable, the class laughed louder and louder. My manner of speech apparently amused the entire class. And my outfit didn't help matters any. In my attempt to look American, I wore cowboy boots and a large belt, similar to the one boxers receive when they win a match. Huge and shiny.

"Mary? What about Obtunde or something like that? What? Did you change your name at the airport?" one student yelled out.

"You speak English good for an Afkan," another student quipped. Doesn't she mean, "I speak English well?" I thought to myself.

I became a piñata for the class's questions and insults. "What did you do with the tree you lived in when you left Africa?" I remember one student yelling.

Hoping to return control to the class, Ms. Smith interrupted. "So, Mary, what are your dreams? What do you want to be in the future?"

Blinking back tears, I answered, "A rocket scientist." Once again the class exploded into laughter.

"Oh dear! That's like saying you want to be the Easter Bunny! You ought to study something like physical education, where you get a chance to swing around, just like back home. Besides, you gotta be real smart to be any kind of scientist!" Ms. Smith was now having her own fun with me.

Soon after, the bell rang and everyone dispersed. I sat frozen for a few minutes, feeling numb, filled with disbelief. Later that day,

I met with the guidance counselor and things grew worse. Without giving me any evaluative tests, she concluded I wasn't smart enough to take classes like physics and calculus. The counselor's words were the final jabs through my soul. In an instant, all my dreams seemed to go down the drain.

Although I had completed physics and calculus courses in Ghana, I was put back into basic algebra. Teachers and counselors told me my primary focus should be getting rid of my African accent. I felt hopeless. If they were right, if my IQ really was low, what could my future possibly hold?

After graduation, I left South Carolina for New York and got a job at McDonald's. I knew I could flip burgers and mop floors, but I wanted to be so much more. After hearing a commercial, I enlisted in the Air Force and served for almost five years, earning enough money to attend college full-time. I studied hard, received an additional scholarship and headed off to Syracuse University to study electrical engineering.

Several years later, I found myself trudging through the brutal Syracuse winds, arms and legs frozen cold from the icy snow. It was time for my senior design review, the event every engineer dreads. The design review panel consists of a couple of professors and representatives from the engineering industry, and they can be an intimidating bunch.

We stood in the back of the class, squirming impatiently, as we watched the review panel approach our lab stations one by one. I was reminded of Don Shaw, our lab instructor, and the inspections we had endured for semesters. During Don's inspections, he would always stop at Lab Station 10 and ask, "Do you know whose lab station this is?" He'd then answer his own question with a mouth full of theatrics. "This is the lab station of Eileen Collins, the first space shuttle commander! Yes, this is the station that Eileen used." Even though I had used Lab Station 10 for more than three years, everyone still called it the Space Commander's Lab Station.

As the review panel approached Lab Station 10, the head of the panel asked in a booming voice, "Whose lab station is this?" I could hear my heart pounding as I made my way to the front of the class-room. This time the question would have far greater implications than ever. I hesitated for a few seconds, biting my lips, tears not far from my eyes, and I answered their question with these words, "Ahem... mine." I glanced over at Don Shaw, wondering if he had a better answer for the review board. Smiling through tears of his own, he nodded in encouragement.

The panel drilled me about my design. I tried to remain calm throughout the endless torture. I spoke slowly, answering their questions, but soon the words flowed with the inspiration and reason behind my senior design project. My words were not perfect, but this time I knew they were beautiful. I felt it. Everyone in the room did.

In that instant, nothing else mattered. The African had spoken; this time they were proud. They were happy to see her. I felt the unique reverence for life that only a death-defying (or life-defining) moment can create. I didn't want to stop speaking. I wanted to be heard forever.

Then came the announcement that I'll never forget: "Congratu-lations, you are this year's winner of the IEEE (Institute of Electrical and Electronics Engineering) Design and Implementation Award!" The class cheered. People came over to talk to me. Some people asked me questions about the project, while others asked me about things they had been dying to know since our freshman year. Still others expressed their deep respect and admiration. Later that week, I learned I would be graduating number one in my electrical engi-neering class. It was an honor and a blessing.

After leaving Syracuse University, I continued on to Georgia Tech for graduate studies in deep space communications. I have since worked on heat-seeking probes for the NASA SETI (Search for Extra-terrestrial Intelligence) program, designed orbits for rockets bearing communication satellites, sent a rocket into space with my signa-ture on it, and engineered technology that allowed George Lucas to deliver Star Wars episode II digitally. The Boeing Company recently bought and patented four of my inventions in deep space science.

Ms. Smith was right. The Easter Bunny and a rocket scientist do have something in common: the unbelievable. Today, I walk through life proud of the African heritage of which I was once ashamed. Who knows what that class back in South Carolina felt in the instant they almost crushed my dreams? Maybe, through the teasing, they caught a glimpse of the woman I would ultimately become: Mary A. Spio, independent inventor and American rocket scientist. Something unbelievable.

—Mary Spio
Chicken Soup for the African American Soul

A Better Message

*It doesn't matter if you try and try and try again, and fail. It does matter if
you try and fail, and fail to try again.*
—Charles Kettering

My senior year of high school, I wanted to be a social worker like my older sister, Lynn. She had really inspired me. I
wanted to help people, to make a difference in their lives,
just like she was doing.

I knew I had work to do because I hadn't really applied myself in high
school. It was more social for me than anything else. But I was looking ahead
to my future, and I knew that if I really wanted to do this, I was going to
need help. I made an appointment to see a guidance counselor, Mr. Shaw.

He listened to my inspired rap as I went on and on about the
wonders of a helping career. I could actually help make a difference
in the world! Mr. Shaw looked back at me in disbelief. "You're not
college material," he said clearly and deliberately. It felt like my heart
stopped... frozen in the moment of those icy words.

That evening I broke the news to my parents. Seeing how dis-
traught I was, and how sincere I was in really wanting to go to college,
they offered to help. They found a small college that would take me
if I could manage to get a C average during the current semester. It
was too late. I had goofed around too much, and even my best efforts
could not bring up my grade point average.

My parents were so wonderful and supportive. They found

another small college whose financial status would permit anyone to attend. In other words, they would take anyone with a pulse. I felt like such a loser. Mr. Shaw's resounding words came back to me: "You're not college material." And I was beginning to believe it. So much so that I was flunking out—even at this college.

I gave up. I believed Mr. Shaw was right about me. After I left college, I moved home again and starting working part-time jobs. Maybe college wasn't for me. But deep down in my heart I knew that I truly wanted to be a teacher or social worker, and... that would require a college degree. No getting around it.

What would I do? I simply had to try again, I had to believe in myself even if no one else did. With all the courage I could muster, I enrolled in a community college nearby and took one course in their night school. I was shocked when I received my grade. I got an A. Maybe it was a mistake or some sort of fluke. I took another course and earned another A. Wow.

I made an appointment to see one of my professors. Things were turning around, and I needed guidance. Dr. Sarah Cohen, my professor in child psychology, told me to relax and enjoy my experience; I was doing very well by all standards. She also said that I was fun, bright and could do anything I put my mind to. Here was an educational expert with a different message. I felt empowered. I was on my way.

I graduated from that community college with honors and went on to earn my B.A. in psychology and my M.A. in psychology from New York University. The very same degree the illustrious Mr. Shaw holds. I felt vindicated.

I realized that choosing who you believe in can change your life. When I believed Mr. Shaw, my life fell apart and there was no way I would ever realize my dream. But when I believed in myself and persevered through seemingly insurmountable odds, I encountered more people who inspired and supported me the way Dr. Cohen had.

As Henry Ford once said, "If you think you can, or if you think you can't... you're right."

—Carol Grace Anderson
Chicken Soup for the College Soul

The Neighbor Lady

Some people come into our lives and quickly go. Some stay for a while,
leave a footprint on our hearts, and we are never, ever the same.
—Flavia Weedn

When I was in grade school, I used to have a dream that Mrs. Paxton's house next door had fallen down the hill with Mrs. Paxton in it. If that imagined event had actually come to pass, I was sure my life would get much better.

We lived then in a suburb of Pittsburgh—a family neighborhood with lots of kids. It was ideal: big yards, lots of little wooded lots, safe streets, hills for sledding and a few dangerous places to explore. Everything a boy could want. Except for Mrs. Paxton, our neighbor lady.

She was a small, thin woman, who wore spectacles on a black cord around her neck. She had a receding hairline and a ring of gray curls high on her forehead that looked, from a distance, a little like a halo. She never had kids of her own, which seemed to us a lucky break because Mrs. Paxton was any kid's worst enemy: a nosy woman who not only watched us more closely than our own mothers, but reported what she saw.

From her upstairs bedroom window Mrs. Paxton had a view of our backyard, our hillside and the street below. So she could see almost everything we did. Sometimes when we got into fights, she would tap on the glass with a pencil; you would be surprised how far

that sound carries. Other times, if we were into something dangerous like hopping curbs on our bikes, she would tell my parents and
I would get a lecture... at least a lecture.

Our only respite from Mrs. Paxton's constant intrusion on our
privacy was on Thursday afternoons in the summer. Then three cars
would pull into her driveway, and music teachers from my school
would file into her house.

That got my attention because I thought teachers made themselves cocoons or something and just hibernated in the summer.
But there they were carrying instrument cases, and after a while we
would hear the sounds of a string quartet coming though the open
windows.

Mrs. Paxton herself played the viola, and I often listened more
attentively when her instrument had the melody. I'd begun piano
lessons a few years earlier and had gotten good enough to know how
to really listen to music. Still, there was something about the sound
the string quartet made, sounds that got to me in a way the piano
couldn't. When Mrs. Paxton played, she made a warm, sweet sound
like a song—sweet and mellow as summer.

Quartet day was good news because it meant that Mrs. Paxton
was not at her upstairs window, and we could do the things we did
not want our parents to hear about. So my friends and I would head
down the hill to the drainage ditch. My own mother said it was "a
filthy sewer," but really neat salamanders lived there, so I liked it a lot.
Sometimes we would crawl into the forbidden burned-out house—
still standing because of some legal tangle. We would peel back water-
stained wallpaper looking for hidden messages or sift through ashes,
looking for coins.

If we did any of these things unaccompanied by the sounds of
string quartets from Mrs. Paxton's house, our parents would know
about it immediately. Mrs. Paxton knew everything about our neighborhood and told everything she knew to some grown-up or other. I
couldn't imagine why she was like that. Was it because she never had
kids of her own that she didn't like us?

By the end of summer, I entered the eighth grade, and signed up for the school orchestra. I got up the nerve and went to see the orchestra director about the possibility of learning on one of the school instruments. But Miss Wagner told me all of the stringed instruments had already been signed out. She said she'd love it if I could help out in the percussion section, though.

That was a long way from what I had in mind, so I moped around the house for a few days. My parents could not afford to buy me an instrument, and I did not want to beg for it. Though I spent more time than usual running with my friends, I could not get the idea of making music out of my head.

Then one day I came in from riding bikes with my friends to find Mrs. Paxton sitting in our very own living room talking with my mother. I tried to step slowly backwards out the front door, but my mother had already seen me and told me to come in. Mrs. Paxton had something she wanted to say to me.

I felt my body get sort of heavy, and I shuffled into the room. I sat down on a straight-backed chair across the room from Mrs. Paxton. She patted the seat next to her on the couch and told me to come sit beside her. I would rather have been told I had to play with my sister's friends. I delayed moving, and my mother shot me one of her looks—the kind that get you out of your seat in a hurry.

I considered sitting at the far end of the couch, but I knew my mother would consider that noncompliance. So I sat cautiously down next to Mrs. Paxton. To my surprise, Mrs. Paxton smelled like lilacs. She immediately began to quiz me about music, of all things. She wanted to know what I liked and if I really wanted to play a stringed instrument—somehow she even knew that.

I looked at my mother to see if she had blabbed it, but she shook her head telling me she had not. I did not know what to tell Mrs. Paxton about why I wanted to play in the orchestra so badly. I had become obsessed with making a kind of music that was like singing.

But that's just not the kind of thing you say, not even to your own mother. Still, something inside told me to just say it anyway and let everyone laugh if they wanted to.

I said, "I want to play something with strings because you can make them sing the way a voice does."

Mrs. Paxton's eyes widened. She looked at me very curiously as though I had somehow said the magic words. Then she lifted a long black box from the floor and placed it between us on the couch. She opened it, turned back the green velvet cover, took out her viola and held it in her lap. Sort of like the way my mother held babies.

It was the instrument of my dreams. The honey-colored viola glowed and shone. She stroked it gently with her hand and then handed it to me. "I want you to have this. It is a loan until you have your own someday."

I didn't know what to do. I stared at her and then the viola. I couldn't move. She took my hand in hers, which was strangely soft and warm, and put my fingers around the neck of the instrument. I looked at her. She smiled. I looked at my mother. She smiled. I started to shake a little and was really afraid I might cry or do something else disgraceful. But somehow I kept hold of my self-respect.

She did not stay long after that. I wanted to say something really nice to her, but I was so used to hating her I couldn't think of anything at all to say except, "Thank you very much." It seemed lame somehow, considering what the instrument meant to both of us.

Later, I accused my mother of telling Mrs. Paxton about my wanting an instrument. But she swore she hadn't done anything of the kind. "Mrs. Paxton just knows things," she said.

"But why would she do this?" I asked, still amazed by my good luck.

"Well, she never had children of her own. I think she just loves you." I looked at my mother as though she had lost her last marble. "When you're older..." I was out of the room before she finished that dumb line I knew by heart.

Over the years I often thought about Mrs. Paxton and the mystery of why she gave me the thing she loved most in the world. I eventually got good enough to play in a string quartet of my own, to tour Russia, to play in an orchestra in Carnegie Hall, to become principal violist of the Florida Philharmonic.

And after all this time, I see that Mrs. Paxton knew more about me than I ever imagined, knew me almost as well as my own mother.

I think she watched out for me and cared about me just as she might have done for a son of her own. And I think that if she had been able to have children they would have been very lucky. She would not only have watched over them, but she would have opened doors they never knew existed, opened doors to joy and happiness and the immeasurable pleasure of finding the thing you loved to do most in the world—just as she had done for me.

So now as I get ready to begin Fort Lauderdale's Beethoven at the Beach concert, I put on the festival T-shirt that the orchestra wears for these performances. And I hope that my playing will have a sound like singing, a sound I heard long ago coming from Mrs. Paxton's open windows on a summer afternoon.

—Michael McClelland
Chicken Soup for the Mother's Soul 2

90

Joe Camel

Unless someone like you cares a whole awful lot,
nothing is going to get better. It's not.
—Dr. Seuss

"I don't believe it. They are actually taking it down!"

"We really do make a difference!"

As we sit in the bleachers of our high school stadium, we're feeling elated as the huge Joe Camel billboard, positioned directly in sight of our school, is being disassembled—and we did it!

Have you ever raised your hand simply to be part of something, and then have it turn into a life-altering event? That's exactly what happened to Eddie, Marisol and me. We belong to a school club called Friday Night Live, which promotes alcohol- and drug-free friendships and activities. It's not easy resisting the temptation to drink and smoke when, wherever you turn, advertising companies are using big money trying to hook us into using their products. The message is loud and clear: Use this stuff and you are cool, beautiful and popular.

During one of our FNL meetings, Eddie said, "It really makes me mad that everywhere I go on this campus, I can see the Joe Camel billboard, and yet the big tobacco companies tell everyone they are not targeting teens. Yeah, right!"

There are other billboards, but this is the only one you can see from our school. Our counselor, Ms. Bambus, asked if anyone would be interested in writing to the billboard company and asking them to take it down. What followed was an amazing process that landed us on the Today show, CNN and many local TV shows.

We did some research and found out that there was a group called Human Health Services. We asked them if there were any other groups that had done this before and what they did. They gave us a few examples and recommended writing a polite letter to the billboard company. It seemed as if it would be more fun if we just marched over and ripped up the billboard, but logic won out and we contacted the company and simply explained our concerns. We also cited the code that does not permit tobacco and alcohol advertisements within sight of a school. The vice president of the company said he couldn't see that the billboard was doing any harm.

Eddie wrote an article about it for the school newspaper, which was picked up by the local city paper. From then on, we had national media coming to our campus. One day, when I was on my way to lunch, Channel 10 came up to me and said, "Irene, we've been looking for you. We heard you and your friends are taking on Joe Camel." They asked for permission to film us talking about how we got started and what we hoped to accomplish.

Five months after all the excitement, the billboard came down. It was replaced by an ice cream advertisement. We were glad that it was all over and were looking forward to getting on with just being teens.

During the time we were involved with this, my grandfather—a smoker who started in his teens—was diagnosed with cancer. Maybe there was a higher power calling me to raise my hand to help write the letter that day. I believe if we help people not to start smoking, that's one family that won't have to watch a loved one die from it. That's a big deal!

—Meladee McCarty
Chicken Soup for the Teenage Soul II

91

Winners Never Quit

I had been swimming competitively for about five years and was ready to quit, not because I had satisfied my desire to swim, but because I felt I was horrible at it. I was often the only African American at a swim competition, and our team could not afford anything close to the great uniforms the other teams were wearing. Worst of all though, and my number one reason for wanting to quit, was that I kept receiving "Honorable Mentions" at each competition, which simply means, "Thank you for coming. You did not even rank first, second or third, but we don't want you to go home with nothing, so here is something to hide later." Any athlete knows that you don't want to have a bookshelf or a photo album full of "Honorable Mentions." They call that the "show-up ribbon;" you get one just because you showed up.

One hot summer day, the very day before a big swim meet, I decided to break the news to my grandma that I was quitting the swim team. On the one hand, I thought it was a big deal because I was the only athlete in the family, but on the other hand, because no one ever came to see me compete, I didn't think it would be a major issue. You have to know my grandma—she stood on tiptoe to five-feet-two-inches and weighed a maximum ninety-five pounds, but could run the entire operation of her house without ever leaving her sofa or raising her voice. As I sat next to my grandma, I assumed my usual position of laying my big head on her tiny little lap so that she could rub it.

When I told her of my desire to quit swimming, she abruptly pushed my head off her lap, sat me straight up facing her and said, "Baby, remember these words: 'A quitter never wins and a winner never quits.' Your grandmother didn't raise no losers or quitters. You go to that swim meet tomorrow, and you swim like you are a grandchild of mine, you hear?"

I was too afraid to say anything but, "Yes, ma'am."

The next day we arrived at the swim meet late, missing my group of swimmers in the fifteen/sixteen age group. My coach insisted I be allowed to swim with the next group, the next age older. I could have just as easily crawled out of the gym. I knew she was including me in the race so our long drive would not be wasted, and she had no expectations whatsoever that I would come in anything but eighth— and only that because there were not nine lanes.

As I mounted the board, I quickly noticed that these girls with their skintight caps, goggles and Speedo suits were here to do one thing—kick my chocolate butt!

All of a sudden my grandma's words rang in my head, Quitters never win and winners never quit, quitters never win and winners never quit.

SPLASH!

Quitters never win and winners never quit, quitters never win and winners never quit.

I was swimming harder than I'd ever swum before. As I drew my right arm back, I noticed I was tied with one person. I assumed we were battling for seventh place and I refused to finish dead last, so I added more kick on the last two hundred yards.

Quitters never win and winners never quit, quitters never win and winners never quit.

I hit the wall and looked to the left and to the right for the swimmers who had beat me, but no one was there. They must have gotten out of the water already.

I raised my head to see my coach screaming hysterically. My eyes followed her pointing finger and I couldn't believe what I saw. The other swimmers had just reached the halfway point of the pool! That day, at age fifteen, I broke the national seventeen/eighteen-year-old 400-freestyle record. I hung up my honorable mentions and replaced them with a huge trophy.

Back at Grandma's, I laid my head on her lap and told her about our great race.

—Lisa Nichols
Chicken Soup for the African American Soul

92

I Won't Be Left Behind

I run my fastest
But still get beat.
I land on my head
When I should be on my feet.

I try to move forward,
But I am stuck in rewind.
Why do I keep at it?
I won't be left behind.

The harder I am thrown,
The higher I bounce.
I give it my all,
And that's all that counts.

In first place,
Myself, I seldom find.
So I push to the limit—
I won't be left behind.

Some people tell me you can't,
Some say don't.
Some simply give up.
I reply, I won't.

The power is here,
locked away in my mind.
My perseverance is my excellence,
I won't be left behind.

Make the best of each moment,
The future is soon the past.
The more I tell myself this,
The less I come in last.

Throughout my competitions,
I've learned what winning is about.
A plain and clear lesson—
Giving up is the easy way out.

So every night before I go to bed,
I hope in a small way I have shined.
Tomorrow is a brand new day,
And I won't be left behind.

—Sara Nachtmann
Chicken Soup for the Teenage Soul II

Chapter 10

Teens Talk
Growing Up

Making A Difference

*They may forget what you said,
but they will never forget how you made them feel.*
—Carl W. Buechner

The Greatest Audience

I was sixteen years old, and like many other teenage boys, I was in a band. We played a mix of hard rock and heavy metal, covering our favorite bands. We weren't great, but we were good enough to come in third place at our school's talent show, so we decided to see if we could get some local gigs. When we found out we'd gotten booked for a charitable event at a large rehabilitation hospital, we were ecstatic. It wouldn't pay much, but it was our first real job. For two weeks we practiced hard, getting together every day after school to hone our skills and learn enough songs to fill a one hour show.

The day of the concert, we showed up early in order to check out the stage. It was nerve-wracking to stand there and look out at the hundred or so chairs lined up below us. To my eyes it seemed like those chairs went on forever. We set up and did a quick sound check, then went backstage to have a soda and rest, anything to calm our nerves. While we were back there, the hospital's entertainment director came over to talk to us.

"Okay, boys, I just want to fill you in on a couple of important details," she told us. "A lot of the people in the audience are suffering from severe physical and/or mental disabilities. Also, many of them are older, in their sixties and seventies. Don't let that alarm you. These patients have very few chances to see live entertainment of any kind, so they enjoy any kind of musical talent that we can bring in. Just play your regular show, and you'll do fine." With that, she left, going into the auditorium to help the volunteers and staff that were assisting the patients to their seats.

Soon enough it was show time. We made our way through the thick, dusty curtain that separated the backstage area and stepped out onto the creaking wood floor of the stage. As we picked up our instruments and plugged them in, we got our first real look at the audience. I think to one degree or another we all felt a kind of nervousness that had nothing to do with how we would perform.

The auditorium was packed, and there were at least two or three rows of wheelchairs in both the front and the back of the big room. The majority of the people watching us had either been seriously injured in accidents or born with major congenital birth defects. Many of them were missing limbs. Some were talking quietly among themselves, but most were just sitting there, intently watching the stage. The quiet was unnerving, especially to a group of young men used to rowdy, energetic audiences.

Tommy, the lead singer, signaled us to start the first song, and we broke into the opening chords. Everything was perfect, and we played probably the best show of our lives. We hardly missed a note on any of our songs, even the ones that we'd only recently learned. My guitar solos seemed to flow effortlessly from my fingers, and I felt surrounded by a wall of music. I knew I was getting a taste, just the merest glimpse, of what real musicians must feel when they're on stage. Unfortunately, we couldn't enjoy our performance.

As each song finished, there was a short pause, maybe three or four seconds, before we launched into our next number. This was the time when the audience would normally applaud. Now, we were realistic enough to know that even at our best, we weren't professional musicians by any means. We didn't expect thundering applause or standing ovations. No illusions of greatness here. But polite applause is usually a given, even if the audience doesn't like you. We were getting nothing. Zero. If there was anything there, it was Zen applause— the sound of one hand clapping. To say it was disheartening would be an understatement.

The deafening silence only made us more determined to win

the audience over. We played each successive piece stronger, more furiously than the last, striving for perfection. Loud songs, mellow songs, it made no difference. Each time we concluded a number the audience just continued their imitations of statues. After forty-five minutes we decided to end our set early. Why bother finishing when no one was appreciating us anyway?

We unplugged our instruments and went backstage. A moment later, the entertainment director ran back and confronted us. "What are you doing?" she asked. "I thought we agreed that you'd play for an hour!"

"Well, that was before we realized that the audience was going to hate us," Tommy replied, disgust and embarrassment evident in his tone.

"What are you talking about?" asked the director. "They love you. Get back out there and finish your show. You can even play some extra songs if you want."

"Love us?" exclaimed Pete, our bass player. "That's the worst audience I've ever seen!"

"You don't understand," the director continued. "Most of these people don't know they're supposed to clap. In fact, many of them can't. I've been out there talking to them, and they can't believe how good you are. They'll be so hurt if you don't finish."

The four of us looked at each other. None of us really believed her, but we decided that we should honor our word and finish the show. Returning to the stage, we played our final three songs—and added two more for good measure.

Finally, the show was over and we gratefully began packing up our instruments. We had still received no applause, not even when we said good night. Backstage the director told us, "When you're done packing up, please come back inside the auditorium. Some of the patients want to thank you for coming."

We didn't want to do it, but hey, we felt obligated. I mean, after all, it was a charity event. Of all the things I expected, what happened next shocked me more than anything. At least fifty people, ranging in age from ten to seventy, had gathered by the stage. All of them wanted to thank us; some shook our hands, and one small girl even asked me for my autograph. Several told us that we were the best band that had played for them in years. We couldn't believe it. The director had been right all along; they loved us! We ended up staying there for more than half an hour, saying hello to people, telling them about ourselves and talking about music.

While I knew I was never going to end up having a career in music, I did play a few more small shows with different bands. But no matter how much the audience cheered, I never felt as good as I did that one special night.

—Greg Faherty
Chicken Soup for the Teenage Soul IV

94

Black Jellybeans

People who love cats have some of the biggest hearts around.
—*Susan Easterly*

I've never read an official study on the matter, but I've noticed that in animal shelters, black cats are the most overlooked. Black seems to be the least preferred of cat colors, ranking below all combinations of white, orange, gray, spotted and striped. Black cats are still stereotyped as Halloween cats, creatures of bad luck, more appropriate on a witch's broomstick than curled up on your pillow. To make matters worse, in cages, black cats become close to invisible, fading into the dark shadows in the back of a stainless-steel cage.

For eleven years, starting when I was ten years old, I volunteered at an urban animal shelter. It always struck me as particularly unfair that, time after time, I'd get to know affectionate, adorable black cats, only to watch them be passed over by adopters merely because of their color. I assumed there was nothing that could be done.

One day, many years into my work at the shelter, I spent a few minutes petting a sweet, black half-grown kitten, who had been found as a stray and brought to the shelter. The slender thing purred warmly at my attention, gently playful as she patted my hand with one paw. I thought about what a shame it was that the kitten was already too big to be adopted on baby-kitten appeal alone, and so solidly black that most people wouldn't even pause in front of her cage. I noticed there was no name written on the informational card on her cage. Since volunteers were welcome to name the strays that came to the shelter, I thought for a moment about what I could name this black kitten. I wanted to think of a name that could give the kitten the kind of appealing "color" that might encourage an adopter to take a second look. The name Jellybean popped into my head, and I wrote it on the card, just as I'd named thousands of cats in the past.

I was taken entirely by surprise when, later that afternoon, I overheard a woman walking through the cat room say, "Jellybean! What a wonderful name!" She stopped to look more closely at the kitten, now batting at a piece of loose newspaper in the cage. She asked me if she could hold Jellybean, and, as I opened the cage, I sheepishly admitted that the kitten didn't know her name, as I'd named her just hours before. I lifted her into the woman's arms, and the kitten leaned into the woman, looking up into her eyes with a purr of kitten bliss. After a few minutes, the woman told me that she'd like to adopt this black kitten, and, when the paperwork was approved a few days later, she took Jellybean home.

I was pleased, of course—adoptions were always what nourished my soul—but I chalked it up to a lucky break for one black kitten, and moved on.

I was surprised again a few weeks later when the woman came back to the shelter. She found me refilling water bowls in a cat room and said, "You were the one who helped me adopt that black kitten a few weeks ago, remember? Jellybean? I know you were the one who named her, and I've been wanting to stop back to thank you. She's the sweetest thing—I just love her to pieces. But I don't know if I would have noticed her if she hadn't had that great name. It just suits her perfectly. She's so bouncy and colorful—I know that sounds crazy. Anyway, I wanted to say thank you."

I told her I was touched that she had stopped by and thrilled to hear that Jellybean was doing well in her new home. Then I explained how I thought black cats were often unfairly overlooked and admitted the name had been my conscious attempt to get someone to notice a cat who would probably not have been adopted otherwise. She said, "Well, it worked! You should name all the black cats Jellybean."

I smiled politely at the suggestion, thinking to myself that this woman knew nothing of the harsh realities of animal shelters. Just because I named one kitten Jellybean and it had gotten adopted didn't mean anything—it had just been a stroke of luck. Black cats were still black cats, after all, and most people didn't want them.

As the day went on, I kept thinking about the woman's advice: "You should name all the black cats Jellybean." As crazy as it seemed, I decided I had nothing to lose. Pen in hand, I walked along the cages, looking for a black cat without a name. There was only one, a small black kitten alone in a cage, sleeping. I wrote "Jellybean" on its cage card. Later that afternoon, someone came along and said they'd like to adopt that little Jellybean. Well, I thought to myself, that wasn't really a fair test—it was so cute and tiny.

A few days later, a nameless black cat came along, fully grown. I named it Jellybean. It was adopted. Days later, another. Adopted. The process repeated itself enough times that, after a while, I had to admit that maybe there was some magic in the name, after all. It began to seem morally wrong not to name black cats Jellybean, especially ones who had a bounce in their step and a spark of joy in their eyes. Although I'd usually refrained from using the same name for more than one cat, after a while, my fellow volunteers ceased to be surprised when they came across another of my Jellybeans.

Of course, we'll need more far-reaching solutions to ensure that every cat has a home. But for my black Jellybeans, sitting in sunny windows, sniffing at ladybugs walking across the kitchen floor, snuggling in beds with their adopted people, a name made all the difference. "Jellybean" allowed some humans to see beyond a dark midnight coat into the rainbow of riches in a cat's heart.

—Dorian Solot
Chicken Soup for the Cat Lover's Soul

95

The Seal

Obstacles don't have to stop you. If you run into a wall, don't turn around
and give up. Figure out how to climb it, go through it, or work around it.
—Michael Jordan

At the age of fourteen, I landed one of the most sought-after summer jobs in Vancouver—I became an attendant at the Stanley Park Children's Zoo. Few of us are fortunate enough to experience the perfect job, but for the next five summers, I did just that.

Zoo designers from around the globe asked for tours because they had heard that our children's zoo was one of, if not the, best there was. The children's zoo, an integral part of one of the world's most beautiful areas within a city, Stanley Park, was ahead of its time. Pits were used instead of cages, and zoo attendants worked hard to make each habitat different and exciting for the animal that lived there.

Orphaned members of the local native wildlife were also brought to our zoo for care. Everything from baby pigeons to owlets, fawns to porcupines were given the best possible attention.

The harbour seal pups in our care were kept in the back building, away from small fingers. Twice a day, we would bring them out to the man-made pond in the contact area and allow them to swim. The pond was at the bottom of a waterfall of fresh, cold water.

One day, as I waded in the thigh-deep, icy water with two seal pups, some people gathered to watch. The pups stayed close to me, surfacing occasionally to catch a breath and look around. I saw a boy, about ten years of age, pointing at one and calling to his mother to come and see.

As I walked around, feeling my legs turning numb, the boy yelled, "Hey! Where's the other one?"

While one of the seals was nuzzling my leg, my eyes scoured the pond for the other, Spica. The water was clear, as well as cold, and it was soon obvious Spica wasn't where he should be. My heart skipped a beat as I realized he had swum under a rock formation, which was there to hide the drain. There was a small, fist-sized hole on one end of the formation, and another hole, just large enough for a baby seal, on the other end. But I was quite certain that the inside area was too narrow for Spica to turn around in.

"Oh no!" yelled the boy. "The little seal is under the rocks and can't get out. He's going to drown!"

Everyone in the zoo came to the edge of the pond to watch the drama unfold. I was terrified and called to another attendant to take the other pup to safety. I dove under the water and felt the small hole. Sure enough, Spica was trying to get through it. I knew that the pond would take hours to drain. I also knew that seals could hold their breath for twenty minutes or longer, but I didn't know if a week-old seal in an agitated state could.

And then, just like a white knight riding to the rescue, one of the men who worked at the main zoo arrived. Ken was a good friend to all of us and often spent his breaks at the Children's Zoo. He ran over, assessed the situation, and whipped off his shirt and shoes. Jumping in, he dove under and tried to reach Spica through the larger of the openings. He couldn't even touch him.

"Okay, Diane," he said to me. "Dive under and push him back as far as you can. I'll try to grab him from this side. Ready? Go!" he commanded.

I held my breath, found Spica's muzzle still near the small opening and pushed as hard as I could. My head throbbed from the frigid water, and my lungs wanted to hyperventilate. Every ounce of my being screamed to get out of that freezing water. It took every thread of strength I had to stay put.

Finally, I could no longer feel Spica, and with my stomach in knots, I stood up. Precious time had gone by, and Spica had been motionless, offering no resistance when I had pushed. The little boy among the spectators was now providing a play-by-play account: "Oh, the poor thing! He is suffering so much! His little lungs are probably exploding. The poor little seal... he's dead by now."

Suddenly, after what seemed like forever, Ken burst out of the water, gasping and coughing. He was holding a very limp body. I looked at Ken, and he lowered his eyes as he shook his head. The crowd, even the little boy, was silent.

And then, Spica raised his head, and in the way of infant seals, cooed at me.

The audience let out a cheer and applauded loudly, generously patting Ken, my new hero, on the back. He handed me the pup and I snuggled the wet, slick fur, revelling in the intense relief.

I glanced around, searching for the boy. I found him, standing perfectly still and absolutely quiet, while tears ran down his face and dripped into the pond.

—Diane C. Nicholson
Chicken Soup for the Canadian Soul

96

Small Girl Learns a Big Lesson

We are each burdened with prejudice; against the poor or the rich, the smart or the slow, the gaunt or the obese. It is natural to develop prejudices. It is noble to rise above them.
—Author Unknown

Auden, my dear grandmother, passed away in 1992. I was only five years old, too young to remember enough about her. But one important life lesson she taught me remains unforgettable.

When Auden was a high school senior in 1940s Chicago, there was a "must-go-to" party after the prom. My grandmother was invited and was eagerly anticipating the big event. That is, until a few days later when she found out that Jennifer, one of her best friends, hadn't received an invitation. Auden's excitement quickly turned to anger when she discovered the reason for the exclusion.

Jennifer wasn't invited because she was Jewish.

Understand, this wasn't just a big party, it was the party of this senior class's high school lives.

No matter. My grandmother didn't take this sitting down.

"I didn't want Jennifer, or anyone, to feel left out," Auden said. If Jennifer wasn't welcome, then Auden wouldn't go either. Instead, she invited Jennifer over for their own small party. A two-person party...

that turned out to be the party of the Class of 1940s young lives as more and more classmates decided to do the right thing.

"Injustice," I remember Auden telling me more than once, "is everyone's battle."

I was only a kindergartner, but I listened, I learned and I remembered.

• • •

As I have grown up, racism is something I have read about in history textbooks, something that happens to other people, in other times, in other places. Certainly I never thought I would witness something so ugly in my small hometown in Southern California. My middle school was largely white, but with a healthy minority mix of Hispanic, Asian and a few African-American students. I have been brought up to notice skin color only the way I might notice someone's red hair or freckles or dimples. I just see people. Human beings. My classmates. My friends.

But one morning I arrived at school to find out my friend Damien had been suspended for getting into a fight with another student. I was shocked. Damien was a kindhearted, gentle person, an honors student, even voted "friendliest" by his eighth grade classmates. He always smiled and said "hello" when you passed him in the hallways. He was popular with the cool kids and also with the less-cool kids because he was nice to everybody. Damien was the last person I would suspect of being suspended.

Throughout the day, the details of Damien's suspension leaked out. At first I was shocked, then perplexed, then, as I gradually pieced together the whole story, furious.

This is what happened. Damien was waiting for his ride home after school when the school troublemaker, a white kid who had already been suspended numerous times and was just a few missteps away from juvenile hall, sauntered up to him, sneered a racial slur (Damien, I should mention, is African-American) and began to push him around. Damien first tried to walk away, then tried to defend himself. When an administrator finally noticed the scuffle and rushed over to tear them apart, it looked as if both boys had been involved in the fight. Both were suspended immediately. Even when the few witnesses said that Damien was just defending himself, school administrators remained firm. Damien had been involved in a fight with another student, and therefore he was suspended.

"Zero tolerance," they said, unaware of the irony. "No ifs, ands or buts about it."

Not only did Damien have to miss school for a few days, as a student who had been suspended he was also barred from any of the remaining school functions: dances, the end-of-the-year field trip to the beach, even the eighth grade graduation ceremony. To me, this seemed unbearably unfair, especially since Damien had merely been defending himself.

I talked to the principal. She remained steadfast in her stance. I passed around a petition at school and drummed up support from more than 400 students, nearly the entire eighth grade class. The administration remained stubbornly firm behind the suspension.

On the day of graduation, Damien sat in the audience instead of onstage with the other graduates. As class president, I was allowed to give a speech at the ceremony. I stood at the podium, tears welling up in my eyes at the sight of Damien sitting amid the crowd of parents instead of onstage with his classmates and friends.

I cleared my throat.

"When I was very young," I began, "an incredibly wise lady, my grandmother Auden, taught me a valuable lesson. 'Injustice is everyone's battle,' she used to say. And I say that it is an injustice that Damien is not up here onstage with us today..."

I wish I could tell you that our principal was affected by the ovation Damien received and invited him up with us. But she didn't. This battle against injustice was lost.

Or maybe not. The smile on Damien's face told me he didn't feel completely left out.

It is now four years later. When I see Damien in the high school halls, he still sometimes thanks me for what I did.

In truth, he should thank my Grandma Auden.

—Dallas Woodburn
Chicken Soup for the Teenage Soul: The Real Deal School

97

My Lollipop

> *Someone's opinion of you does not have to become your reality.*
> —Les Brown

Ice. Snow. Cold. It was the lovely month of February, when everyone was sick of the snow, and spring still felt light years away. The cold air on windows during February, however, always did make for good pictures in the stream of my breath.

As I drew a heart on the window, something outside caught my eye. It was a girl. She wore designer clothes and had a pretty face. She is the type who wakes up at 5:30 to leave enough time to fix her makeup, even though school starts at 7:25. She was surrounded by a group of her friends, all of them chatting and laughing as they left the school. I envied her. Not because she was beautiful or because she had enough friends to last her a lifetime. I envied her because it seemed as if she knew exactly who she was and where she wanted to be. The arrival of a white Camry interrupted my thoughts. Her ride was there. She waved goodbye to her clique as she climbed into the front seat, and the car door slammed.

The car door brought my mind back to the night before. It sounded just like my bedroom door had after I slammed it in an effort to escape from my mother's angry voice. Her screams followed me to my room, however, and somehow found a way to penetrate my door. They will remain with me for years to come.

Ten minutes before, I had pushed my four-year-old brother out of my path to reach something. "Get out of my way," I said.

"No!" replied my brother. He has a way of constantly being directly in the way of something I need, and it does no good to reason with him. So instead of wasting my time and energy that night, I just moved him out of the way. This annoyed my mother. She started yelling about how terrible I was with children. Now, in order to understand why this upset me so much, there is something you must know. Anyone who has discussed my career plans with me knows that I love kids. I not only plan on working with them in the future, but I work with them now as well, and I thoroughly enjoy myself. My mother knows this, yet she continued to scream herself hoarse. "You have the worst personality when it comes to children. You had better start changing your plans quick!" This stung. It was probably the worst thing she could have said to me.

I sighed as I managed to pull myself from the window. The room started to come back into focus. On one side, there were tables with chairs and a blackboard. The other side was more interesting and was separated into little kitchen areas. Spoons were set out on the counter, along with bowls and plastic molds. Chocolate would appear later, ready to be molded into candy.

As I examined the pictures carved into the plastic molds, Mrs. Festa came in with more supplies. She is the advisor of a club called Helping Little Hands. The club's mission is to help and plan activities for underprivileged children.

I heard another car door slam outside, but this time I was too busy to be looking out the window. Mrs. Festa and I had started to melt the chocolate. Within seconds of hearing the car door, eager feet could be heard pounding down the hallway. The children had arrived.

Every year, we invite the children to our club to make cookies or chocolate at holiday times. The children are always excited to come back and have memorized the rules by now. They all know to get an apron and to wash their hands before touching anything. After those things are completed, the children wait for instructions. (I have a sneaking suspicion even those have been memorized as well.)

We explained how to spoon the different-colored chocolates into the heart-shaped molds, and the kids jumped right into the project, even the youngest ones, too short to reach the counter. There were quite a few kids to lift that day.

Whenever I am with children, I do my best never to pick a favorite. However, there are always one or two kids I find especially interesting. On this day, there was a certain boy I was drawn to. He was ten, but his attitude and the aura of toughness he was trying to uphold told the story of a boy who had been hardened by the world and all the trouble it had caused him. His face looked much older than ten.

I especially noticed the lollipop he was making. Most of the children had finished with their projects. There wasn't much chocolate left. He took the remaining spoonfuls of all the different colors, so jumbled that a person could not see where one color started and the next ended.

Over two hours had passed. It was time for everyone to go. Each of the children was given a bag, and they all split the candy amongst themselves to take with them. The ten-year-old boy came back over to me after he had gotten his share of candy. He noticed my hands were empty. "Why didn't you take any?" he asked.

"I wanted to make sure there was enough for everyone else," I said.

"Oh," he replied, but I could see he didn't really accept my answer.

As everyone got ready to leave, I was occupied with buttoning coats and didn't see the boy staring at me. I got a hug from each of the smiling children as they slipped out the door.

"Terrible with children," my mother had said. As much as the previous night had made me angry, now her words saddened me. It dawned on me that my mother didn't just say that because she was angry. She said it because she really believed it was true. It made me sad that my own mother hadn't taken the time or energy to know anything about who I really am.

My ten-year-old friend was the last to go. By now, I had noticed the little tough guy looking at me. He came up to me again, this time slowly, looking around to make sure no one was watching.

"This is for you," he said, as he handed me a piece of candy. It was the last lollipop he had made, the heart-shaped one with all the different colors mixed together. I smiled as he motioned me downward with his finger. As I bent over, he whispered into my ear, "You're my favorite grown-up." For a second, his tough, hardened face broke into a wide, childish grin.

I kept that lollipop, that piece of chocolate made by a child's hands, for months afterward. With all its colors in disarray, the stick on it chipped and the ribbon frayed, that lollipop remains a special treasure. I may never know exactly who I am or where I'm supposed to be, but however insignificant it is to anyone else, I do know one thing: I am his favorite grown-up, and for now, that is all that matters.

—Andrea Mendez
Chicken Soup for the Christian Teenage Soul

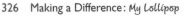

98

Food from the 'Hood

I was in junior high school when the verdict came out: The four policemen filmed beating Rodney King were acquitted. South Central L.A. exploded in riots. I was outraged at the looting and burning that took over our city. I thought, Why burn your own neighborhood?

At the age of fourteen, I had experienced some tumultuous times myself. My mother had always been in and out of jail. There were times I didn't know where my next meal would come from. But I had never been driven to the point of violence. The events of that spring made no sense to me.

The next fall I enrolled at Crenshaw High School, one of the most notoriously gang-ridden high schools in South Central L.A. One day, my biology teacher, Tammy Bird, asked a few students to meet her during lunch hour. She introduced us to Melinda McMullen, a business executive who was looking for a way to help rebuild our community. Together, they proposed that we turn the abandoned plot of land behind our classroom into an organic garden. With Ms. Bird offering extra credit and Melinda offering pizza, it was an offer too good to refuse.

For the next few weeks, about a dozen of us spent our time after school cutting down the weeds in the garden, most of them taller than we were. The ground was so hard and dry that we had to take an extra Saturday to prepare the soil. Then we planted herbs and vegetables. Before long, we were growing more than we could eat—so the idea of selling our bounty was a natural.

In September of 1993, we held our first official business meeting. We named ourselves "Food from the 'Hood" and decided to use our profits to fund college scholarships.

That April, we took our vegetables to Santa Monica's Farmer's Market, which is in a pretty ritzy part of Los Angeles. At first we felt out of place. People ignored us. I don't think that they knew what to make of a bunch of Latino and African-American teenagers at a vegetable stand touting "Food from the 'Hood." Finally, one of the guys bounced out of the booth and walked up to people saying, "Hi, I'm Ben Osborne from Crenshaw High. We've grown some organic veggies that are just too good to pass up!" People started buying our produce like crazy. For the rest of the school year, we had sell-out weekends.

But even with the success of our farmer's markets, we ended the school year with a profit of only $600 to put toward the scholarships. (Farming is so expensive!) It was clear we had to find an additional route to profits if we wanted to go to college. That's when we decided to go into the salad dressing business. After all, as my friend Karla Becerra said, "We grow ingredients for salads, so why not make what goes on top?"

Our next step was to develop a recipe. Our first priority: low sodium. High blood pressure is a serious issue among minorities in our community. Our second priority: low fat. We wanted to make people healthy, as well as make money!

That December, we got a tremendous surprise. Rebuild L.A., a nonprofit organization formed out of the riots, gave us start-up funding of $50,000. Armed with our "seed" money, we found someone to manufacture our dressing and made our first large batch. We also used the money to buy office equipment and set up shop in a storage room near the garden. Also, we hired Aleyne Larner, one of our adult volunteers, to be the company's full-time advisor.

I'll never forget our first sales call. It was with the senior vice president of Vons, one of the largest grocery store chains in California.

The room was full of men in suits and us—a group of kids from South Central! We told them about our product and how well it would sell, and they agreed to stock it! Other large grocery chains also decided to carry our dressing.

On April 29, 1994, on the second anniversary of the Los Angeles Uprising, we announced to the community that Food from the 'Hood's Straight Out of the Garden salad dressing was available in 2,000 supermarkets. No one had ever dreamed we could be so successful.

Soon after that, we heard that England's Prince Charles would be visiting Los Angeles. Carlos Lopez, our fourteen-year-old PR manager, wrote and invited him to visit us. We didn't know it at the time, but Prince Charles is a huge fan of organic gardening and has his own company that helps build economic empowerment in the inner cities of England. No one thought that he would come. But a few weeks later, we got a call from a representative of the British consulate saying, "The prince would be delighted."

Three weeks before the prince was due to arrive, our office was vandalized. All of our computer equipment, fax machines and telephones were stolen or destroyed. Some of us burst out crying. But Ben said, "Whatever doesn't kill us makes us stronger." We decided to come back stronger than ever. Many people from the community helped with repairs, and a few businesses donated money to replace the stolen equipment. Our school district even donated a telephone. We were back in business.

The day of the prince's visit finally came. I shook hands with the Prince of Wales! Karla, who used to be really shy, showed him around our garden. There were lots of reporters trying to crowd around, but Prince Charles waved them back and said, "I'm afraid you're trampling on their lettuce." He had lunch with us and ate an entire plate of salad with our salad dressing on it. Then he said, "Your garden is truly remarkable." After the prince's visit, the British consulate gave us a gift: a company delivery truck. We call it the Chuck Wagon.

Today, Food from the 'Hood is seven years old and the biggest success ever seen at Crenshaw High School. Our salad dressings—we now have three flavors—are sold in grocery and natural food stores in twenty-three states. To date, we've had more than seventy student-owners participate in Food from the 'Hood. Most have gone on to pursue higher education. This year, many of us are graduating from colleges all over the United States, including UC Berkeley, Stanford and San Diego State.

I feel like I owe a lot to that quarter-acre plot in back of my old classroom. We all do. The garden is where it all started. Ms. Bird always said one of the most important things about gardening is composting—how you can take leftovers and garbage and turn them into fertile soil for growing great things. Well, truer words were never spoken. I've never seen a bigger waste than the riots—and look what great things we grew out of that!

—Jaynell Grayson
Chicken Soup for the Gardener's Soul

The Power of a Smile

aiting tensely in the small, single room of the Portland Blanchet House, I could hardly control the knot of nervous excitement forming in my gut. It was my first time here with the church youth group to help feed the homeless, and I'd been given the hardest job of all. Nineteen tables in careful rows crowded the room, and it was my job to stand in the center, where I could see every table, telling new people to come in and fill the seats as they emptied.

I was thrilled and eager to be actively doing something directly to help people in the community, but I was also very nervous and curious. What would these people be like? I knew I was doing good and that I could learn a lot from hands-on work, but along with that zealous enthusiasm to broaden my perspective there tugged the urgent voice of a sheltered little suburban girl, whispering for me to hide.

There was no turning back now; it was time. People trudged in, a huddled line of bundles and packs. Red or blue patches of near frozen skin showed here and there beneath ragged scarves and overcoats, muffled eyes peered around the room with an air of bewilderment.

The seniors, who were always the first to be served, quickly occupied the seats farthest from the draft coming from the open door. They immediately started filling the complimentary plastic bags with portable food items such as cookies and rolls. I watched with a kind of naive awe, searching their faces, wondering what were their reasons for living this way, imagining what it would be like to live on the city streets twenty-four hours a day.

I was fidgety, having little to do at this point except wait for the first round of people to finish their meal, so I focused on the advice of the house director: "Lots of 'em come here as much to see a friendly face as to eat the food, so don't be afraid to smile."

This I could handle. Smiling the warmest, most sincere smile I could muster, I caught the eyes of every person I could, and though few smiled back, I felt good about it.

One old man with flyaway tufts of white hair kept looking at me with an expression of far-off wonderment. Vague gray-blue eyes shone amidst the wrinkled sandpaper of his face, and a not-quite-all-there smile beamed out with childlike simplicity. I was greatly touched by his evident pleasure at alternately swallowing a spoonful of ice cream and staring at my face. When he motioned me to come over closer to him, I was only a little alarmed. His speech was slurred and gentle, and he appeared mildly senile. As he reached out one thick-skinned hand to take mine, I felt no threat in his grandfatherly presence.

"I just wanted to ask you," he murmured sweetly, "how much do I owe you for your smile?"

In a laughing rush, I told him, "nothing," and that aged smile grew even more wide and amazed.

"Well, in that case, may I have another?"

I complied with a helpless blush. He told me that as long as he remembered that smile, he'd be doing just fine.

I thought, Me, too. Sometimes that's all it takes.

—Susan Record
Chicken Soup for the Teenage Soul II

Just Being There

Music washes away from the soul the dust of everyday life.
—Berthold Auerbach

It was my junior year of high school, and I needed to knock out twenty hours of community service—and fast. My ethics teacher had given us months to get it done, but with everything else I had going on, I'd managed to procrastinate right down to the last two weeks of the semester.

Lucky for me, there was a convalescent home a few blocks down the street from my school. To be honest, I wasn't looking forward to it. I'd always had an aversion to hospitals and convalescent homes. Still, I needed the hours—and how bad could it be? I could walk over after class let out, spend a few hours there, and voila, obligation fulfilled in no time.

On my first afternoon there, one of the nurses introduced me to a group of wheelchair-bound ladies playing penny-ante poker out in the central courtyard, under the shade of a gazebo. They always met to play poker at that same time each afternoon, so I became a member of their bunch. They couldn't walk, but their minds were sharp. We'd joke and share stories between each hand.

My last day of volunteering at the convalescent home was a Friday. I was in high spirits as I arrived that afternoon. As much as I enjoyed the sassy grandmothers and their stories, I was still a teenager. I had other things I wanted to do and people my own age with whom to hang out.

But the gazebo was empty. A nurse explained that the physical therapy sessions earlier that day had put everybody's normal schedule out of whack. There'd be no poker under the gazebo that afternoon.

I asked the nurse what I should do. Not having anything specific for me, she led me to the lounge reserved for the residents with Alzheimer's. It was a gloomy, cavernous room. Those within sat quietly on couches or trembled from place to place with no specific destination. It was age, sickness, loss of mental faculties and impending death. It was, in short, everything that frightened me about the idea of growing old.

There was a small, old-fashioned organ sitting in the corner. There was no rhyme or reason to it being there. The nurse noticed me looking at it.

"Why don't you play for them?" she said.

"But I can't play the organ," I protested. "I can't even play piano!"

"They won't know the difference," she said, leaning in confidentially. Before I could reply, she'd turned and walked out.

So there I was—seventeen years old, surrounded by Alzheimer's patients and not a clue as to what I should do. I looked around the room again, hunting for that one face, that one pair of eyes that wasn't adrift in a sea of memories. I didn't find it.

Suddenly, that organ was looking pretty good.

I sat down at it and fiddled with the different keys, buttons and levers. After that, I tried to plunk out simple songs, one key at a time. "La Cucaracha" and "Daisy" had never sounded so bad. If that organ could think, it would have crawled away in shame.

Halfway through my off-season rendition of "Joy to the World," I noticed movement out of the corner of my eye. I looked over and saw an old man in a bright red sweater shuffling toward me. He walked slowly, but with purpose.

"Hey, young fella," he said, wiping at his wet mouth with a shaking handkerchief. "You play pretty good."

"No... I mean, thanks, but... I'm just messing around...."

"It's a good job, playing piano. That, and plumbing."

"Yeah... I guess."

"Plumbers and piano players, fella. They can find work anywhere. No matter where they go in the whole wide world, they'll find work."

"I hadn't thought of that."

He patted me on the shoulder with a hand that was gnarled and dry with age.

"You keep up with that piano playing, young fella. It'll take you places. Piano players and plumbers. They work anywhere—you remember that."

With that, he turned and shuffled away, as randomly as he'd appeared in the first place.

As soon as he was gone, the nurse hurried over to me. I didn't realize she'd been watching. Not knowing what I'd done wrong, I panicked.

"Was he talking to you?" she asked.

"Yeah," I said.

She stared at me.

"I'm sorry," I blurted. "I didn't mean to cause..."

"Sorry? You didn't do anything wrong." She looked over at the old man. He was sitting on one of the couches at the other end of the room, a faint smile on his lips. "He and his wife got sick around the same time. They've both lived here for years. She died a month ago. He hasn't spoken a word to anybody since then. Until now. What did you say to him? How'd you get him to open up?"

"I didn't say anything. I didn't do anything. I was just here."

Sometimes that's all it takes.

—Patrick Seitz
Chicken Soup for the Teenage Soul IV

The Yellow Birds

Today, give a stranger one of your smiles. It might be the only sunshine he sees all day.
—*Quoted in P.S. I Love You, compiled by H. Jackson Brown, Jr.*

I was in the prima donna, self-centered phase of age seventeen, and my motives were simple—to enhance my final Health Assistant grade. To accomplish my goal, I volunteered at the nearby convalescent center.

For weeks, I grumbled to my boyfriend, "I can't believe I'm stuck with tending to old people for free." He agreed.

I soon realized that the bright yellow uniforms we were required to wear made matters even worse. On our first day at the center, the nurses took one look at our bright apparel and nicknamed us the "yellow birds."

On the days I was scheduled to work, I complained to the other "yellow birds" about how emptying bedpans, changing soiled linens and spoon-feeding pureed foods to mumbling mouths were not things any teenager should have to do.

One long and tedious month passed before I first met Lily Sturgeon, an eighty-seven-year-old resident who would change my life. I was given a tray of food and sent to her room. As I entered, Lily's bright blue eyes appraised me.

After talking with her for a few minutes, I realized why I hadn't noticed Lily before that day. I had walked past her room numerous times, but, unlike many of the other residents, Lily was soft-spoken and congenial. From my first day at the center, I learned that the nurses had their favorites, usually those who had outstanding characteristics. From joke-tellers to singers, the loud and rambunctious received more attention.

There was something about Lily that I liked immediately. Strangely, I began to enjoy our talks.

One rainy afternoon she smiled and said, "Come here, Karen. Sit down. I have something to show you." She lifted a small photo album and began to turn the pages. "This was my Albert. See him there? Such a handsome man."

Her voice softened as she pointed to a pretty little girl sitting on top of a fence. "And that was our darling Emmy when she was eight years old." Suddenly, a teardrop landed on the page.

I quickly turned to Lily. "What is it?" I whispered, placing my hand on hers. She turned the pages silently, and I noticed that Emmy was not in any of the other photographs.

Then Lily broke the silence. "She died from cancer that year," Lily said sadly. "She'd been in and out of hospitals most of her life, but that year her little body just couldn't take any more."

"I'm so sorry," I said, not knowing how to comfort her.

She smiled slightly as she turned to the last page. Inside the worn album was one more faded picture of a middle-aged Lily standing on tiptoes and kissing a clown's cheek. "That's my Albert," she laughed, recalling happier memories. "After Emmy died, we decided to help the children at the hospital. We were disturbed by the dismal surroundings while Emmy was hospitalized."

Lily stopped briefly to look at the photograph one more time. "That's when Albert decided to become 'Smiley the Clown.' Emmy was always smiling, even in the worst of times. I scraped together what fabric I could find and sewed this costume for Albert." She smiled and clapped her hands in joy. "The children loved it! Every weekend we'd volunteer at the hospitals to bring smiles and gifts to the children."

"But you said that you were poor," I reminded her. "How'd you manage that?"

"Well," she grinned, "smiles are free, and the gifts weren't anything fancy." She closed the album and leaned back against her pillows. "Sometimes the local bakers donated goodies. When we were really hurting for money, we'd bring a fresh litter of pups from our farm. The children loved petting them. After Albert died, I noticed how faded and worn the costume was, so I rented one and dressed as Smiley myself... that is, until my first heart attack, about ten years ago. Smiley was then forced into retirement."

When I left Lily's room that day, I couldn't think of anything but how generous she and Albert had been to children who weren't even their own.

Graduation day neared and, on my last day, I hurried to Lily's room. She was asleep, curled into a fetal position from stomach discomfort. I stroked her brow and worried about who would take care of her the way I did. She didn't have any surviving family members, and most of the staff were too busy to give her the extra love and attention I had grown to so willingly share.

At times, I wanted to proclaim Lily's virtues to the staff. She would stop me and remind me that the good things she'd done were done without thoughts of self. "Besides," she would say, "doesn't the good Lord tell us to store our treasures in heaven and not on this Earth?"

Lily must have sensed my anguish that day as I stood by her bed. Opening her eyes, she asked in a concerned voice laced with pain, "What is it, dear?"

"I'll be back in two weeks," I responded, explaining about high-school graduation. "And then I'll visit you every day. I promise."

She sighed and squeezed my fingers. "I can't wait for you to tell me all about it."

Two weeks later, I rushed back to the center with a bouquet of lilies in my hand. As I stepped into her clean, neat, unoccupied room, I searched for an answer to Lily's whereabouts. My heart already knew the answer.

I threw the flowers on the bed and wept.

A nurse came in and gently touched my shoulder. "Were you one of the yellow birds?" she asked. "Is your name Karen?"

I nodded, and she handed me a gift-wrapped box. "Lily wanted you to have this. We've had it since she died because we didn't know how to get in touch with you."

It was her photo album. Clutching it tightly to my chest, I quickly left.

Three weeks later, my horrified boyfriend stood before me. "You can't be serious!" he said, pacing back and forth. "You look ridiculous!"

As I tried to look at myself in the mirror, he blocked my reflection. "You can't be serious!" he repeated. "How in the world did you pay for that thing anyway?"

"With my graduation money," I answered.

"What?" he exclaimed, shaking his head. "You spent the money that we saved for New York on that?"

"Yep," I said. "Life is more about giving than receiving."

"This is just great," he muttered, helping me tie the back of my costume. "And what am I supposed to say when someone asks me what my girlfriend's name is? Bozo?"

Looking at my watch, I realized I needed to hurry if I wanted to make it on time to the Children's Hospital. "Nope," I answered, kissing him on the cheek. "Tell them it's Smiley... Smiley the Clown."

—Karen Garrison
Chicken Soup for the Volunteer's Soul

More

Chicken Soup for the Soul®

...

Chicken Soup for the Soul

Share with Us

We would like to know how these stories affected you and which ones were your favorite. Please write to us and let us know.

We also would like to share your stories with future readers. You may be able to help another teenager, and become a published author at the same time. Please send us your own stories and poems for our future books. Some of our past contributors have launched writing and speaking careers from the publication of their stories in our books!

The best way to submit your stories is through our web site, at

www.chickensoup.com

If you do not have access to the Internet, you may submit your stories by mail or by facsimile.

Chicken Soup for the Soul
P.O. Box 700
Cos Cob, CT 06807-0700
Fax 1-203-861-7194

Chicken Soup for the Soul®

Teens Talk Tough Times

Our 101 BEST STORIES

Stories about the Hardest Parts of Being a Teenager

Jack Canfield
& Mark Victor Hansen
edited by Amy Newmark

Being a teenager is difficult even under idyllic circumstances. But when bad things happen, the challenges of being a teenager can be overwhelming. This book contains the best stories from Chicken Soup's library on tough challenges and issues that you and your friends face. Think of it as a support group that you can carry in your hand!

*C*heck out the other books in the

Chicken Soup for the Soul

for the Soul.

Our 101 BEST STORIES

Teens Talk Relationships

Stories about Family, Friends and Love

Jack Canfield
& Mark Victor Hansen
edited by Amy Newmark

Being a teenager is hard but you are not alone. Read stories written by other teens just like you, who face the same problems and issues. Read how other teens met the challenges of new friends, new love, and changing family relationships.

Teens Talk Series

More books for Teens!

Chicken Soup for the Teenage Soul

Chicken Soup for the Teenage Soul II

Chicken Soup for the Teenage Soul III

Chicken Soup for the Teenage Soul IV

Chicken Soup for the Teenage Soul on Tough Stuff

Chicken Soup for the Teenage Soul Teen Letters

Chicken Soup for the Christian Teenage Soul

Chicken Soup for the Teenage Soul Journal

Chicken Soup for the Soul: The Real Deal School

Chicken Soup for the Soul: The Real Deal Friends

Chicken Soup for the Soul: The Real Deal Challenges

Chicken Soup for the Teenage Soul on
Love & Friendship

More of Our 101 BEST STORIES for Teens & Preteens!

Chicken Soup for the Soul: Preteens Talk
Inspiration and Support for Preteens from Kids Just Like Them
"Our 101 Best Stories" series
978-1-935096-00-9

Chicken Soup for the Soul: Christian Teen Talk
Christian Teens Share Their Stories of Support, Inspiration and Growing Up
"Our 101 Best Stories" series
978-1-935096-12-2

Upcoming for Teens & Preteens!

Chicken Soup for the Soul: Teens Talk High School
101 Stories of Life, Love, and Learning for Older Teens
978-1-935096-25-2

Chicken Soup for the Soul: Teens Talk Middle School
101 Stories of Life, Love, and Learning for Younger Teens
978-1-935096-26-9

Chicken Soup for the Soul: Teens Talk Getting In...to College
101 Stories of Support from Kids Who Have Lived Through It
978-1-935096-27-6

About the
Chicken Soup for the Soul
Authors

Who Is
Jack Canfield?

Jack Canfield is the co-creator and editor of the Chicken Soup for the Soul series, which Time magazine has called "the publishing phenomenon of the decade." Jack is also the co-author of eight other bestselling books including *The Success Principles™: How to Get from Where You Are to Where You Want to Be*, *Dare to Win*, *The Aladdin Factor*, *You've Got to Read This Book*, and *The Power of Focus: How to Hit Your Business and Personal and Financial Targets with Absolute Certainty*.

Jack has recently developed a telephone coaching program and an online coaching program based on his most recent book *The Success Principles*. He also offers a seven-day Breakthrough to Success seminar every summer, which attracts 400 people from fifteen countries around the world.

Jack is the CEO of the Canfield Training Group in Santa Barbara, California, and founder of the Foundation for Self-Esteem in Culver City, California. He has conducted intensive personal and professional development seminars on the principles of success for over a million people in twenty-three countries. Jack is a dynamic keynote speaker and he has spoken to hundreds of thousands of others at more than 1,000 corporations, universities, professional conferences and conventions, and has been seen by millions more on national television shows such as The Today Show, Fox and Friends, Inside Edition, Hard Copy, CNN's Talk Back Live, 20/20, Eye to Eye, and the NBC Nightly News and the CBS Evening News.

Jack is the recipient of many awards and honors, including three honorary doctorates and a Guinness World Records Certificate for having seven books from the Chicken Soup for the Soul series appearing on the New York Times bestseller list on May 24, 1998.

To write to Jack or for inquiries about Jack as a speaker, his coaching programs, trainings or seminars, use the following contact information:

Jack Canfield
The Canfield Companies
P.O. Box 30880 • Santa Barbara, CA 93130
phone: 805-563-2935 • fax: 805-563-2945
E-mail: info@jackcanfield.com
www.jackcanfield.com

Chicken Soup *for the* Soul

Who Is
Mark Victor Hansen?

Mark Victor Hansen is the co-founder of Chicken Soup for the Soul, along with Jack Canfield. He is also a sought-after keynote speaker, bestselling author, and marketing maven. For more than thirty years, Mark has focused solely on helping people from all walks of life reshape their personal vision of what's possible. His powerful messages of possibility, opportunity, and action have created powerful change in thousands of organizations and millions of individuals worldwide.

Mark's credentials include a lifetime of entrepreneurial success. He is a prolific writer with many bestselling books, such as *The One Minute Millionaire*, *Cracking the Millionaire Code*, *How to Make the Rest of Your Life the Best of Your Life*, *The Power of Focus*, *The Aladdin Factor*, and *Dare to Win*, in addition to the Chicken Soup for the Soul series. Mark has had a profound influence in the field of human potential through his library of audios, videos, and articles in the areas of big thinking, sales achievement, wealth building, publishing success, and personal and professional development.

Mark is the founder of the MEGA Seminar Series. MEGA Book Marketing University and Building Your MEGA Speaking Empire are annual conferences where Mark coaches and teaches new and aspiring authors, speakers, and experts on building lucrative publishing and speaking careers. Other MEGA events include MEGA Info-Marketing and My MEGA Life.

He has appeared on Oprah, CNN, and The Today Show. He

has been quoted in *Time*, *U.S. News & World Report*, *USA Today*, *New York Times*, and *Entrepreneur* and has had countless radio interviews, assuring our planet's people that "You can easily create the life you deserve."

As a philanthropist and humanitarian, Mark works tirelessly for organizations such as Habitat for Humanity, American Red Cross, March of Dimes, Childhelp USA, and many others. He is the recipient of numerous awards that honor his entrepreneurial spirit, philanthropic heart, and business acumen. He is a lifetime member of the Horatio Alger Association of Distinguished Americans, an organization that honored Mark with the prestigious Horatio Alger Award for his extraordinary life achievements.

Mark Victor Hansen is an enthusiastic crusader of what's possible and is driven to make the world a better place.

Mark Victor Hansen & Associates, Inc.

P.O. Box 7665 • Newport Beach, CA 92658

phone: 949-764-2640 • fax: 949-722-6912

www.markvictorhansen.com

Chicken Soup for the Soul

Who Is
Amy Newmark?

Amy Newmark was recently named publisher of Chicken Soup for the Soul, after a thirty-year career as a writer, speaker, financial analyst, and business executive in the worlds of finance and telecommunications.

Amy is a graduate of Harvard College, where she majored in Portuguese, minored in French, and traveled extensively. She is also the mother of two children in college and has two grown stepchildren.

After a long career writing books on telecommunications, voluminous financial reports, business plans, and corporate press releases, Chicken Soup for the Soul is a breath of fresh air for Amy. She has fallen in love with Chicken Soup for the Soul and its life-changing books, and found it a true pleasure to conceptualize, compile, and edit the "101 Best Stories" books for our readers.

The best way to contact Chicken Soup for the Soul is through our web site, at www.chickensoup.com. This will always get the fastest attention.

If you do not have access to the Internet, please contact us by mail or by facsimile.

Chicken Soup for the Soul
P.O. Box 700
Cos Cob, CT 06807-0700
Fax 1-203-861-7194

Acknowledgments

Chicken Soup for the Soul

Thank You!

We would like to thank the entire staff of Chicken Soup for the Soul for their help on this project and the 101 Best series in general.

Among our California staff, we would especially like to single out D'ette Corona, who is the heart and soul of the Chicken Soup publishing operation, and who put together the first draft of this manuscript, Barbara LoMonaco for invaluable assistance in obtaining the illuminating quotations that add depth and meaning to this book, Patty Hansen for her extra special help with the permissions for these fabulous stories and for her amazing knowledge of the Chicken Soup library, and Patti Clement for her help with permissions and other organizational matters.

In our Connecticut office, we would like to thank our able editorial assistant, Valerie Howlett, for her assistance in setting up our new offices, editing, and helping us put together the best possible books for teenagers.

We would also like to thank our master of design, book producer and Creative Director, Brian Taylor, at Pneuma Books LLC, for his brilliant vision for our covers and interiors.

Finally, none of this would be possible without the business and creative leadership of our CEO, Bill Rouhana, and our president, Bob Jacobs.

—Chicken Soup for the Soul